BLACK PERFORMANCE THEORY

BLACK
PERFORMANCE
THEORY / Thomas F. DeFrantz AND Anita Gonzalez, EDITORS

Foreword by D. Soyini Madison

DUKE UNIVERSITY PRESS   DURHAM AND LONDON   2014

© 2014 Duke University Press
All rights reserved
Printed in the United States of America on acid-free paper ∞
Designed by Heather Hensley
Typeset in Minion Pro by Graphic Composition, Inc.

Library of Congress Cataloging-in-Publication Data
Black performance theory / Thomas F. DeFrantz and Anita Gonzalez, editors ;
foreword by D. Soyini Madison.
pages cm
Includes bibliographical references and index.
ISBN 978-0-8223-5607-3 (cloth : alk. paper)
ISBN 978-0-8223-5616-5 (pbk. : alk. paper)
1. Blacks in the performing arts. 2. African Americans in the performing arts.
I. DeFrantz, Thomas. II. Gonzalez, Anita.
PN1590.B53B53 2014
791.089'96073—dc23
2013045755

Frontispiece: Amy Papaelias, "Navigations of Blackness—2," 2013. Courtesy of the artist.

CONTENTS

Black performance theory (BPT) helps us decipher the imperatives of blackness. Translating the meanings of blackness by excavating the enlivening enactments that sustain blackness, theory does the labor of translating the thick ontologies of what black imperatives are by locating them within the generative forces of performance. With each generation, perhaps with each turn of a phrase, we stake a new claim within a new world order for the nature and significance of blackness. Black performance theory complicates old claims of blackness, because life is change and the world keeps turning, demanding new vocabularies and new actions. Blackness is born and reborn as something uniquely itself, in stark difference against that which it is not, and in comforting familiarity with those things that are itself. To say something different and new about blackness, about it having a nature or a decipherable core, is serious work because it is head spinning in its contradictions and contingencies. Black performance theory shows us how each unfolding or iteration of what blackness is can be constituted by performance and revealed within unlimited performance frames.

This volume transforms black ontologies and imperatives into the lived realms of time, space, and action: bodies, machines, movement, sound, and creation now culminate within temporalities of struggle and renewal. Black performance theory shows us how subjects and subjectivities animate blackness across landscapes that are all spectacularly excessive in the cause and effects of African dislocation, imperialist trade, capital accumulation, human violence, and black abjection as well as circum-Atlantic expressions, black labor, Africanist retentions, black diaspora movements, the politics of black is beautiful, and more.

In deciphering the imperatives of blackness, BPT becomes an oppositional move within a matrix of disciplining powers reigning over the black body. Because it deepens the details of black expressivities and transgressions within the abiding contexts of disciplinary histories and circulations of inequality, BPT translates all of this within fluid rubrics of performance, performativity, and the performative. If *performance* constitutes forms of cultural staging—conscious, heightened, reflexive, framed, contained—within a limited time span of action from plays to carnivals, from poetry to prose, from weddings to funerals, from jokes to storytelling and more; if *performativity* marks identity through the habitus of repetitive enactments, reiterations of stylized norms, and inherited gestural conventions from the way we sit, stand, speak, dress, dance, play, eat, hold a pencil and more; if the *performative* is the culmination of both in that it *does something* to make a material, physical, and situational difference—then BPT speaks to why all this matters to blackness and to contested identities. Black performance theory helps us realize performance. In this performance/theory coupling what is revealed to us is how performance performs *and* how theory performs *us* through its realizations, claims, and possibilities. It works to translate and inspire, to politically interrogate and sensually invoke, how realms of performance struggles and troubles illuminate black agency and subjectivity within reimagined spaces of being.

Black performance theory is high stakes because it excavates the coded nuances as well as the complex spectacles within everyday acts of resistance by once known a/objects that are now and have always been agents of their own humanity. Black performance theory is oppositional because it honors the subaltern, rhetorical roots of black symbolism that survive and break through the timeworn death wish cast against black expression. The theorist attends to performance histories, aesthetics, and orders of belonging governed by multifarious modes of un-freedom as well as the radical performances that violent constraint has invoked. But, as much as black performance theory is about politics, entangled within history and power, it is also an enterprise and labor of the senses. The gift of performance theory is its distinct attention and indebtedness to the sensory as the senses actualize temporality, enliven desire, and embrace beauty across the poetics of bodies and the aesthetics of their creations. Performance theory honors and heightens the gravitas of the senses as gateways to the symbol-making body, its sonics, and its existential truths wrapped in art and purpose.

If the genealogy of black performance extends like a rhizome to cross its dense continental roots and budding diasporic expressivities in the culmination and continuum of endless circum-Atlantic performances, then black performance theory inherits an ethics commanded by the performatives of Africanist multitudes. Because black performance is born through and sustained by circum-Atlantic epochs and its (dis)concordant expressivities, it follows that black performance *theory* is indebted to the truth of this Africanist inheritance that constitutes the fact of blackness. Africa/Africanisms/

Africanist symbols, meanings, and lives have been the prototype of abjection. Therefore, the political stakes and sensory affects of black performance theory require an intellectual rigor that elucidates and disentangles the complexities of these Africanisms and the haunting terrors of their degradation. Black performance theory also requires an ethics of engagement that begins with, but moves from, economies of dislocation and disciplinary power to futures of what black performatives *do* and its instructive elaborations on futurity. Black performance theory offers up something beyond what we already know, because it is an ethics that does not stand in iterations but intellectually thrives in thick performatives of kinesis and invention: for life's sake.

This volume is a palimpsest of black performance histories, practices, affects, and ideologies. In this contemporary moment, what surfaces and leaves its imprint upon BPT is the demand for new imperatives, expanded notions of black ontology, fresh meditations on black abjection, and renewed dialogues on how performance can generate it all. This claim goes further in enunciating that race is both a fundamental constant and a "resistant" factor in the infinite and boundless reaches of black performance, its sensibilities, and its analytics. I am reminded of Harry Belafonte's lament of how black artists have turned their backs on black social responsibility, adding, "Give me Bruce Springsteen, and now you're talking. I think he is black" (Zawia). Herein the notion that cultural politics trumps race. From Toni Morrison's noted comment about Bill Clinton being the first black president to the controversy over the meanings of post-black, the point is that race is a fact of blackness within racially boundless articulations and performatives that rise from this fact. This volume illuminates the constant of blackness *and* its abiding boundlessness.

Exceeding iterations of ready-made blackness and overcooked theories of performance, this volume honors the charge to theorize outside the expected and to say something new. It does this with each essay. Theorizing is a real commitment. It is hard, good, interventionist work. Blackness makes theorizing even more complicated, because it makes theory expand and reach into histories and economies that are layered by abjection and subjugated spaces. Black performance theory, with heartfelt commitment and sharp-tongued intellect, deepens the expanse and reach of this interventionist work to offer up black imperatives of politics, beauty, and the senses.

D. SOYINI MADISON

ACKNOWLEDGMENTS

Black Performance Theory is a project of Slippage: Performance|Culture| Technology, Thomas F. DeFrantz, director.

MIT Office of the Provost, MIT SHASS Dean's Office, and especially Philip S. Khoury, who funded Slippage and *Black Performance Theory* as we wound our way around the country.

All of the participants in the Black Performance Theory working group over the years, and especially the "witnesses" who held productive silence and participated in the working group via the stamina of sustained gestures of stillness.

The outstanding emotional generosity of Venus Opal Reese, Sandra Richards, and Mae G. Henderson, each of whom helped us conjure this work forward in her own special way.

D. Soyini Madison, whose writing inspires us all.

The many artists who performed at the various BPT working group sessions: Thaddeus Bennett, Thema Bryant, Mark A. Davis, Kim Fowler, Amatul Hannan, Adrienne Hawkins, Craig Hickman, Thomasi McDonald, Carl Hancock Rux, Pamela Sneed, and Cristalyn Wright.

The hosts of the BPT working group from 1998 to 2015: Richard C. Green, Thomas F. DeFrantz, Ananya Chatterjea, Annemarie Bean, E. Patrick Johnson, Daphne Brooks, Stephanie Batiste, Omi Osun / Joni L. Jones, Tavia Nyong'o, Awam Amkpa.

Courtney Berger, and the staff at Duke University Press, for an unprecedented responsiveness.

Colleagues at Duke University, especially Dean Srinivas Aravamudan and Vice Provost for the Arts Scott Lindroth.

And most important, Richard C. Green, who created the inciting space for this event through his startling scholarly imagination, and encouraged us all to vibrate in another key.

FROM "NEGRO EXPRESSION" TO "BLACK PERFORMANCE"

Black Performance Theory reflects upon and extends twentieth-century intellectual labors to establish black expressive culture as an area of serious academic inquiry. Here, we bring forward a wealth of critical paradigms that illuminate the capacities of black performance and black sensibilities to enable critical discussions of performance histories, theories, and practices. Authors here are less concerned with errors of omission in a historical genealogy of performance studies than a project of revelation, one in which the capacity of black performance is revealed as a part of its own deployment without deference to overlapping historical trajectories or perceived differences in cultural capital from an elusive Europeanist norm. Black performance theory emerges now, as we are convinced of the endurance of black performance even in a world that daily realigns the implications of race, ethnicity, gender, sexuality, location, ability, age, and class. As we attempt to capture the field through definitions, dialogues, or performative writing, we discover two important truths: that black sensibilities emerge whether there are black bodies present or not; and that while black performance may certainly become manifest without black people, we might best recognize it as a circumstance enabled by black sensibilities, black expressive practices, and black people.

To uncover a history of black performance, we begin by considering naming—the mechanisms used to designate black presence. For example: African, Ethiop, Negro, colored, black, African American. These monikers demonstrate shifts in thinking about black identity and representation. Each label represents a context for packaging ideas about black people in particular places and during particular historical time periods. African or Ethiop suggests originary locations and routes of black migration—whether free or enslaved. Negro and colored were terms of patriarchal domination, popular in the nineteenth through the mid-twentieth century. Black and African American represent resistant, dissident self-namings that emerged in response to political activism of the latter part of the twentieth century. And by now, in the twenty-first century, black has stabilized an international identity of diasporan consciousness.

The naming of black people allowed authors in different historical eras to categorize black practices of performance according to the racialized beliefs of the time. Colonial and nineteenth-century authors often described "African" and "Ethiop" performances as demonstrations of foreign, or primitive, cultures.[1] In the early twentieth century of the United States, an undeniable growth in professional black performance by "Negro" and "colored" artists generated increased commentary. While some authors considered these performances as mere entertainments, theoretical writing concerned with black performance as artistry began to emerge at this time. Strikingly, the most powerful examples of this genre of writing came from African American artist enclaves.[2] In New York, authors of the Harlem Renaissance wondered at the efficacy and impact of black expression as they produced plays, visual arts works, dances, and musical compositions. Their early theorizing established that black performance styles and sensibilities were not merely verbal or aural, but also included visual symbolic codes that communicated and commented in-group. These authors and artists began to question how black expression translated to outsider audiences. Among these authors, Zora Neale Hurston emerged as an originary theorist concerned with aesthetic composition of black performance.

Negro Expression

Hurston wrote a prescient short article for the groundbreaking anthology *Negro*, published in 1934 (Hurston). She offered a taxonomy of African American performativity titled "Characteristics of Negro Expression" that referenced sites, modes, and practices of performance. The essay, and its placement alongside the creative writings of other artists and researchers of the Harlem Renaissance era, predicted a broad interest in understanding African diaspora performance. The implications of Hurston's short essay still stand: black performance derives from its own style and sensibilities that undergird its production. And black performance answers pressing aesthetic concerns of the communities that engage it.

Working from her fieldwork observations, Hurston theorizes Negro performance of the American South of the early twentieth century in provocative, unabashed style. She proclaims Negro talk to be "dramatic" and notes a characteristic willingness to use "action words"—words that paint pictures—as a stabilizing point of entry to understanding the expressive aesthetics of black language and gesture. Perhaps the most important quality that Hurston includes in her explicit taxonomy is the "will to adorn." Here, language pushes forward toward an unprecedented space of expressiveness. For example, the word "syndicating" to refer to "gossiping" demonstrates metaphor and simile; the double descriptives "low down" or "high tall" elaborate meaning; and verbal nouns such as "funeralize" or "jooking" capture action in language. Following Hurston, we can conclude that black expressive performance springs from the need to communicate beyond the limited events of words alone.

Hurston's essay also highlights dancing, dialect, folklore, culture heroes, imitation, and "the Jook"; each section confirms Negro Expression as its own source and subject of possibility. Perhaps this is Hurston's grand achievement: she allows black performance to be in dialogue simultaneously with itself, the world around it, and the lives of black people. Negro Expression is an act of confirmation that is aesthetically motivated and foundational to understanding the community that practices it.

In its first iterations, Negro Expression was routinely aligned with vernacular and folklore studies, areas that allowed for uncomplicated readings of fixed social practices without resource to aesthetic or literary theory. In time, editors and researchers, including activist Nancy Cunard, folklorist Alan Lomax, musicologist Eileen Southern, dance researcher Lynne Fauley Emery, anthropologist Lawrence Levine, literary theorist Houston A. Baker Jr., cultural theorist Kobena Mercer, and historians Shane White and Graham White, offered volumes that attested to the resiliency of black cultural expression.[3] Eventually, disciplinary affiliations including anthropology, musicology, dance, theater, and the literary and visual arts created mechanisms for the consideration of black performance that sought to account for its structural complexity and diversity.

Flash Forward Thirty Years: Africanist Aesthetics and Civil Rights

1966: Art historian Robert Farris Thompson publishes "Dance and Culture, an Aesthetic of the Cool: West African Dance" as prelude to his magisterial catalogue *African Art in Motion: Icon and Act in the Collection of Katherine Coryton White* (1974), and LeRoi Jones publishes "The Revolutionary Theatre" in a collection of writings titled *Home: Social Essays*.

Thompson's work considers the aesthetic value of West African dance and song: "West African dances are key documents of aesthetic history;

they are nonverbal formulations of philosophies of beauty and ethics; and they furnish a means of comprehending a pervasive strand of contemporary American culture" (85). Thompson's theorization of performance includes a taxonomy of four shared traits of West African music and dance: "the dominance of a percussive concept of performance; multiple meter; apart playing and dancing; call-and-response; and, finally the songs and dances of derision." These shared traits became the foundation for an aesthetic ideology surrounding Africanist performance as a family of practices.

From Thompson's essay, a possibility to theorize black performance in terms of its own ontologies emerges. Thompson's writings built upon fieldwork that he conducted on the continent; he was explicitly seeking out connections among performance modes and art practices in various groups. In taking this "long view," as Hurston had done in her tours of the American South a generation earlier, Thompson confirmed aesthetic commonalities, and *imperatives* that guided creative communications among black people.

The turn to West African values and aesthetics marked a general interest in Afrocentric thought that was a by-product of increasing interest in narratives of origins. Thompson's work coincided with black political activism in urban locations that generated art inspired by social change. Theater artists and activists including Amiri Baraka (LeRoi Jones) described their performance priorities in terms of revolution. Baraka's essay "The Revolutionary Theatre" conceived of black performance as continuing, evolving, ritual and experimental work that could evoke the imagistic world of spirit and dreams.[4] His call for a "theatre of world spirit" opened possibilities for defining black performance as process rather than product.

While Hurston documented what she saw among the folk, and Thompson created terminology that could categorize Africanist aesthetics, Baraka called for a deployment of theatrical imagery that could connect an idea of blackness across time and space. He wrote, "The imagination is the projection of ourselves past our sense of ourselves as 'things.'" He encouraged revolutionary black performers to incorporate intangible aspects of black life in their art: rites of passage, guttural moans, ritual chants, and improvisational riffs. His insistence on an imaginary space of possibility created an intercultural and intertextual articulation of black performance, one that explored an essential *soul* of black folk.

Flash Forward Thirty Years and Counting: Working Together to Define Black Performance

1995: The Black Public Sphere Collective publishes *The Black Public Sphere* (University of Chicago Press), a coedited volume; 1998: Michele Wallace and Gina Dent offer *Black Popular Culture* (New Press); and in 2005, Harry J. Elam Jr. and Kennell Jackson's volume *Black Cultural Traffic: Crossroads in Global Performance and Popular Culture* (University of Michigan) appears.

Television and Internet replicate black acts. Media amplify and accelerate the distribution of performance, and an ever-widening global populace comes into contact with Africanist aesthetics in motion. Black performances are embodied by people of color and, importantly, others who have access to the constellation of gesture and word that had previously emerged in black communities. Academic definitions of performance broaden, to recognize affinities and differences among the location and experience of "black life" in a fragmented, postmodern world. Concepts of hybridity, public spheres, the postcolonial, queer black sexualities, and de-essentialized identities enter discussions of black performance, emphasizing complexities of theoretical analysis.

Collectively, the three volumes above established community dialogues of academics working on black performance. These curated projects brought together scholars who consistently considered a "public" for performance more broad than the audience in any room. Their discussions situated performance not only as folklore or political identity, but within the interdisciplinary spheres of global popular culture and mediated expression. Taken together, they confirmed an institutional legitimacy for advanced, nuanced discussion of black performance as artifact and artistry.

Post 9/11, a proliferation of perspectives exploring black performance theory decentralizes academic inquiry. Feedback and talkback loops among artists, authors, and audiences explode boundaries between making and writing about work. New literary formats confirm playful, and serious, modes of engagement with theory. In this moment, the present volume proceeds, and we parse the terms "black," "performance," and "theory."

Parsing Black

DeFrantz: For me, black is the manifestation of Africanist aesthetics. The willingness to back-phrase, to move with a percussive attack, to sing against the grain of the other instruments, and to include the voices of those gathered in the fabric of the event—these are the elements of black that endure and confirm. Yes, it can be the grain of the voice or the sway of the hip; a stutter call that sounds like an engine starting or an unanticipated reference to political circumstances: these elements mark the emergence of black in time and space. This black is action: action engaged to enlarge capacity, confirm presence, to dare.

Gonzalez: By way of contrast, I understand black as a response to histories that extend beyond Africa and its aesthetics. Black performance expands, synthesizes, comments, and responds to imaginations about black identity as much as to its own inherent expressions. If black identity is constructed and articulated by those outside of the "race" then performances of blackness are created in response to these imagined identities as well as to cultural retentions and Africanist histories. Cultural infusions from other parts of the world collect and mingle with the multitude of African performance genres to create a great diversity of styles. I view black as a dialogic imagination—an outsider response to the very existence of people from Africa who carry their own shifting cultural ideologies and metaphysical worldviews.

Parsing Performance

Anita: Performance for me involves enactment, re-creation, or storytelling. Performers present humans in relationship to the exceptional circumstances that surround them. Even as performance centers in living beings and concrete experiences, it is also a metaphoric, or symbolic, iteration of life. In performance, the vocal physical expressive body becomes a conduit, or cauldron, of expressive potential that recycles emotion, spirit, behavior. Performers use metaphoric or symbolic content to communicate perspectives about life.

TommyD: Performance, as I imagine it, involves the excitement of breath to create subject or subjectivity. In other words, performance emerges in its own conscious engagement, and it is created by living people. Of course, some will argue that "texts perform," or "music videos perform," which may be true, but for my sensibility, performance involves subjectivity occasioned by action born of breath. People make performances happen, whether they be in the nightclub, in church, in the classroom, on the job, or on a stage. Importantly, performers need to recognize their own performance in order for it to be valuable. It needs to be conscious action, conceived or created as performance.

Parsing Theory

Male-Identified Queer High Yellow Duke University: Theory, in this formation, is the mobilization of practice toward analysis. The taking stock, or noticing, of action to recognize its component parts and its implications, and the extension of that noticing to construct a way to understand, or interpret, what is happening there. Theory assumes action and practice already in motion; theory might be the realization of that noticing translated into text, or music and motion. Surely theory doesn't have to be written in order to become manifest, but just as surely theory has to be shared among people to be a valuable analytic.

Afro Southern Caribeña now in Ann Arbor: Theory is not limited to academic or intellectual inquiries. Theories develop through evaluative processes initiated by artists in the moment in which they assess what "works" about a performance. Performance theory can be delivered through a hand gesture or sketch, embedded in a lecture, or disseminated within the pauses of a sound score. Artists articulate thoughtful analyses in a multiplicity of ways. Post-performance discussions easily take the form of active breath or performed actions that comment and expand upon originating concepts, relocating the performance practices within new theoretical contexts. This is theory manifest: an articulate response to a performance. All theory, and certainly the best theory, is subjective—a unique and personal response to the performance act that helps the reader or viewer to perceive in a new or unexpected manner.

Black Sensibilities

From Madison, WI: I remember defending my dissertation with Sally Banes, the prolific and innovative dance scholar, at the University of Wisconsin in 1997. After a lengthy oral defense in which I argued passionately about the "relative construction of blackness" and the need to recognize variable types of blackness based upon historical and social circumstances, Sally turned to me with a deadpan face. "Well then, Anita," she said, "What are you going to teach?" Her point was that if black is relative and variable, then how do we talk about it/theorize it? In an attempt to diversify blackness, I had removed blackness from the equation. My desires to articulate blackness within paradigms of postmodernism were realized through participation in the Black Performance Theory working group.

Black performance theory came into being as a "think tank" about black performance at a moment when blackness had been successfully deconstructed as a social and literary category without fixed contents. And yet black performance remained a palpable aspect of being in the world. Many of the scholars involved in early meetings of the group were the first of their families to attend primarily white educational institutions and to immerse themselves in theorizing black performance within integrated academic institutional contexts. In these circumstances, we were forced to describe, articulate, and validate our blackness. Many of us wondered, "Are we black enough?"

From Cambridge, MA: I began my first tenure-track job at the Massachu-

setts Institute of Technology in the late 1990s, and immediately felt the isolation of professional academic work. Each institution is encouraged to have "one" of everything, so of course I arrived as the only scholar-practitioner working in dance and African American studies, as well as media and popular culture studies. We launched BPT at MIT and Duke to create community that could nurture the working-through of concepts and performance ideologies in a group model that resonated with our sense of Africanist structures of communal labors.

Unlike their progenitors, the authors of BPT emerged from environments that wondered at an ontology of blackness that extended beyond race. We wondered, if blackness was no longer stable, what are its performative markers? How can black performances be theorized toward their own ends, even as those ends are dispersed across geographies and historical eras? The writers and artists of BPT embraced the notion of "black sensibilities" as a way to capture ideas of black performativity. Black sensibilities—the enlivened, vibrating components of a palpable black familiar—demonstrate the microeconomics of gesture that cohere in black performance.

Few will argue that black sensibilities do not permeate contemporary life, arising in fragmentary moments of personal relationship or in sustained performance practices. For example, hip-hop, conceived as a flexible platform incontrovertibly black at its root, has become an engine for expressive discovery and marketplace situatedness embraced globally. Gospel music has become a defining mechanism for the circulations of Christian ministries of several denominations. Black strategies of "talking back" to everwidening hegemonic mainstreams of sexualities, religion, class consciousnesses, and even race are engaged regularly in terms of fashion, language, physical stance, and the expansive mutabilities of "being black." Questions about the impossibilities of purity within always-shifting black identities were recounted nearly daily during the early presidency of Barack Obama. In all of these maneuvers, black sensibilities—stylized ways of being in relation to each other and our environments—become wellsprings of creative tactics employed consciously and subconsciously as resources of strength, resistance, and unexpected pleasure.

In a remarkable essay published in 2006 that provides an overview of black performance studies, E. Patrick Johnson cogently explains the fraught terrain of blackness as a manifestation of the epistemological moment of race, one that "manifests itself in and through performance in that performance facilitates self- and cultural reflexivity—a knowing made manifest by a 'doing'" (Johnson, "Black Performance Studies," 446). In the essay, Johnson argues many modalities in which blackness "offers a way to rethink performance theory by forcing it to ground itself in praxis, especially within the context of a white supremacist, patriarchal, capitalist, homophobic society." Wondering that the two categories are already in opposition—black and performance—Johnson wryly notes that in this context, "black performance has the potential of simultaneously forestalling and enabling social change" (Johnson, "Black Performance Studies," 446). Forestalling, within a larger context of white performance; and enabling, as a seemingly endless capacity for all people to emerge into presence through performance.

Johnson also notes that while black performance "has been a sustaining and galvanizing force of black culture and a contributor to world culture at large, it has not always been recognized as a site of theorization in the academy" (Johnson, "Black Performance Studies," 447). *Black Performance Theory* seeks to offer examples of how that theorization happens and to predict where we may go from here.

Some may wish to define what black performance is by reflecting upon what it is not.

Black performance is not static, contained, or geographically specific. There is no locale that designates the origin of "black" sensibilities because skin colors have always been global and relative. The very notion of black is conceived within political/social economies of power defined by historical circumstances. And yet the circumstances multiply or diffuse the instant that they create a distinct entity that we want to delineate as "black." Authors in the volume theorize the web, the spirit, the ecstasy, the ethnosphere, and the thermodynamics of decidedly undetermined modes of expression that communicate within black realms or across political or aesthetic or social boundaries. Race is both a defining paradigm for blackness and a resistant frame for understanding the unbound nature of the field. Clearly black performance is not ending, but rather transforming in response to technology, and ever-changing transnational settings.

Black performance contains history and racism, but it is not about either of those things. Black performance injects itself into pertinent political discussions like those surrounding the death of Trayvon Martin, a teenager shot in 2012 while walking and wearing a hoodie within a predominantly white Florida neighborhood. The Martin tragedy demonstrates how markings associated with black performance—such as a hoodie—can be deadly. Clearly, theorizing black performance is imperative in the present moment.

While deployment of feminist theory might point toward the resistant capacities of black performance as a site of opposition, the authors in this volume explore performance largely as an ever-present feature of human exchange. In this formation, performance may be resistant, affirmative, or several states in-between and simultaneously; it may underscore oppositional aesthetics or collude with creative practices far removed from the lives of black people. Here, the terms of performance are expansively imagined to allow for subversive and normative simultaneity: cross-rhythms of rupture and coherence amid shifting landscapes of intervention and virtuosity. In this way, narratives of domination and oppression that often circumscribe depictions of black performance arrive alongside considerations of presence and activity as their own means and ends.

Rather than constrain performance as public or private, live or mediated, historical or contemporary, theorists in this volume allow slippage between these areas to go unedited. Recurrently, queering the capacities of theoretical intervention arrive as an urgency in this work: the authors here wonder, repeatedly, at the productive work of disidentification that produces the synchronous singularities of black performance.[5]

On Performative Writing

Some postmodern performance theorists describe intertextuality as a post-1960s phenomenon.[6] However, we find its roots in earlier renditions of black aesthetic writing. Performative writing might be the writing that Hurston refers to at the beginning of her essay, when she writes of the black performer that "his very words are action words. His interpretation of the English language is in terms of pictures. One act described in terms of another" (Hurston). Hurston's writing demonstrated "black talking back"—rich portrayals of nuances of Negro form. Her willingness to be playful in her writing also predicated the performative scholarship offered here. Talking back playfully confirms a black mode of intertextual and interstitial writings that enliven analyses of black performance.[7]

Black Performance Theory includes chapters that demonstrate how experimentation with form and ingenuity are part of what has been called "the black aesthetic." When authors use words to create unexpected interpretative spaces, they replicate the open structures of jazz, speech, and motion. Four overlapping terrains suggest routes of exploration: Transporting Black, Black-en-Scène, the Black Imaginary, and Hi-Fidelity Black. Arching over all of these imaginary regions is a meta-discourse of diaspora, the homeward-tilting, impossible concept that continuously binds concepts of blackness, performance, and theory. In constructing the volume, we deliberately include writings that move across the page as they communicate. To introduce the concepts of the chapters included here, as well as the organization of the volume, we offer riffs on the concepts that undergird the volume.

Riffing Diaspora

Diaspora is continual; it is the unfolding of experience into a visual, aural, kinesthetic culture of performance. Like skin, it is porous and permeable, flexible and self-repairing, finely spun and fragile. And like skin on a body, diaspora palpably protects us. We wrap ourselves in its possibilities, and they remind us of impossible connectivities. In this reminding—this bringing into consciousness of the intangible experience of a mythic past—we wear memory on our bodies; we see each other in skins that go together or sometimes belong apart. The connective skin of diaspora offers us protection from the coldness of individual isolation.

Maybe this is a way to think of the damage that the individualistic push of Eurocentric cultures does to communal, Earth-based cultures of an African diaspora. Surely black people can live each alone in the world. But we thrive in concert and call-and-response, in vibrant communication through a relationship to diaspora. In this way, diaspora becomes a very real process, one that can be experienced in the interplay of ideas that performance cultures bring forth.

Diaspora also serves as a process of unification. It brings together collective experiences around particular issues, forces, or social movements. Like all alliances, it is strategic. Most fascinating in current diaspora studies are the shifting points of origin for groups of folk designated as black. Does the journey begin in Africa, or the Americas, or the Caribbean? Does it end where you, the artist-scholar, has landed? Even as we define an African diaspora as expressed through the skin that may be marked black—through its gestures—the texture and color of these skins keep shifting through new alliances, new ways of codifying our collective experiences. Performance becomes a dialogue between ourselves and others as we "make sense" of diasporic journeys.

The volume begins with Transporting Black, where authors write about diasporic notions of black identity that travel across continental borders, even into intergalactic terrains. Anita Gonzalez and Nadine George-Graves use metaphors of navigation and spidering to unravel matrixes of thoughts and ideas that supersede geographic boundaries. Gonzalez situates black identities as a call-and-response of images within a grid of circulating international representations. By exploring traffic in minstrel tropes from Liverpool to North American Afro-Mexican settlements, Gonzalez documents diasporic circulations of performance and its representational capacities across cultural groups, geographies, and historical eras.

George-Graves investigates the trickster character of Anansi as an embodiment of the fluidity of African agency across unstable narratives. Hershini Bhana Young discards the imaginary of location and instead utilizes theoretical writings by Alexander Weheliye, Fred Moten, and Kodwo Eshun to reconsider the imagistic manipulation of alienness in the work of the Afro-futurist graphic artist John Jennings. Explorations of "see-jaying" and transport by alien spacecraft demonstrate black strategies of making impossible space tangible.

Finally, Melissa Blanco Borelli writes across the pages of personal and theoretical journeys as she examines the impact of the hip on *mulata* performance and reception in Cuba and New Orleans. Her elegiac rendering of the mulaticized *rumbera* as a commodity linked to exports of a Cuban imaginary conveys the melancholia that out-of-body transmissions of black performance routinely evoke. She aligns the phenomenological hauntings, always present in black representation, with a new historiography of mulata dance worship.

Black-en-Scène

Theater lies in the word, they say. However, in black performance, where the vernacular and the non-textual carry pertinent meanings, "text" is danced, mediated, literary, or contained within the enactment of sexuality. Uncovering these meanings within black performance—at times half-conscious, double-conscious, or fully conscious—is the task of authors in this volume. Lynching dramas and modern dance provide fuel for musings about how artists communicate multiple meanings through performance texts.

Plays are templates for performance, therefore play scripts deliberately allow many possibilities of interpretation. Dramas about black life reveal the potentials of inclusion and omission in theatrical circumstances. Plays about lynching enact and imply the terrorizing mob action too readily summoned in the United States. Koritha Mitchell argues that the emergence of this genre of dramatic literature confirmed complex negotiations of literacy, performance, and corporeal presence that resisted prevalent conceptions of African American capacity onstage and off. Her reading of early twentieth-century lynching plays offers a challenge to smooth recitations of American theater history, suggesting the broad reach of performance/texts as evidence of performance ideologies constantly in revision.

Queer texts of black performance arrive in implicit abundance, often as gestures or subtext of omission.[8] Carl Paris mines the enactment of "spirit" as a conduit for sexual and communal presence in work by choreographers

Ronald K. Brown and Reggie Wilson. For Paris, the performance of spirit grounds complex choreographic texts so that they might convey *ashé*, or the power to make things happen. In each of these chapters, the authors assume a broad theoretical reach in performative operation at the level of textual, or semiotic, analysis.

Rickerby Hinds offers evidence of an unexpected extension of black popular culture representations in the re-performance of seminal hip-hop artist album covers. For the emerging black performance artists who populated these gallery presentations of *Uncovered: A Pageant of Hip Hop Masters*, "performing the representation" surely acquired a frisson that exceeds the limits of these photographs.

Black Imaginary

Metaphorical spaces fragment presence across geographical and temporal sites. And yet where black performance may be mobilized, we find confirmation of black presence. Authors discover spaces of possibility in science fiction flying, or walking through devastated urban terrains. Soyica Diggs Colbert's spaceships allow Africans to fly where they have never—and have always—been, suggesting possibilities of diaspora beyond measure. Her exploration of work by Toni Morrison, George Clinton, and Kanye West attests to aural, visual, and conceptual affiliations within black performance across genre.

Evocation, provocation, mediation. Wendy S. Walters draws us a map of black persistence that is as journalistic as it is conceptual. Evocatively, she siphons off moments of geographical space and political events, always leaving it to the reader to map their placement and impact. In elegant performative writing, Walters renders an impossible complexity of black performance by its cartographical dimensionality. But what, and where, do we remember about black performance? Anna B. Scott's meditation pursues the geography of a cityscape that contains the rhythms, sounds, and pulses of black movements. For Scott, when we revisit terrains of familiarity, we are inevitably disappointed that the return is made strange in old steps done new. And yet we have to walk that walk again.

Hi-Fidelity Black

Sounds permeate skins, as rhythmic impulses career the body. Keens and rumbles erupt to demonstrate the emotional states of the performer. Guttural languages click off tongues encountering foreign dialects. Black performance is reinvented within the cacophony. Writing about sound challenges equations of skin color with cultural knowledge even as it reinforces that there can be—must be—some connection between the adversity of living black and the possibilities of ecstasy.

Collectively the writings here press against the brain's inner ear to reconfigure notions of aurality. When we read about sound, multidisciplinarity takes control of the experience. When we know the sounds being referenced by a literary text—"know" the sound, in the deep way of having lived with it and its progenitors—we experience the text at hand in unexpected arousal. Black performance theorists write about black sound with a velocity of affect and expectation. We expect our best music to speak to its own history and the histories of its sonic families. These families of affect are indeed of the skin and sinew, even as they are of the inner ear, the intellect, and the dance.

Tavia Nyong'o begins his scrutiny of Little Richard's sound with an autobiographical account of the singer's physical disability and its queering capacities. Within Little Richard's family, queer physical presence predicts the queer performance affect that became his hallmark. Jason King wonders at the fantastical aura surrounding Michael Jackson's final film performance. Citing a performative presence that surpasses Jackson's oversized celebrity, King interrogates the sensuality of an entirely mediated black performance, at once fragile, spontaneous, and magical. For Daphne A. Brooks, feminist praxis suggests a familial of sound to align a stellar array of performers whose "new black feminist noise" pursues nothing less than a new world order. Framing her close exploration of Nina Simone and Adrienne Kennedy's sonic futurism with discussions of celebrities Moms Mabley and Butterfly McQueen, Brooks imagines the outrageous impact and presence of things not heard. Thomas F. DeFrantz queries the relationships of "cool" to an emergent global hip-hop habitus that ties black performance to adolescent physicalities across geography. He asserts that contemporary corporealities become more and more recognizably black in their physical manifestations, as a global cohort of youth mature via the sonic imperatives of popular hip-hop musics.

The chapters in this book confirm the expanding presence of creative labor expended in theorizing black performance. Building on a varied literature in motion, we hope to contribute to the library of writings that offer varied and unexpected elaborations of performance and its urgencies, capacities, and the terms of its recognition. Surely there might be dozens of texts theorizing aspects of black performance rather than only a handful.[9] If theory encompasses unexpected ways to organize information and mobilize tools of analysis, the present volume demonstrates that black performance theory has only begun to uncover its resources to inspire creative intellectual practice.

Notes

1. Among many publications concerned with black performance in this era, see Bean, Hatch, and McNamara; Chude-Sokei; Elam and Krasner; and Lindfors.

2. Critical writing by artists and authors emerged in magazines and journals, including the *Crisis* (magazine) and the *Liberator* (magazine); and in the black press, such as the *Chicago Defender*, the *Philadelphia Tribune*, and the *New York Amsterdam News*.

3. See Baker; Cunard; Emery; Levine; Lomax; Mercer; Southern, *Music of Black Americans*; White and White.

4. Written in 1964, the essay was republished in 1966. Jones, "Revolutionary Theatre."

5. Jose Esteban Muñoz effectively defines and parses the concept of disidentification in his book *Disidentifications*.

6. Theorist Julia Kristeva inspired engagement with the concept of intertextuality. See *Desire in Language*.

7. See especially Madison, "Performing Theory/Embodied Writing"; and Pollock.

8. See especially Johnson and Henderson.

9. Among recent offerings that explore black performance theory, see Batiste; Brody, *Punctuation*; Brown; Catanese; Chatterjea; Jackson, *Real Black*; Jones, Moore, and Bridgforth; Moten, *In the Break*; and Young, *Embodying Black Experience*.

PART I   /   Transporting Black

1 / Anita Gonzalez

NAVIGATIONS

Diasporic Transports and Landings

An aerial grid of cultural migrations in 1840 might show a satellite hovering over the Atlantic Ocean, recording data as boatloads of Africans land on various shores of a circum-Atlantic landscape. Once grounded, African migrants would begin to enact performances of social disenfranchisement. Both historically and in contemporary contexts, these transatlantic voyages, and their corresponding landing points—New York, Jamestown, Hispaniola, Cuba, Rio de Janeiro, Amsterdam, Liverpool—have become sites for negotiating new identities with other ethnic and social groups. Historical maps depict transatlantic slave migrations as triangle voyages. Ships laden with textiles travel to Africa, where they buy and sell. Ships of enslaved workers travel to the Americas and empty their loads. Finally, ships of sugar and/or cotton travel back to Europe. Economy, transport, and territory are part and parcel of this international exchange of blackness. In the colonial worlds of the sixteenth through the twentieth centuries Africans were just one of many economies of goods and services that moved across the seas. Each destination was a new beginning—a new origin point—for a diaspora experience.

Now imagine the aerial grid realigned so that the destinations—points outside of mainland Africa—are origin points for negotiating new social and political experiences. As conversations about the African diaspora broaden, it is impossible to ignore the complex interactions and transformations that constitute the field. "Recognizing that diasporic connections are made and remade, undermined and transformed means that they are neither universally constituted nor static" (Clarke and Thomas, 19). Too often,

FIGURE 1.1. Amy Papaelias, "Navigations of Blackness—1," 2013. Courtesy of the artist.

African diaspora performance is read as a response to Euro-American or white frames of reference. This stance ignores the complex interplay of African descendants with other ethnic groups in the panorama of social identities. Jacqueline Nassy Brown simplifies this notion, asserting: "Diaspora is better understood as a relation rather than a condition" (38). The interplay of ethnic communities at each local site is what constitutes transnational experiences of diaspora (Fryer; Small; Nassy Brown). Concepts about blackness are developed within the subject "blacks" and also constructed by others in response to the presence of Africans and African descendants.

Performances of blackness were unnecessary before African encounters with other ethnicities and their social practices. In the absence of common languages, performance—physical, vocal, and emotional—captures the ongoing negotiation of social status. This means that points of origin, claims of authenticity, national or racial inclusion, are all relative. This chapter examines two case studies, one contemporary and one historical, in which black performance is part of an ongoing and evolving dialogue with other ethnicities for economic and social status. My project focuses on local mediated practices that are responses to African presence. At two distinct geographic sites—Liverpool, England, and Oaxaca, Mexico—non-black performers use African identities as cultural collateral for a social acceptance that approximates whiteness. I call this process of negotiating with blackness a social navigation. Performers of all ethnicities learn the social codes of power and subservience, and then use performance to jockey public opinion as they steer a path toward upward mobility. In Liverpool, transplanted Irishmen use minstrelsy to distance themselves from the rapidly growing African and Black Caribbean community. In Oaxaca, the Chontal Native Americans impersonate the rebellion of their Negrito neighbors. In both cases, "black performance" requires a masquerade in which layers of applied makeup, or the impermeable surface of the physical mask, substitute for inferior social status. Social whiteness or mainstream acceptance is the ultimate goal for each of these ethnic communities that seek to distance themselves from negritude.

Smoked Irish and Whiteness

Whiteness studies of Irish heritage generally focus on the mid- to late nineteenth century, a historical time period when Irish populations migrated en masse to mainland England and consequently to the United States. The potato famine that ravaged Ireland between 1845 and 1855 was a direct impetus for this relocation. Poor Irish migrants congregated in ghettos and slums—the North End in Liverpool and Little Five Points in New York, where the transplanted "white Negroes" and real Negroes rubbed shoulders and became nearly indistinguishable. Stereotypical representations of Irish, while fictional, circulated and perpetuated ideas about Irish lifestyles. The Irish, like the African Americans in the United States, were associated with rural practices and agricultural communities. Irish were commonly referred to as "niggers turned inside out," while blacks were called "smoked Irish." Noel Ignatiev, in his foundational text *How the Irish Became White*, describes how constructs of race were used by the Catholic Irish to move from their status as an oppressed "race" to an oppressing group within the Americas. Nineteenth-century racial notions fixed the Irish at the lowest rung of the Caucasian hierarchy so that "by the 1860s the 'representative Irishman' was to all appearances an anthropoid ape" (Curtis, 2). Stigmatized but not subjugated, the Irish, especially in Liverpool, were far from passive victims of such prejudice. The *Emerald*, "the first Irish Magazine ever brought out in Liverpool," drew critical attention to "Irish misrepresentations, for the vulgar stage representation of them has contributed more than even their own worse conduct has done toward making our countrymen in England objects of contempt, or of a condescending patronage (like the humoring of a lunatic or wayward buffoon) which is far harder to bear than down right contempt" (Belchem, 14).

Irish presence within newly formed urban enclaves of the nineteenth century provided a site for the alchemy of racial transformation. Trapped within unsanitary ghettos without food or running water, the two ethnicities, Irish and African, competed for jobs requiring unskilled labor. They drank and caroused together, and gave birth to mixed-race children, who further confused the racial categories designed by British and American social codes. Liverpool's "Black People of Mixed Origins," like Americas's mulattos, were ostracized through social codes and purged from mainstream cultural lives of both England and the United States with national laws that chose not to distinguish between the "filth" of its lowest-class citizens (Small, 515). As poverty persisted, how were the Irish to socially advance and overcome their racial stigma? Penal codes prevented them from voting, holding public office, or living within the boundaries of incorporated towns (Ignatiev, 34). Progressive movement toward social acceptance was a fraught path for the new settlers.

Performance was a strategic, vernacular way of publicly demonstrating the differences between the two immigrant groups. Over a one-hundred-year period, Irish residents strove to assimilate into the white working class and to advance within the social cauldron of the United States and British politics. Performance tropes captured the evolving social realignments that characterized this collective shift. Pubs and street corners were cultural breeding grounds for ongoing exchanges of performance activities in which song and dance competitions, fiddling, brawls, and drunken sea shanties pitted performers against one another. The dance competition between John Diamond and William Henry Lane (also known as Master Juba) exemplifies this type of performance exchange. This widely publicized dance battle of rhythm and foot clogging traversed the Atlantic Ocean as the two dancers competed in both London and New York. Their competitive performances were but one of many types of ethnic trade-offs. In 1841 Charles Dickens witnessed jig competitions at the black-owned Almack's club on Orange Street in the Little Five Points district of New York (Anbinder, 173). Five Points housed many dance clubs and drinking establishments. In both singing and dancing exchanges the stakes were high. Successful entertainers received monetary awards of as much as $500 and were given the chance to travel and perform in Liverpool, London, and other British cities. The dance traditions of the immigrants—Africans and Irish, like the ethnicities of its practitioners—were conflated and considered indistinguishable. However, competitive trade-offs could ensure that one ethnicity was the victor over the other. Later, more structured entertainments like touring acts and variety shows would popularize the vernacular dances. Local audiences began to attend public spectacles, and the spectacles became forums for distinguishing between blacks and whites.

Liverpool Trading

Liverpool, England, and New York City are potent points for discussion of Irish and African American/black British exchanges because both cities served as entry points to their respective countries. The itinerant nature of industry, coupled with the backbreaking labor and isolating lifestyles, created a kind of lawlessness within the dock communities. At the same time, for the ambitious worker, there was the possibility of using the sailing life as a way to learn about new places, acculturate, or perhaps settle in on either side of the "water." Men and women of the ports established camaraderie with one another. Social networking allowed workers to exchange knowledge of neighborhoods, opportunities, dangers, and alliances on both sides of the Atlantic. Performance was a mechanism for information exchange as well as a justification for moving from place to place. As workers became migrants, immigrants, and citizens, the lawlessness of the ports were muted by civic organizations that established moral codes and cultural policies.

Liverpool is a port city with a long history of multicultural encounters. In 1664, the small village was merely a shipping stop along the rugged western coast of Great Britain. One hundred years later, as the physical infrastructure of the port improved and more sailors migrated into the area, Liverpool was poised to become the major slave port of the English-speaking world. The docks evolved into a multilingual site of cultural meetings. Local merchants prospered through the exchange of human cargo for agricultural goods. The working class excelled at sailing, stocking, and building ships for cross-Atlantic transport that fueled local and colonial economies. The docks needed laborers, and the Irish—poor and living in close proximity to the port—were the preferred choice for workers. Once settled in Liverpool as in New York, the Irish lived side by side with enslaved and free African people. Even after the decline of the slave economy, black seamen and sailors continued to live within mixed-race communities. Indeed, Stephen Small describes Liverpool as an anomaly within England because of its unique racial and racialized "half-caste residents." However the passionate, insular social practices of Liverpudlian "Scousers" excluded black "Scousers" from employment opportunities (513, 517). Historically, free and partially skilled black workers were an economic threat to struggling Irish immigrants. As a result, African descendants, traveling between Liverpool and the United States, formed their own network of transatlantic alliances.

There are several examples of African diaspora theatrical exchanges that were spawned by the Liverpool trades. Perhaps the most well known is the case of Mr. William Brown, who founded the African Grove Theater, the first African theater company in the United States, in 1821. Mr. Brown came to know about the art of theater through his service on ships that sailed between the Caribbean, New York, and Liverpool. James Hewlett, the actor he hired for performances in his summer African Grove, was also a steward along this line. Hewlett's skills as a tailor, coupled with his firsthand knowledge of British Shakespeare performances, allowed him to introduce theatrical performances to the "free colored people" of New York (McAllister, 43–47). Another excellent example of a Liverpool exchange was the appearance in 1866 of Mr. Hague's Slave Troupe of Georgia Minstrels. Hoping to build upon the successes of the "real negro impersonator" companies in the United States, Mr. Hague decided to bring a troupe of emancipated African Americans to Liverpool. The results were disastrous. When they traveled to Liverpool in 1866, the black entertainers were not well received. The heavily Irish city of Liverpool preferred to see interpretations of blackness designed and performed by whites. The entrepreneur eventually fired his black actors, leaving several behind to become integrated into the black Liverpudlian community (Southern, "Origin and Development," 10).

Minstrelsy Archetypes

North American minstrelsy, or blackface performance, was introduced by the Virginia Minstrels in 1842 and expanded upon by dozens of other performance companies throughout the nineteenth century.[1] Minstrel shows in the United States were variety revues that included comic skits, political stump speeches, sentimental songs glorifying life on the plantation, and dance numbers. The art form was a precursor to vaudevillian entertainment. When innovative white performers like the Virginia Minstrels developed blackface minstrelsy, the Irish working class in both England and the United States embraced the genre as a mechanism for distancing itself from popular imagery personifying the Irish as poor, uncouth, immigrant, outsiders to the civiliz(ing) nation. Minstrelsy was ideally suited for this transformation; its revue-style performance format could be utilized for political ends. Not only could the show's contents be adapted for local social commentary but the genre itself, by ridiculing southern African American lifestyles, served a political purpose. The ignorant and uncouth manners of the southern Negro provided strong contrast to the humanity and relative whiteness of the Irish immigrants.

Perhaps a word needs to be said about the efficacy of stereotypes and archetypes in promoting social standing. Africans in the Americas have long been subject to external exaggerations of racial qualities. Phenotypes—

physical characteristics—have evolved into stereotypes, which in turn have evolved into archetypes. In the United States, I would identify the Uncle Tom figure as an example of this evolution. Under systems of slavery in the United States, African workers were infantilized and assumed to be less-than-human beings. African men in particular were expected to take on servile roles and to acknowledge the superiority of the white slaveholders. Often, fearing punishment, the African men would perform tasks with heads bowed, or take action without question in compliance with their master's wishes. Nineteenth-century texts like *Uncle Tom's Cabin* by Harriet Beecher Stowe popularized images of the southern servile Negro. With time, this stereotypical image of the compliant, servile black man became a cultural icon—an archetypal representation of black identity. Today, the remnants of this iconography are visible on commercial products like Uncle Ben's rice.

Minstrel shows cast African Americans as ignorant creatures content with the slow and lazy life of the American South. These portrayals complemented perceptions of the Irish that had long circulated in derogatory cartoons that depicted the Irish as animalistic creatures, "bog trotters," ogres, or pigs. The political efficacy of minstrelsy was manifest on both sides of the Atlantic. John Belchem writes that in Liverpool "blackface minstrelsy became an Americanizing ritual, offering socially insecure Irish migrants a sense of superiority over the blacks with whom they were once identified (labeled respectively as 'white negroes' and 'smoked Irish') and from whom they were able to distance themselves by parody" (148). Spectators in the United States viewed early minstrel acts as a way of presenting the manners of "real Negros." Northern audiences in particular, who were unfamiliar with the lifestyles and circumstances of southern agricultural plantations, turned to minstrel shows as a popular form of reality cultural exchange. Liverpudlians used the minstrel format differently. Black representations were not designed to demonstrate the reality of foreign cultural lifestyles; rather, they were utilized by Irish performers to demonstrate the superiority of Irish cultural practices over the backward manners and mannerisms of the black American / black British resident. Because the Liverpool Irish had long been exposed to Africans and African cultural practices, they were familiar with both the nobility of continental Africans and the misery of enslaved Africans. This new character—the partially civilized black clown—fulfilled a Liverpool Irish cultural need to redefine black identities in such a manner as to construct a cultural wall between black Brits and their Irish neighbors. Histories of Irish discrimination in Liverpool partially justify such practices.

Belchem describes how the Irish community of Liverpool incorporated the tropes of blackface minstrel performance into neighborhood performance halls. "In a bewildering process of cultural and commercial fusion and borrowing, 'negro entertainment' spread beyond the professional stage to become the main attraction in the lecture halls and meeting rooms of Irish and Catholic associational culture. One of the most popular troupes, the Emerald Minstrels, adjusted the Christy-style format to conclude with a one-act tableau suitably transposed from the conventional setting, an idealized paternalist plantation in the Deep South, to a warm and welcoming Irish domestic scene" (149). By incorporating the tropes of minstrelsy into the community gathering spaces of the Liverpool Irish, Emerald Minstrels were able to distance themselves from grotesque characterizations of their own ethnicity while at the same time subjectively situating the African American/black characters as socially and culturally inept. These altered representations of the underclass undoubtedly boosted the self-esteem of the local cultural associations. Meanwhile, black minstrel acts continued to appeal to audiences who, in later decades, supported African American revues and musicals that included many of the same stereotypical characters. Touring presentations continued to include performance styles particularly associated with African American "old slave life"—cakewalks, buck dances, and sand dances. In effect, minstrel performances set a precedent for ongoing exchanges of musical revues and song and dance acts. In the realm of black musical theater, one of the earliest all-black efforts of this kind to make its way to England was an unusual variety show with an oriental as well as an African tinge, a production called Oriental America. During the 1897–98 season a Liverpool critic described it: "The ludicrous mirth-making Negro sketch called The Blackville Derby epitomising in very large degree the true type of Negro fun, character, frolic and pastimes, was given at the Court Theatre on Monday with considerable success" (Riis, 52). African American minstrel tropes peaked with the tour of the musical *In Dahomey* in 1903. Irish appropriations of blackface minstrelsy enabled the Irish, a population clearly segregated from the mainstream of Protestant British society, to resist ostracism by publicly impersonating a presumably lower form of humanity—the black African. The Irish, by establishing themselves as the "middlemen" of cultural production, could ascend the social ladder in a strategic move toward whiteness.

Native American Renditions of Blackness

In a similar way, middlemen in Mexico on the other side of the Atlantic have used impersonations of African identities to distance themselves from the lowest echelons of Mesoamerican society. Today, in the twenty-first century, Native American community members, who live in close proximity to Afro-Mexican settlements, stage annual festival events in which they wear black masks to represent their darker-skinned neighbors. These dances, called Negritos, capture archetypal beliefs about the moral codes and behaviors of African descendants in Mexico. Within this psychological landscape, residues of blackness are assigned, appropriated, and utilized for social commentary. Each appearance of the Negrito in Mexican community dances marks a history of relationships between neighboring populations. In some cases the dancers wear jet-black wooden masks with exaggerated features: red lips, wild woolly hair, chiseled features. Representations like these capture archetypal beliefs about black personalities. Even though the masks depict retro stereotypical phenotypes, the facial features lie in stark contrast with contemporary outfits—urban suits and T-shirts that the dancers use as costumes. It is the contemporary nature of the characters that adds to the vitality of the performance commentary; the costumes reflect a reality of ongoing encounters that residents have with local Afro-Mexican communities. Patricia Ybarra describes this use of dialogic performance when she writes: "Performances use stage and civic space, juxtapose textual and embodied actions, and orchestrate various media such as dance, music, and narrative so that their audiences and participants may see and experience their *productions* of identities and political uses in process" (10).

Violent encounters between slaves and masters, and between blacks and indigenous communities, are peppered throughout Mexican history. The eastern shores of Mexico experienced the first maroon community of the New World when Nyanga Yanga founded a settlement near Córdoba, Veracruz, in 1580. The community maintained its independence for thirty years by raiding trade caravans and intermarrying with local Native American residents. Spaniards overtook the town in 1609. However, after Yanga made an impassioned plea in which he defended his raids as compensation for what had been denied him as a slave, he was eventually allowed to maintain the community under the name of San Lorenzo de los Negros. Today the town, renamed Yanga in 1932, is one of the few Mexican sites that celebrate Afro-Mexican heritage.[2] Similar maroon communities were established in parts of the states of Guerrero, Colima, and Oaxaca, where slaves were imported to work in the mines and in the fishing industry.

There were also relatively isolated communities of black workers in the central Mexican states of Michoacán, Guanajuato, Querétaro, Nuevo León, Tabasco, and Tamaulipas. In sixteenth-century Guanajuato, for example, archival documents indicate that Afro-Mexicans were employed as cattle ranchers, muleteers, and domestic servants as well as overseers and foremen of Native American and African mine workers. Black servants in this region labored on small ranches, in agriculture, and occasionally as house servants in the newly formed colonial villages. Colonial residents who could afford domestic slaves gained prestige and social status and frequently willed their human property to their descendants.[3] The two types of social arrangements for blacks, as domestic ranch hands and as escaped renegades, explain in part the types of characters that appear and reappear in dances about blacks. For example, Totonac Negrito dances in Papantla feature a black woman who cures her son from a snakebite while a line of dancers help her to complete the ritual. This representation references the *bruja* or *curandera* figure that is a part of Santería practices on the eastern coast of Mexico. In contrast, the Chontal Negrito dances that I describe here present violent gangster-like blacks who invade the town and demand a fair share of community recognition. In Michoacán, the Negrito dancers are tall, stately figures. They wear ribbons and appear to have power and stature (Toor).

The dances described here represent the Afro-Mexican as a disruptive outsider who disturbs the peace of the local Chontal indigenous community. Historical events explain, in part, the images that circulate about Afro-Mexicans. Francisco Camero Rodriguez writes that blacks, in response to their social status, from the moment that they set foot in New Spain, began to struggle for their freedom and wrote their actions in brilliant pages of bravery, audacity, sacrifice, and organization.[4] These actions, which went against existing societal laws, were construed as violent and immoral. When blacks were successful at establishing and maintaining separate settlements, they used warfare and violence to maintain their strongholds. This is especially true of the Costa Chica, where maroon communities interacted and intermingled with indigenous communities, using armed resistance to hold their territories. Later, in the twentieth century, the isolated mountains of Guerrero and Oaxaca became asylums for rebels, insurgents, military or police defectors, and drug lords. Paulette Ramsay describes "bands of soldiers" that were formed to combat the violence of the *guachos* (army) and *la motorizada* (military police) (Ramsay, 446–64). Music and dance performances memorialize the valor, violence, and resistance of the coast. Characters like the active devil or the cantankerous bull express a continuing stance of rebellion on the coast. *Corrido* songs in particular describe the exploits and fighting abilities of coastal figures. Both historical storytelling songs like "De la Entrada de Juarez" or "Corrido de los Zapatistas de San Nicolás" and contemporary emotive songs like "Cuando yo Haya Muerto" glorify the fiery, valiant personality of the renegade warrior.[5]

Spaniards also used blacks to control the natives. When the Spaniards arrived in the New World, they were already familiar with using African labor. The wars against the Moors had brought many African people into Spanish territories. Some of these Africans were familiar with horses and knew the Spanish language. It was natural for them to be assigned the task of overseeing indigenous workers. Peter Stern writes that "they [blacks and Indians] were either neutral towards each other or they joined together in mutual opposition against European control. Where blacks were placed over Indians, relationships were usually antagonistic" (189). Interestingly, Afro-Mexicans also served in the militia of the Spanish viceroyalty. Ben Vinson III has an excellent book that provides extensive historical documentation of the activities of the free colored militia during the late eighteenth century. By 1793 Mexico's free colored people represented almost 10 percent of the colony's population (Vinson). Colored militias, concentrated along the coastal rim of New Spain, maintained positions of authority and privilege within the emerging colony. "Service in the *pardo* militia did not offer a means to escape the confines of race; rather, it better allowed them the ability to negotiate race's meaning" (Vinson, 225). The black military leader was a unique combination of Spanish values and African physicality. Indigenous and mestizo communities viewed the black militia with trepidation and at times enacted legislation to contain it.

The Spaniards created a complex system of castes and racial categorizations to keep domestic blacks within limited social categories (Stern). They were present within the "civilized" ranks of Spanish society, but forbidden from intermingling. As a result, the reasons that Native Americans "dance black" are as varied as the historical circumstances that bring Afro-Mexicans in close proximity to indigenous and mestizo communities. Here I would like to examine archetypes of blackness that are appropriated within a Native American community in the state of Oaxaca. In one annual festival in the village of Huamelula, masked performers play the roles of Turks, blacks, and an alligator in order to reexamine the social order of the community. The Huamelula ritual is a performance that allows the community to reinvestigate its relationship with external and internal histories. Black masking—the adoption of a black mask to represent the lowest echelon—is utilized in a more nuanced way than in the spectacles of minstrelsy.

The Huamelula Ritual

The theatrical reenactment begins with the arrival of wealthy foreign visitors known as the Turks, who enter the town square in a rolling float decorated to look like a boat. Their pompous entrance speaks to their high status. They wear long-faced yellow masks with painted beards and perform pretentiously, speaking with a Spanish accent that would be similar to the sound of a British accent on American ears.[6] Once the Turks are ensconced within the landscape of the town, the Black men or Negritos arrive. These characters arrive in a disruptive way wearing red bandanas wrapped around their heads, bandanas that punctuate and contrast with the pitch-black masks. While the bandanas capture the idea that the invaders are workers or gang members, the characters also wear suit jackets and casual street attire that give them an air of relaxed urbanity. The black invaders represent a cross between urban ghetto youth and coastal laborers. The Negritos disturb the peace of the community as soon as they arrive. On the village streets they block the road with sticks, claiming their territory as they prevent others from entering the town. After seeing the disorder that the blacks bring to the village, the Turks, the elite outsiders, go to the mayor and ask him to allow them to punish the blacks for their conduct. The mayor reluctantly gives his consent for the Turks to discipline the Negritos. The actions of the blacks and the Turks in this dramatic enactment underscore the idea that the Chontal regard the Negritos as a part of their community. Although they do not approve of their disruptive behavior, they consider the Negrito side of the story before agreeing to have them punished for their actions. With the consent of the mayor, the Turks gather up the black men and bring them, with ropes, to the town square, where they suspend them, individually, upside down from a tall pole. Symbolically they are being murdered—hung upside down like the Antichrist. Once the killings begin, a group of Negritos goes to the mayor and complains about the executions taking place on the town square. The mayor is surprised. He says that the Turks were to punish the blacks, not kill them. He gives the Negritos permission to punish the Turks. The blacks, now vindicated, gather up the Turks and throw them into the town jail, where they are punished for their inhumanity.

The "black" performance of the Chontals in Huamelula captures a perceived relationship with Afro-Mexicans at a particular point in time. Representations change each year and with each set of performers. "Acting out" Chontal relationships with Afro-Mexican communities is just one component of a much larger scenario in which the community reimagines group encounters and alliances. In some ways, the dances capitalize on global stereotypes about African identities; yet in other ways they uniquely embody a specific local history.

Most societies create stereotypes about their poorer or more marginal residents, and in Mexico, preconceptions about Afro-Mexicans abound. Amranta Arcadia Castillo Gómez, in a study of language and perceptions on the Costa Chica, found that mestizo and indigenous residents consistently described blacks as lazy, unreligious, violent, argumentative, and heavy drinkers (Castillo Gómez). These assessments are negative stereotypes, and the perceptions are reflected in the language the people speak when they reference Afro-Mexicans. Dances also reveal these types of negative attitudes—particularly those in which performers impersonate blacks in an unflattering way, as criminals or thieves. In part, these character descriptions are designed to differentiate the "us" from the "them"; to distinguish between ethnic and social communities. By associating blacks, the "others," with negative traits, the communities are able to attest to their own "goodness." Again, the Castillo Gómez study indicates that Mixtecs, for example, describe blacks as opposite of themselves. Mixtecs work hard, but blacks are lazy. Mixtecs are very religious, but blacks are not religious. There are black/Mixtec marriages, but they are looked at disdainfully (277). In effect, the Mixtecs describe the Afro-Mexicans as "not-us," a social designation that impacts the self-esteem of Afro-Mexicans who reside in the area.

In contrast, the Nahua people who live in the mountains just inland of the coastal areas have created a festival dance called Los Costeños in which Afro-Mexican Negritos dance as fisherman. The Nahua dances present somewhat positive images of Afro-Mexicans. The Negritos first challenge and then stalk and kill an alligator. The capture of the alligator represents an act of valor. In effect, the Nahua people wear the mask of blackness in order to evoke the valor of their neighboring Afro-Mexican communities. What is interesting about the Mexican performance model is that Native American community members cover their faces with solid masks of blackness as they impersonate their neighbors. Completely hidden behind the mask, they use active gesture to act out their own unique understandings about Afro-Mexican culture. In contrast to minstrelsy, where characters are fixed, the Mexican performances do not re-create a static imaginary about who blacks are. Rather, each masked character that appears within the local community dances is performed in response to local assessments of the Afro-Mexican character.

Coda—Masking Out

Black Liverpudlian Laurence Westgaph walks the streets of Liverpool narrating historical sites that demonstrate an ongoing African diaspora presence within Liverpool, the "European cultural capital" of 2009. With political astuteness, he uses his slavery walking tour to insert black presence into a whitewashed landscape of monocultural history. Yet the history in Liverpool, like the history in New York, has always included a contested response to African diaspora presence. Slavery tours, a spin-off of the Slavery Museum that opened in 2007, are popular in 2012. Their interpretation of Liverpudlian histories relegates African presence to the colonial era and negates the ongoing, contested mixed-race histories of Liverpool's residential areas. In a similar way, performers in the indigenous and mixed-race communities of western Mexico pace through the dusty avenues of local villages re-creating a history that is responsive to local myths and imagery about blacks. In each case interpretations of the social spaces respond to ongoing negotiations of black presence within multiracial settings. Chontal and Nahua communities take on black identities to comment upon and construct identities within their own locales, while nineteenth-century Irish minstrel performers, in response to Irish stereotypes, distanced themselves from tropes of primitive blackness by replacing Emerald minstrelsy with blackface minstrelsy at Irish community centers. Collectively, these acts of black performance demonstrate a flexible restaging of blackness that mediates the status of disempowered populations at each diaspora site.

Notes

1. These volumes provide overviews of minstrelsy in the United States: Bean, Hatch, and McNamara; Hill and Hatch; Stearns and Stearns; and Woll.

2. Historians prominent in the field of Afro-Mexican studies who have documented maroon communities include Carroll, 90–92; Jiménez Román, 8–9; Palmer, *Slaves of the White God*, 128–30; Cruz Carretero, Martínez Maranto, and Santiago Silva, 11–41.

3. Domestic ranch hands played an important role in the settlement and anticolonial activities of Mexico. See Guevara Sanginés, 156–57; MacGregor and García Martínez, 172–75; Martinez Montiel; Martinez Montiel and Reyes G.; Nettl Ross, 116–21.

4. "En cuanto a su proyección social, desde que puso los pies en la Nueva España, el negro inició su lucha para liberarse, escribiendo con sus acciones, páginas resplandecientes de valor, audacia, sacrificio, y organización" (Rodríguez).

5. The lyrics to these corridos are printed in Rodriguez; and Ramsay.

6. This information comes from the photographer George O. Jackson Jr., who photographed the Huamelula feast during 1990 and 1991.

DIASPORIC SPIDERING

Constructing Contemporary Black Identities

Diaspora: global dispersion of Africans due to the transatlantic slave trade
and the subsequent fallout.

Anansi: a folkloric trickster figure; a spider. Also a god, a man, and sometimes a woman.

Web 5.0: a way of searching for information in the new millennium.

Diasporic Spidering: The multidirectional process by which people of
African descent define their lives. The lifelong ontological gathering of
information by going out into the world and coming back to the self.

The complexities of the spiderweb interest me and draw me to the
figure of Anansi. Anansi was/is a god, man, sometimes woman
and spider. Like the signifying monkey described by Henry Louis
Gates Jr., he is at times a trickster but at other times the one tricked.
He rarely works for his food, which leads some to call him lazy. Yet
he always manages to eat, which leads some to call him resourceful.
In most of his tales, Anansi manages to procure food and shelter
by deceiving unwitting animals and humans. And even in those
tales where his plans backfire, Anansi manages to survive to play
his games another day. In Ghana, Anansi is a messenger god existing as a liminal presence for the purposes of unsettling organized
society. In Jamaica, he becomes a freedom fighter and a symbol of
survival, at nearly any cost. His godhead is sacrificed for the benefit of more humanly practical pursuits. This complex character is
at once a revolutionary hero and a petty thief. He does not always
represent the morally correct path and moves readers/audiences
to consider him beyond binaries of good and evil. However, his
saving grace is that he uses ingenuity rather than brute force and

more often than not triumphs. As Emily Zobel Marshall claims, "It is vital to remember that Anansi is a master of transformation and metamorphosis and therefore *resists* fixed definitions and interpretation" (11).

Anansi stories have significant reach, occurring throughout the traditional African diaspora (West Africa, Europe, the Caribbean, and the Americas). They span the globe like a giant game of cultural telephone, taking on local nuances influencing and being influenced by other stories (e.g., the Cherokee Tar Wolf story) while maintaining diasporic similarities to other Anansi stories. Two stories in particular, "Anansi Becomes the Owner of All Stories" and "Anansi and the Pot of Wisdom," have Anansi negotiating with Nyame, the sky god, for sole proprietorship of vital qualities—history (or memory) and knowledge. These quests articulate projects crucial to critical race theory, for in addition to denying life, liberty, and the pursuit of happiness (and/or property) the transatlantic slave trade and the resulting systems of slavery and oppression also denied heritage and education to slaves. Anansi's strategies in these two stories are foundational to the theories of Diasporic Spidering.

In "Anansi and the Pot of Wisdom," Anansi has been given all of the wisdom in the world by Nyame. Anansi, wanting to keep all of the wisdom for himself, puts it in a large pot and looks for a place to hide it so that no one else will have any knowledge. He finds a tall silk-cotton tree, attaches the pot around his waist in front of him, and attempts to climb the tree to hide the pot in the branches. Even though the trunk is very slippery, Anansi is sure that he can climb it since he has eight legs. Several times he tries and each time he falls back down to earth. His son Kuma, who had been watching, asks his father why he doesn't just tie the pot to his back instead of his front so that he can get a better grip on the tree. When Anansi hears this he becomes enraged that clearly Kuma has some wisdom and he, in fact, does not have all the wisdom in his pot. In his anger, Anansi throws the pot, which smashes, releasing the wisdom. Because of this, Anansi is said to be responsible for wisdom being everywhere in the world (even the animals have some). Like Pandora and Eve, Anansi's actions allow knowledge into the world through a fatal flaw. The message, however, is clear—no one has all of the wisdom, so it must be sought in multiple places. Also, no one should deny or be denied knowledge.

In "Anansi Becomes the Owner of All Stories," Anansi desires to be remembered even though he has no heroic accomplishments. Instead, he figures that if he can get all of the stories to be "Anansi stories" then he will have to be remembered whenever anyone tells a story. In some versions he goes to Tiger, who owns the stories under the title "Tiger Stories," but in others it is Nyame. In both versions, Anansi must bring back three conquests: the snake, the bees or hornets, and the fairies or dwarves (some versions say a leopard). In order to capture these prizes, Anansi, the deceptively simple spider, must use his wits rather than strength since he is no match for the speed and power of his adversaries. In some versions his wife gives him his strategies; in others he goes it alone. When he succeeds, Nyame gives him all of the stories. The staying power of Anansi stories all over the world attests to his prize. Diasporic heritage survives despite the odds, and Anansi's processes of journeying, gathering (wisdom and memory), gaining insight, sharing, and connecting are Diasporic Spiderings.

I first encountered Anansi stories as a child on one of many trips to Jamaica to visit my maternal relatives. My Aunt Gerry, a schoolteacher in Spanish Town, bought for me, from the Spanish Town library, *African Folk Tales* (a compendium that had a number of Anansi tales in it) as well as a copy of *Anansi and Miss Lou*. The African folktales book is clearly a colonialist project published by Oxford University Press in the 1950s. Even though it makes reference to the African origins of Anansi tales, it is not written in dialect and the cadence of the writing is distinctly British. My young mind, of course, did not process this complex intercultural relationship. But for me, Anansi was a distinctly Caribbean figure tied up in my experiences in Jamaica, connecting with family and contrasting with my white suburban Catholic school teachings. Surely my extended family wanted me, the first member of the family born in the United States, to know something of my "authentic" Jamaican roots. Yet at least half of my initial cultural encounter with Anansi was presented through the lens of cultural hegemony and colonialism. The *Anansi and Miss Lou* book, written by Jamaican storyteller Miss Lou, was written in dialect and on the surface seems the more "authentic" set of folktales. But if I had only that book, I would not have considered Anansi African. The concept of authenticity in African American cultural production has been well rehearsed, so I'll resist the theoretical traps of piecing out authentic representations of Anansi and accompanying value judgments. However, this story points to the complexity of cultural identification that is too often oversimplified. Recent work in African American humanities and social sciences touches on these ideas and helps me articulate the significance of my proposed reimagining of African diaspora through performance. Particularly useful are some of the theories of Kwame Anthony Appiah, Paul Gilroy, Daphne Brooks, and others. Building on their arguments challenging us to reconsider black identity as an active process, I hope to prove that a concept of spidering that is distinctly performative is a valuable tool for scholars of African American, diaspora, and performance studies.

Though I do not adopt all of their arguments wholesale (particularly their utopian moves), both Appiah and Gilroy articulate a vision for the future that positions blacks as both grounded in cultural specificity and open to larger global implications and experiences. Appiah's "rooted cosmopolitanism" advances a way of globalizing human rights as citizens of the world. "Cosmopolitanism imagines a world in which people and novels and music and films and philosophies travel between places where they are understood differently, because people are different and welcome to their difference" (258). Gilroy, through an unfortunately un-detailed vision of "planetary humanism" and "strategic universalism," hopes for an end to raciology and the color line in a future-oriented project. I, too, take on the idea of hope to rechart the schematic of black identity though I resist a progressivist project that leads to the ultimate end of the color line. While I hope to more fully take on these theories in a larger book project, I want to emphasize the call for overhauling our visions of race. Here I'll argue that performative acts of spidering are important steps in this work.

Daphne Brooks's work on popular music demonstrates the analytical richness of attending to varied cultural influence beyond judgments of authenticity. Her short book about Jeff Buckley's album *Grace* is in part a deeply personal biography cum love letter to a white male pop music icon. In it she not only describes the man and his music but also interrogates her position as a black female scholar vis-à-vis his music. She digs the Africanist presence in his work but also allows him to be a white male artist who profoundly influences her as a black woman. She broadens this to critique the racialization of Generation X. As she claims, African Americans were never the face of Generation X, though the cultural nostalgia so important to Xers was often laid out along racial lines. She interestingly finds these presences in the postmodern hybrid, juxtaposition, and multiple influences of Buckley's work. I argue that the Anansi trope fosters similar intricate work and what Brooks is describing is a type of spidering. In fact, in the complicated processes described by Appiah and Gilroy as well as Brooks, we can see Anansi finding ways to survive by redefining himself and the terms of his existence. The web of stories that Anansi spins serves as a metaphor for the ways in which we remain connected to people over time, geography, cultural differences, and so forth.

I posit the term "spidering" to describe the Anansi metaphor for contemporary diaspora. In addition to inspiration from Anansi, I have borrowed the term from a cyberspace practice in which a program travels the Internet looking for data. (The most familiar use of this technology is the Google search engine.) A web spider or web crawler is a program or automated script that systematically browses the Internet in order to provide up-to-date information and copy URLS. A list of these URLS is called the crawl frontier and is recursively visited and adjusted. The architecture of the web changes in time, and different nodes reference how other sites refer to each other. To extend the metaphor, identity therefore shifts in response to how other identities are shifting in a look by an individual, less to the past than the present and future. Information is sought, gathered, and constantly added to the larger "World Wide Web," enriching and complicating the matrix and thus making this process never static and never entirely reliable. This "movement" is dynamic and serves a presentist agenda. Applying this theory to the story of African descent, the Middle Passage becomes one of many diasporas. Diasporic Spidering allows for many different points of intersection and modes of passage to be woven together around a central core—the individual searcher/journeyer. Rather than describing a fixed moment in time, African diaspora (and black identity) in this sense becomes also a contemporary active process—an act, a performative.

Further, Diasporic Spidering assumes an individual with agency (though no one has total control over the elements that define him or her) who creates a life based on experiences. It is a performativity in flux as new information is continually incorporated. This articulation allows for the intercultural complexities of ethnic identities, validating the retentions as well as new information. It resists the fatalism of Afro-pessimism, the historical locking of the traditional concept of African diaspora, and challenges the uncritical glorifications of Afrocentrism.

One may contrast this theory with Alex Haley's (and others') search for "roots." The concept of African roots provides the stability of "knowing where one came from." It is grounded, earthbound, and solid; certainly necessary at a time when heritage was denied and African Americans were deemed to have no past. It is a geographical image emerging from the agrarian South, reaching down/back to an African past. By focusing on the image of a family tree, and more narrowly the roots, African Americans become stable beings with history, but they are also rooted, or locked, and the only significant aspect of identity comes from those roots, the past. There is little room for anything else to go into defining a person or building a life in this closed system. Spidering, on the other hand, is tied to the Internet generation. It is overwhelming, messy, and intangible. It can be both comprehensive and meaningless, and it focuses on the present and future. It does not deny the past but is not locked to it. Building a life becomes an open system, and individual agency is privileged. There is still a beginning place—the center of the web (the individual at a given time and place in his or her personal journey)—but one may move from it in many directions, not just up and down as in the tree metaphor.

The systematic process of web crawling also provides an important metaphor for contemporary diaspora. The automated, and distinctly inhuman, web crawlers have directives and direction and attempt to assemble a mass of information to create a whole or at least a richer database. Likewise, I believe that many contemporary people of African descent assemble a life based not only on inherited traditions but also on individual "searches" that may or may not have something to do with the traditional African diaspora. Of course the process is more human but not necessarily more directed. This process indeed may have been occurring robustly throughout history, but it is only from the late twentieth century on that analysis can zoom out and focus on more than the usual binaries (Africa/America, black/white, good/evil). This conceptualization allows for multiple narratives and experiences to be assessed. In the past, the binary served a sociopolitical purpose, which, though vital, must be interrogated alongside other more complicated configurations.

To return to Anansi for a moment . . . like many folk traditions, most Anansi stories have no known original author. Many modern interpretations are defined as "retold by . . ." New stories, of course, are subject to copyright laws, but the trope in general resists notions of ownership while it moves toward building community. Anansi stories cast a web through performance that has global and historical reach. Memory has been the web of the African diaspora connecting the points along the map, and the fear of the loss of heritage has haunted African American history. Anansi's desire to be remembered through storytelling points to the importance of how we create links. In the twenty-first century, these methods have taken new shape and will result, no doubt, in new concepts of identity.

An example of spidering can be seen in the contemporary ways in which some African Americans search for their heritage. The search for connections and the implications for black identity and subjectivity have always been part and parcel of the African diaspora. African Americans from Alex Haley to Oprah Winfrey have embarked on personal journeys to discover self through history. The roots are genealogical, geographical, biological, real, imagined, and performed. The language contains essential *and* constructed memories. A number of contemporary scholars and artists have participated in acts of "identity tourism" in search of answers, questions, and inspiration in new and significant ways. Though cognizant and wary of the proffered myths of long-lost children returning home, most admit to hopes for personal insight. Most African Americans have refused the tabula rasa theories of cultural identity that posit the loss of everything along the Middle Passage. Instead, personally constructed identities around ontologically slippery notions of blackness fill the void of census records. This spidering is performative in this construction. Some have reached to African name books to redefine themselves, shedding slave names for ones tied to a notion of Africa. Self-determined identity is an act of agency, albeit a limited one. There are only so many "authentic" connections to Africa that any African American can forge. For example, Saidiya Hartman, on her recent journey to Ghana to retrace the Atlantic slave route, quickly recognized herself as the Obruni, stranger, that the locals called her. Her journey began as the "proverbial outsider," and her work in *Lose Your Mother* is a reckoning with that legacy. She claims, "Secretly I wanted to belong somewhere or, at least, I wanted a convenient explanation for why I felt like a stranger" (4).

Also at the root of these journeys is the vexing legacy of not only the European and American tyranny in the transatlantic slave trade but also the complicity of Africans in the sale of other Africans. What implications does this hold for the connections African Americans have been searching for during the past four hundred years? As Hartman reminds us, "Africans did not sell their brothers and sisters into slavery. They sold strangers: those outside the *web* of kin and clan relationships, nonmembers of the polity, foreigners and barbarians at the outskirts of their country, and lawbreakers expelled from society" (5, my emphasis). I highlight her use of the term "web" as key to understanding my position on racial performativity. Though the tyranny of the European and American slave traders overshadows the role of Africans selling other Africans, this part of the history is narratively vexing and is therefore often omitted.

Not only is reliance on narrative and geography unstable but biology also occupies an untenable position in measuring drops of blood and, most recently, strands of DNA. Indeed, the DNA spirals and the hoped-for spiritual and emotional connections they might make can be seen as a kind of spidering. Hartman argues that this leads to people of African descent feeling more lost. The success of Henry Louis Gates's recent project of helping black people test their DNA and discover the geographical regions to which they biologically "belong" will be the litmus test of Hartman's theory. Already there exist accounts of African Americans dealing with the "fact" of being more European than African according to DNA tests or not belonging to the African tribe with which they had so long self-identified. For example, in *Af-*

rican American Lives, Gates's film about the DNA testing of several prominent African Americans, Oprah Winfrey discovers that she is not Zulu despite her previous claims. (A few years before being tested by Gates, Oprah announced in Johannesburg, "I went in search of my roots and had my DNA tested, and I am a Zulu.") Oprah has built her identity based in part around a narrative of her personal ancestors being Zulu despite the fact that the likelihood of an African American being Zulu is extremely slim given that few of the South African Zulu were part of the West African slave trade. Again, the narrative was more important than geography to creating the Oprah we know (or rather the Oprah she knows). The Zulu are known to be fierce warriors, fighters, and not victims. Clearly, Oprah wanted/needed that ancestry. In the absence of certainty, Oprah created that part of her heritage, and her devastation at finding out the "truth" points to the power of her spidering. She made herself Zulu (and by extension one of the richest and most powerful people in America). Would she have had the success she has had if she knew "the truth"? Perhaps. But it is important to interrogate the tenuous connections between who one is and will be to who one's biological ancestors were.

Like previous biological definitions of identity (eugenics, phrenology, bloodlines, the one-drop rule, social Darwinism, primitivity, etc.), DNA's prospects of being the scientific panacea for identity crisis are already suspect. Performance through spidering, on the other hand, resists the project of finding "an answer." It is not stuck in the past and can allow Oprah to maintain a connection to the Zulu. This, of course, presents its own slippery slope. I do not mean to suggest that anyone can become any ethnic identity by searching for information and making connections. For one, performance will always be met with reception, and we are far from color-blind. Rather, because spidering is less concerned with biological essentialism and allows for composite, present, ongoing, and changing identity formation, Oprah Winfrey's inspiration from her conception of a Zulu fighting spirit can be maintained. At the same time, the information gathered from Gates, that she is actually descended from the (perhaps less inspiring) Kpelle tribe of Liberia who were taken in battle and then sold to or stolen by U.S. slavers, can also be a part of who she is.

The Haley, Hartman, and Winfrey stories betray a persistent obsession with Africa as the sole or main definer of identity for descendants of the West African slave trade. Even as the Gates project (see theroot.com) shows that many African Americans have less "African" DNA (and many Caucasians have more) than they perhaps would like to believe, biologic binaries are still overprivileged. There have always been alternative models and people who either resist or don't fit the neat stories. As more examples gain attention, old models will have to be reimagined. Spidering is a valuable site for that discourse and analysis as people assemble lives, define themselves, are defined by others, and resist simple definitions. Two recent examples from different arenas help me demonstrate my point: Stew's autobiographical musical *Passing Strange* and the public life of Barack Obama.

The award-winning and critically acclaimed musical *Passing Strange* traces musician Stew's early years. Feeling stifled by his black Baptist, middle-class 1970s LA life, the young Stew embarks on a textbook geographical journey to find himself—he goes looking for "the real." His soul-searching takes him to Europe, specifically Amsterdam and Berlin, where he gains new perspective on his ethnic identity through his various "passings." He challenges his mother's gospel musical tradition and embraces punk among other influences. The tragedy of the story occurs in the end when after ignoring his mother's repeated requests for him to come home, he finds out that she has died. The message is not subtle. He feels he must leave home, rejecting his past in order to find an "authentic" self elsewhere. Importantly, though, he does not go to Africa, but to Europe. The tragedy of the story is not in his European excursions but in the fact that his past and present could not coexist. These trappings and contradictions don't exist in spidering. Eventually, Stew comes to realize that he is an amalgamation of all of the influences in his life.

Volumes could, and no doubt will, be written about the performance of ethnic identity and the image of Barack Obama. Space limitations prevent a full exploration here, but even a cursory examination proves my point. This example is valuable not just for the myriad ways one might claim Obama presents himself but also for the ways in which others perceive and define him. As a politician he of course has needed to walk a fine line, both in articulating his personal identity and in allowing many different people to claim or deny him, sometimes using justifications of mind-boggling convolution. For example, on February 8, 2007, Debra Dickerson, *Salon* columnist and author of the book *The End of Blackness*, went on the Stephen Colbert show, *The Colbert Report*, to define Obama. When asked if Obama was black, she said: "No. He's not. In the American political context, black means the son of West African . . . the . . . the . . . uh . . . descendant of West African slaves brought here to labor in the United States. It's not a put-down. It's not to say he hasn't suffered. It's not to say that he doesn't have a glorious lineage of his own. It's just to say that he and I, who am descended from West African slaves brought to America, we are not the same."

She goes on to claim that he is not white either and gets even more caught up in her own rhetoric, calling him an African African American and, sarcastically, "as black as circumstances allow." She reassures the joking Colbert, who is disappointed that he won't be able to say that he voted for a "black guy," by saying he could say that he voted for "an American of . . . an African African American, an American of African-immigrant stock. And he is also a person who has adopted, ah, the role of being black. So he's not my . . . he is a brother but he is an adopted brother. . . . He's a beloved adopted brother."

The entire five-minute interview progresses in a fascinating twisting of meaning and definition to the point where Colbert denies he is white and Dickerson claims that he's gotten her "so confused." The humor of this satirical talk show is a valuable forum for highlighting the depths to which we will dig holes at the attempt to discover "the" answer to ethnic identity. Interestingly, Colbert doesn't ask Dickerson if Obama is African American, which might have produced a different but perhaps equally intricate answer. He is not the descendant of slaves brought over on the Middle Passage, but he is a person of African descent born in America. He is "closer" to Africa, being only one step removed. By almost every litmus test (except Dickerson's somehow) he is black by some percentage. By denying Obama the status of being black, Dickerson seems to be articulating a theory of black identity as an exclusive club that Obama doesn't get to join. Blackness for Dickerson is a privilege, and she takes pride in her slave heritage and African American history. She and Obama might have had more common "lived" experiences as black people in America, but she still denies Obama black status because his ancestors do not share her ancestors' exact history. Her main point, however, seems to be critiquing white self-congratulation "of saying we're embracing a black person." In other words, she wants to deny white people the story of historically voting for a black man. Though she nitpicks over geography and biology, she is mainly concerned about narrative. Obama's inspiring narrative and his geographical/biological lineage are both at odds with and part of what got him elected as the first not completely white (that we know of) American president (that and his political stance, integrity, hard work, etc.). He is African, Hawaiian, African American, Indonesian, a Harvard Law grad, *Harvard Law Review* president, grassroots community organizer, Christian, and a Muslim terrorist to ignorant racists. Of course, he is never defined as white even though by extension of the logic of the simplest definitions that allow him to be black, he has just as much claim to whiteness. But the one-drop rule persists. Too, he is rarely considered bi- or multiracial; we have no easy meanings for these terms. Ironically, by disallowing a multiple identity he is able to be nearly all things to all people. But he can't be all of those things at once. For example, when he is "no drama Obama," that is his Hawaiian "side." But Obama himself does not seem to be going through an identity crisis like everyone else. Perhaps that is his Hawaiian side; perhaps he manipulates the political advantage of not distancing himself from any group (except terrorists, of course) or perhaps, like Stew, he can adopt a heterogeneous conception of ethnic identity and move on. He performs himself as extremely intelligent about race (almost waiting for the rest of us to catch up) while he focuses on more important matters. His March 18, 2008, speech on race placated many, but we are still caught up in who he is or how he can or cannot play the "race card." Anxiety abounded in playing the race card during the primaries and presidential campaign, until he won and we could all engage in the self-congratulations that Dickerson warned against in having not only voted for but also elected a "black" man, the first African American president.

These journeys and attempts to forge connections need not be fraught with identity crisis, however. A number of contemporary analytical theories resist the essentialist/constructivist divide of black subjectivity. Michelle M. Wright claims, "Any truly accurate definition of an African diasporic identity then must somehow simultaneously incorporate the diversity of Black identities in the diaspora yet also link all those identities to show that they indeed constitute a diaspora rather than an unconnected aggregate of different peoples linked only in name" (2). Where Wright articulates the negotiation as the production of a common intellectual history, rejecting cultural tropes that reference a West African moment before the fall, I assert that the negotiation is necessarily a current agenda of the individual, not just a historical philosophical and intellectual project. Who are the identity watchdogs that determine whether or not a given set of identities in aggregate is significantly diasporic? This project becomes unsustainable very quickly. The necessarily mediated and contextualized individual hails and is hailed as she builds a life out of personal connections, family history, experiences, group identification, and so forth. Spidering embraces the complex colored contradictions of contemporary negotiations. It is being and becoming and a fluid, ever-changing act of survival. At the end of the day (or life) the meaning of it all is infinitely contingent.

Though Anansi is based in an African diasporic tradition, it is resonant with larger efforts. This project also tells us something about what it means to be black, perform blackness, and be read as black in the twenty-first century. Spidering articulates the complex matrix of networks that maps individual diasporic performativity. It embraces the multifarious and slippery performances of black identity. If the problem of the twentieth century was the color line/the binary, and the project was digging for roots, then the project of the twenty-first century will be spidering/the web, and whether or not it is a problem will depend on how we respond. Some lines of the webs will be color lines; some will break through other lines of wisdom and memory; some will be dead ends; some will become individual paths, some group tours; some will be geographical, some textual, some spiritual, some . . .

Krik?

TWENTY-FIRST-CENTURY POST-HUMANS

The Rise of the See-J

The twenty-first-century post-human borrows heavily from science fiction to tackle head-on, not only the liberal humanism that reinforces the objecthood of black bodies, but also issues of embodiment and technology. But who is this creature that emerges from the break that actively disidentifies with a compulsory humanist notion of real blackness? Who is this demonic post-human subject that insists on re-temporalization and nonlinearity?[1] Stage lights off, then silence until the exquisite music of Thomas Wiggins fills the room.[2] Enter stage left Josephine Baker from graphic artist John Jennings's visual series *Matterz of the Fact*. Bent under the weight of a prosthetic banana, Jennings overlays the traditional image of Baker's body as long-limbed, smooth-toned dancer with that of a plugged-in puppet, jerkily moving to a beat not of her own or Wiggins's making. The experience is uncanny—we are moved, a little afraid of our feelings that stem from this "enchanted encounter in a disenchanted world between familiarity and strangeness" (Gordon, 55). The forgotten social realities around Wiggins's grotesque blackness and around the glossy eroticized images of Baker's body return with a vengeance, and we are haunted by their dual status as object and person, prosthetic and human. We are reminded of their pain as bodies and voice buckle and catch under the shadow of phallic bananas and slave masters who watch from the wings. Through technologies of (hyper)embodiment, these figures reveal the uncanny reinvigoration of modern regimes that render black people as fungible objects, ready for updated forms of consumption. They remember and foresee those events

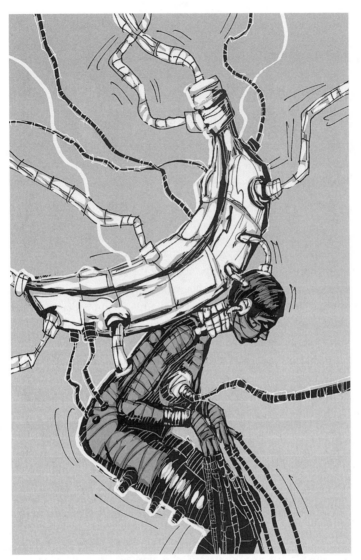

FIGURE 3.1. John Jennings, "Baker's Burden" from *Matterz of the Fact*, 2009. Courtesy of the artist.

and people historically subjugated, refusing any model of reconciliation based on historical amnesia. Josephine Baker and Thomas Wiggins belong not to the past but instead to a post-human world populated by cyborgs, a world of "AfroDiasporic futurism ... a 'webbed network' of computerhythms, machine mythology and conceptechnics which routes, reroutes and criss-crosses the Black Atlantic" in digitalized soundings of pain and desire (Eshun, -006).

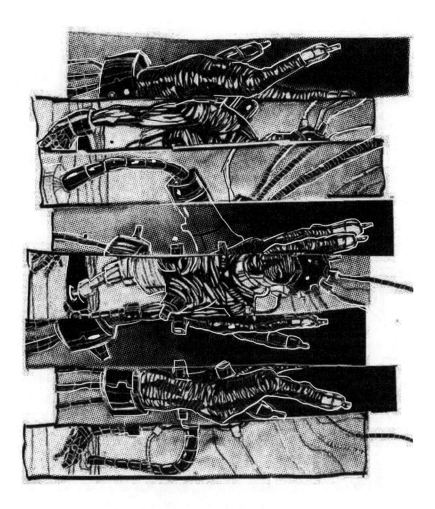

FIGURE 3.2. John Jennings, "Lost Handz Re-mixed" from *Matterz of the Fact*, 2009. Courtesy of the artist.

Though perhaps counterintuitive with its focus on the visual art of graphic artist John Jennings, this chapter turns toward sound theorists such as Alexander Weheliye, Fred Moten, and Kodwo Eshun. For the sonic allows a staging of the black subject as both within and outside of modernity, as excluded from traditional liberal discourses of the human and therefore having a special relationship with the category of post-human. Kodwo Eshun's book *More Brilliant than the Sun: Adventures in Sonic Fiction* (1998) claims that the denial of the black subject's status as human has given her greater access to the category of post-human. A history characterized by the lack of recognition of black humanity, by the denial of human rights, by exclusion, has resulted in the yearning black subject always already turning elsewhere, to alienness and post-humanity. Eshun takes great care to distinguish the intellectual traces of the human embedded within notions of post-human from liberalism's articulations of the human. He insists on "inscriptions of humanity in black culture provid[ing] particular interrogative performances of the human . . . as opposed to mere uncritical echoes of the white liberal humanist subject" (Weheliye, 30).

Weheliye is less quick to jettison notions of the human in favor of the post-human. Examining what Eshun dismisses as the "good for you like Brussels sprouts" humanist elements of black popular music (such as R. Kelly's recorded R&B songs with their valorization of humanist yearning and agency), Weheliye concludes that the complex interplay between these elements and technology actually rearticulates what it means to be human, "provid[ing] different circuits to and through the (post)human. Instead of dispensing with the humanist subject altogether, these musical formations reframe it to include the subjectivity of those who have had no simple access to its Western, post-Enlightenment formulation, suggesting subjectivities embodied and disembodied, human and posthuman" (Weheliye, 40). As an alternative to black bodies being seen as only the victims of technology, we need to move "beyond the binary logic that insists that race and technology are always at odds with each other" (Nelson, Tu, and Hines, 3). The confluence of technology and race, as Harryette Mullen observes, "encodes racial integration so powerfully that it accomplishes otherwise unachieved racial integration through a synthesized synchronicity of images and voices drawn from disparate sources" (86). Rather than only recognizing that slavery rendered black bodies into units of capitalist exchange and mechanisms of labor, the post-human renders more productive the relationship between human, race, and technology. Via its challenge to oppositional notions of the human and machine/slave, the post-human, or cyborg as Donna Haraway calls it, opens out the body to technology's reshaping of it. Like a lover, technology is "pervasive, utterly intimate. Not outside us, but next to us [and inside us]" (Sterling quoted in Foster, *Souls of CyberFolk*, xii). The post-human represents a utopic opportunity to redefine technology and black personhood, particularly in this chapter, through the sonic.

Sound, in its insistence on Sylvia Wynter's nondeterministic "demonic" structure, decenters the ocularcentrism of Western subject formation. The importance and power of the visual gaze to fix the black subject in her own skin appear in numerous black performative texts such as Frantz Fanon's *Black Skin, White Masks* and Adrian Piper's photographs. While I am not suggesting substituting ocularcentrism with the hegemony of the aural, theories of sound provide an indispensable lens to look not just at music but also at the work produced by contemporary diasporic visual artists, in particular for this chapter, John Jennings and to a lesser extent Iké Udé. If we think about the aural as a demonic methodology and not just a phonic materiality, we discover that visual art bears aural substance—it pulsates with sound. An opaque reading would move understandings of the literal meaning of the visual (what Moten calls its ontology) toward a dissonant, improvised reading of the *process* of the visual. Such a sonic reading of the visual would also enable a shift toward non-ontological, nondeterministic readings of the visual animated by sound. As Moten says about a photograph: "You lean into it but you can't; the aesthetic and philosophical arrangements of the photograph—some organizations of and for light—anticipate a looking that cannot be sustained as unalloyed looking but must be accompanied by listening . . . even though what is listened to . . . is also unbearable. These are the complex musics of the photograph" (Moten, *In the Break*, 200). This "seeing that redoubles itself as sound" influences how I look at the post-human in Jennings's work.

Jennings refers to himself as a "See-J" or a "pix-master." By explicitly linking himself to the DJ and the mix-master (those irreverent experts on the sonic cut, scratch, and break), Jennings draws together the sonic and the visual, using graphic art images to create hip-hop. In the manner of DJs who moved understandings of the turntable from a technology that simply played back recorded music toward an instrument with which to reconstruct sound, Jennings reconstructs a circum-Atlantic visuality via the sampling and remixing of familiar images. Recognizable images of Uncle Ben, Whoopi Goldberg, Saartjie Baartman, and nameless bodies with African masks for heads return defaced, spliced, contorted, layered, and demonic in his Afro-futurist series *Matterz of the Fact* and *Rekonekted*. Their truncated torsos, prosthetic limbs, wire tendrils, and replaced heads speak not only to the violence of the transatlantic world that has denied black bodies subjectivity but also to black vernacular works that perform new meanings of the post-human through a co-articulation of black subjectivity and technology.

Jennings's twenty-first-century aliens, in their Afro-futurist stagings of the post-human, focus our attention on the interface between flesh and machine, person and thing. The DJ's hand, placed before the needle of the turntable's arm, blurs the boundary between flesh and technology: "Prerecorded sounds become heard through the hand. The DJ's hand massages the throat to vibrate the vocal trac(k)t. The hand also becomes a motor, twitching inertia in reverse, manually moving, pushing wax up hill. The turntable plays records, yes, but in turntablism the body becomes an engine for the turntable while arms work together to mine beats from the black pits of the groove with a diamond drill" (Guins and Cruz, 230). Similarly Jennings's artistic process, where one hand culminates in a stylus moving across the digital Wacom tablet while the other hand moves the mouse to the beat of black performance, morphs him into a cyborgian "pix-master" and "See-J." His body becomes an engine, pushing, mining, and mixing images of black folk. In *Rekonekted*, Jennings cuts up the images from *Matterz of the Fact* into vertical strips. He tapes these strips from different pieces together, scanning them into Photoshop and using wires, sepia tones, and lines to reconnect the fragments. The reconnection does not result in whole images. Rather the fragments are spliced together in an intuitive process that makes meaning even as it resists containment via an opaque, open-ended sound performance.

It is essential that we be concerned not only with hearing the visual but with what the performance of sound invokes. In other words, what work does sound do? Thinking sonically/demonically about visual art and the artist's process insists that we can't simply excavate the image for teleological meaning. We cannot lay a single deterministic schema over the image to reduce its meaning. "Seeing redoubling as sound" points us away from a singular universality that has excluded black bodies, only including them as the Other-within. The multisensory mode of the visual expresses a longing to journey to another place characterized by a multiple universality that includes black bodies in the category of the post-human. "The discovery of [an image] in the fullness of its multiple sensuality moves in the drive for a universality to come, one called by what is in and around the [image]" (Moten, *In the Break*, 206).

In their utopian longing for a multisensory, open universality, Jennings and Udé bring new black geographies into being by listening to the clamor of ghostly bodies layered like a palimpsest over one another or by sounding the depths of spaces that are seemingly silent. Jennings and Udé thus reanimate and de-animate the processes of surrogation that give meaning to performances of blackness, showing how "the ghosts of the sacrificed still haunt these historic spaces [of the circum-Atlantic]. Effigies accumulate and then fade into history or oblivion, only to be replaced by others" (Roach, 109). For both artists, blackness is not a biological truth performed by skin. In Udé's work the commodity form often replaces the black body by standing in for it, relegating flesh and blood to trace, indent, index. A jacket or a pair of shoes speaks for the wearer who is sacrificed and forgotten, though not gone. Blackness is disembodied, spectral, and sometimes erased. Jennings's work in his series from 2009 *Matterz of the Fact* and *Rekonekted*, by contrast, represents blackness as hyperembodied, newly manifested in post-human forms that meld flesh and machine, the visual and the sonic.

Jennings as See-J attempts to give voice to the commodity. During a close reading of the section called "The Fetishism of the Commodity and Its Secret" that appears in volume 1 of Marx's *Capital*, Fred Moten comments on Marx's insistence that the commodity cannot speak. For Marx, the impossibility of the commodity's speech lies in its inherent lack of value except when participating in a sociality of exchange. The commodity has no use value to itself; it only has value when speaking to other commodities within a system of exchange. Yet what Marx did not take into account was the slave, the commodity on which the modern circum-Atlantic world was founded. The slave's terrible scream, followed by a more terrible hush, insists on the value of the commodity outside of exchange, on her value constituted via the "material reproductivity of black performance." For "this is the story of how apparent nonvalue functions as the creator of value; it is also the story of how value animates what appears as nonvalue. This functioning and this animation are material ... impassioned response[s] to passionate utterance[s]" (Moten, *In the Break*, 18). Black performance reveals and hides this call-and-response, the scream and the hush, forming its essence. Blackness is not about biological sameness performed by skin/hair or a nostalgic return to kinship conceived around the loss of the motherland. Rather it is the sound within black performance of a utopic, improvised desire for freedom that spills from the mouths of objects denied their preexisting value. "If we return again and again to a certain passion ... a protest, an objection, it is because it is more than another violent scene of subjection too terrible to pass on; it is the ongoing performance, the ... scene of a (re)appropriation — the deconstruction and reconstruction ... of value, of the theory of value, of the theories of value" (Moten, *In the Break*, 14). Thus blackness for Moten and Jennings is not only an incantation of violation but also the critical discourse that is produced from and beyond that site of terror.

Turning to the destroyed face of fourteen-year-old Emmett Till, who was beaten, mutilated, shot, and drowned for allegedly flirting with a white woman in Mississippi, Moten poignantly traces the critical, utopic longing manifested in the shudder and moan as black folk mourn yet another victim of racist violence. Just as the leaving open of the casket by Emmet Till's mother, Ms. Bradley, is a performance, our response to the photograph that cannot contain Emmett Till's mutilated body is also a performance of seeing and refusing to see. "So that looking implies that one desire something for this photograph. So that mourning turns. So that the looker is in danger of slipping, not away, but into . . . denial, laughter, some out and unprecedented reflection, movement, murder, song" (Moten, *In the Break*, 201). Staring, as defined by Rosemarie Garland-Thomson, constitutes "intense looking" where the object of the gaze becomes the victim and the starer the perpetrator. Yet the shudder and moan, the gaze and the aversion of the gaze elicited by Emmett Till's mutilated body, activate another politics of looking that moves away from staring toward what Garland-Thomson terms visual activism: "By putting themselves in the public eye, saying 'look at me' instead of 'don't stare,' people . . . practice what might be called visual activism . . . as a three step process: look, think, act" (Garland-Thomson, 192). Can you be black and look at this?[3] Can you be black and *not* look at this?

For Kodwo Eshun, this scratching of looking/not looking "opens up the new plane of Sonic Fiction, the secret life of [commodities], the discontinuum of Afrodiasporic Futurism." It "moves through the explosive forces which technology ignites in us, the temporal architecture of inner space, audiosocial space, living space, where postwar alienation breaks down into the 21st C alien" (Eshun, -003). In *Rhythm Science* Paul D. Miller, also known as DJ Spooky That Subliminal Kid, writes that the "turntable's needle in DJ culture acts as a mediator between self and fictions of the external world" (36). For both Haraway and DJ Spooky, technology grafts itself onto the flesh to create new bodies that interact differently with Afro-futuristic environments.[4] The turntable's arm, like Jennings's digital stylus, forms a technological prosthetic that extends specific human capabilities, altering both the body and the environment in which it performs. This technological prosthetic can be seen as "a repetition with a difference [a black performance] that places recognition of racialization at the center rather than at the limit" (Guins and Cruz, 226).

The performance of the technological prosthetic, in its foregrounding of race, echoes across time and space. Remember the singing voice that accompanied Jennings's Josephine Baker as she jerked onstage. That voice belongs to Thomas Wiggins, a blind boy "owned" by Colonel Bethune, who began performing to increasingly packed houses in 1857 (Best, 55). Tom's brilliant performances stood out in a violent landscape of spectacular black performances at the time. His ability to play any of the music he heard without a score, as well as the exquisite virtuosity of his performances, confused white audiences, caught up in the visual text of his putative grotesque "blubber lips," "coal black" skin, "protruding heels," and shiny teeth that evoked the minstrel shows of the day (Best, 55). White audiences were confronted by the profound contradiction in their positing of slave as commodity and blackness as subhuman and Wiggins's ability not only to perform compositions by white artists such as Verdi that supposedly epitomized the best of human ability, skill, and sensitivity but also to write music whose complex beauty rivaled the best of white composers. If a commodity, and a grotesque commodity at that, could perform with such grace, did it mean that Western aesthetics did not signal the presence of a superior subjectivity or that slaves, in fact, possessed a comparable humanity? The way around this contradiction that shook racism to its core was via the evacuation of meaning from Wiggins's performances. His art was reduced to one of mere imitation, to an unintelligent parroting of sounds. His performance was emptied of deeper meaning, his genius the result of simply duplicating the sounds around him without understanding what they meant. While Stephen Best focuses on the application of intellectual property law to acoustic phenomena as evidenced in such renderings of Tom Wiggins's performances, I want to draw attention to Wiggins as a technological prosthetic. In Willa Cather's labeling of him as a "human phonograph, a sort of animated memory, with sound producing powers" (Willa Cather quoted in Best, 55), one sees evidence of the complex mental gymnastics needed to support ludicrous racist claims about black incapacity and inhumanity/mechanization. Wiggins's performances were seen as mere mechanical reproductions of sound, with his commodified slave body relaying and transferring sound without any true understanding of aesthetic content. "Able to reproduce musical passages with mechanical precision and yet property by the terms of the civil law, he gave off the signs of the phonograph long before its invention" (Best, caption for figure 1, 57). In essence, he melded the body and technology, the commodity and personhood, through his performance of a human phonograph that prefigured the actual mechanism itself. As a prosthetic, he spoke to other commodities, forcing reconsiderations of binaries of human and machine/object in ways that inform and revise the twenty-first-century post-human.

I would be remiss if I failed to mention cyborgs and prosthestics within the context in which they perhaps have the most material resonance: transnational disabled communities. The science of prosthetics, initially developed to provide artificial body parts for male victims of industrial accidents, the Civil War, and World War I, exploded during the 1940s and 1950s due to the social anxieties evoked by the specter of "damaged" veterans unable to be productive citizens. Little attention was paid to how environments create and support normate bodies—rather the failure of fit was displaced onto disabled bodies. This meant that instead of the built environment being significantly altered to accommodate different modes of embodiment, the emphasis was placed on the prosthetic as curative. Numerous design advances were made to prosthetics, which began to be made out of new materials such as acrylic and stainless steel. In the late 1940s, Norbert Wiener, who coined the term "cybernetics," argued that advanced electronics could be applied to prosthetics. Wiener developed the myoelectric arm, also known as the "Boston Arm" or the "Liberty Arm," in his desire to prove that "medical technology could rehumanize the physical body rather than dehumanize it. In creating a group of electronically controlled, self-sustaining artificial limbs that replaced conventional prostheses, Wiener imagined a futuristic body in which applied technical expertise and cybernetic sophistication brought mobility and independence to the nonproductive citizen" (Serlin, 60). However, Wiener's design bypassed the disabled community, ending up instead being heavily utilized in industry. The robotic arm by the mid-1960s was well on its way to displacing manual workers in manufacturing and industrial plants across the United States.

The prosthetic is inextricable from the notion of rehabilitation. This notion of rehabilitation results in a cultural grammar that valorizes a normalized illusory "intact" body and that establishes society's goal as the restoration of the body to its original aestheticized level of functioning. "The practice of rehabilitation 'succeeded in making alterity disappear' and founded a world where [generic] 'identicalness reigns, at least a rough identity, a socially constructed identity, an identity of which citizens can be convinced'" (McRuer, 112). Yet the act of making identical has not been accompanied by the desire to make equal; rather it has enforced compliance, according to Robert McRuer. Noncompliance, an allegiance to alternate embodiments, is not considered an option. The incomplete or failed rehabilitation of people of color whose culture has been pathologized (for example, missing a father instead of an arm) and who refuse to be the same and not equal—must be read as noncompliance. Compliance with the discourse of rehabilitation that underpins the use of the prosthetic can further subjugate black peoples through the dystopic creation of inhuman identical bodies, reduced to their singular mechanized labor function.

Several of the pieces in Jennings's *Matterz of the Fact* and *Rekonekted* insist on tempering our celebration of the cyborg and the prosthetic with its accompanying discourse of rehabilitation and compliance. Alongside Jennings's conceptualization of his artistic process as an Afro-futurist prosthetic performance lies a quiet warning lest we embrace the cyborg too easily without careful attention to historical context. Pieces such as "Lost Hands" and "Wet Nurse" illustrate this tension. "Lost Hands" portrays two elegant black hands severed at the wrists with metallic fingertips. The iron cuffs around the wrists link the hands to cybernetic tendrils that are connected to something or someone outside the frame. "Mammy Outlet" depicts a similarly truncated form, this time of a bare-chested black woman where metallic casing and prosthetic legs replace her lower body, and tendrils pull her head back. Both her arms have also morphed into prosthetics—one is a cybernetic claw with teeth while the other is a machete-like blade. The focal point of "Wet Nurse" is her right breast, which ends not in a nipple, but in a three-pronged outlet. Slavery and imperialism converted the black body into a prosthetic extension of the body of the master—the slave's hands became the master's hands, her breasts his breasts to be used at will. It was the slave's hands that picked the master's cotton, the slave's breasts that suckled his white offspring, her womb that reproduced his workforce in a terrible intimacy. In *Rekonekted*, Jennings splices fragmented images from "Lost Hands" and "Mammy Outlet" together. The resulting piece is over-whelmingly disturbing. Eight strips depicting a black geography of hands connected to pieces of breast, a mess of wires, the corner of an eye. This is the devastating consequence of coerced compliance to the rehabilitatory injunction of the prosthetic as black people became post-human cyborgs, fleshy prosthetic parts of the master's absent though pervasive body. The post-human here does not unite flesh and machine. Rather it turns flesh into machine, person into commodity, life into death. Jennings's images show that disembodiment and/or hyperembodiment, in fact, is not an es-cape from the traumatic consequences of race. The monstrosity of the post-human draws our attention to the monstrosity of the master as he forcibly manipulated categories of the human, converting black people into pros-thetic devices. Slavery and its attendant blackness, Jennings seems to sug-gest, have always been "the comrade of the inanimate, but not by choice" (Ishmael Reed quoted in Foster, *Souls of CyberFolk*, xxv). The cyborg, more often than not, has served conservative agendas instead of the transforma-tive ones hailed by many postmodern theorists. "African-American bodies have historically undergone legal and cultural processes that detached the signs of the humanity from the bodily markers of 'blackness' . . . as Spillers points out" (Foster, *Souls of CyberFolk*, 155).

Yet the power of Jennings's work and black performance in general lies not in their critique or valorization of the post-human but in their existence in the break. Afro-futurist landscapes team with characters whose run-ins with liberal humanism's objectification and commodification of their bodies have given them urgent understandings of what it means to be post-human. Choosing neither a normative, whole embodied humanity that rests on fac-ile binaries of a natural, biological human and object nor a wholehearted embrace of the pervasive intimacy of technology, Jennings's work "moves through the explosive forces which technology ignites in us" (Eshun, -003).

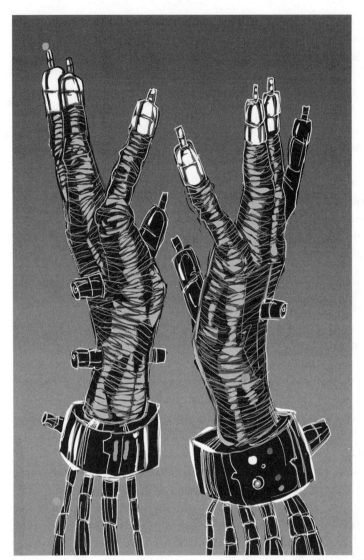

FIGURE 3.3. John Jennings, "Lost Handz" from *Matterz of the Fact*, 2009.
Courtesy of the artist.

Using palimpsestic representations of fungible cyborgs to show the devastated contemporary racial landscape, *Matterz of the Fact* and *Rekonekted* also contain disruptive moments that course through flesh/machine to illuminate unexpressed and perhaps inexpressible longings for freedom. Exceeding traditional flawed progressive narratives of civil rights and formal emancipation, these scratches in the groove perform a "politics of transfiguration" (Benhabib, 41) or what Eshun calls "the secret life of machines which opens up the vast and previously unsuspected coevolution of machines and humans in late 20th C Black Atlantic Futurism" (Eshun, -002).

These disruptive moments are accomplished predominantly through Jennings's use of the trickster. Originally appearing in Jennings's graphic novel *The Hole: Consumer Culture Volume 1*, coauthored with Damian Duffy, Esu-Elegbara limps through its pages in various guises such as White Peter and Papa Legba and reincarnates himself in several of *Matterz of the Fact*'s images. "If the Dixie Pike leads straight to Guinea, then Esu-Elegbara presides over its liminal crossroads, a sensory threshold barely perceptible without access to the vernacular, a word taken from the Latin *vernaculus* ('native'), taken in turn from *verna* ('slave born in his master's house')" (Gates, *Signifying Monkey*, 6). The trickster's characteristics include irony, parody, indeterminacy, "open-endedness, ambiguity . . . uncertainty, disruption and reconciliation, betrayal and loyalty, closure and disclosure, encasement and rupture" (Gates, *Signifying Monkey*, 6). Esu-Elegbara, as god and as metaphorical figure, embodies Wynter's demonic grounds. As such, not only does he live in the break, he *is* the break. Born of, yet prior to, and exceeding the violent commodification of slavery, the trickster strategically mediates binaries. Trickster characters abound: there is the cyborg jungle bunny (Brer Rabbit), coonbot (shifty coon), signifying monkey, and mimicking ape, all of whom visually pun on racial stereotypes, disrupting binaries of flesh and machine. Here humans perform as animals that perform as humans who perform as cyborgs. Jennings uses strategically placed points of light—a red glow, a glint of a prosthetic arm, a blue dot—to suggest possibilities for resistance.

The vibrancy of black trickster characters and See-Js tells us that the instrumentalizing tendencies of power can never be completely successful. Of particular interest is "Back and Forth," an image of two black profiles (sampled from Kongolese masks) with missing bodies, sutured together and onto a metallic casing with umbilical-like wires. One profile has a red eye and bared teeth, the other a brown eye with pensive mouth. This piece makes obvious reference to the Yoruban myth told to me by my godmother in order to illustrate Esu-Elegbara's character. There were two brothers who were very close and boasted that nothing could separate them. Esu-Elegbara decided to put this to the test. He rode past one brother and then rode back past the other. One saw him wearing a red suit, the other a black one. They quarreled and eventually fell out over the color of the suit. Meanwhile Esu-Elegbara had been wearing a suit that was red on one side and black on the other. Both brothers were correct, yet their strict adherence to binary absolutes of right/wrong, red/black, life/death destroyed their bond. "Back and Forth" animates this parable by depicting one post-human as illustrative of person made thing, plugged in, controlled, abject. The other post-human embraces wholeheartedly the "pervasive intimacy" of technology.[5] Yet these two faces, painfully sewn together, speak to an understanding of the cyborg that samples both positions. They refuse "to sacrifice contextual embeddedness or interdependence for a [capitalist] fantasy of autonomous self-control" (Foster, *Souls of CyberFolk*, xx) even while "birthing a new body capable of making a new sound" (Guins and Cruz, 229). The power of these sonic stylings lies in the movement of technology that instead of reifying person and object challenges the naturalness of biology and the artificiality of machine by enlarging what it means to be post-human in an apocalyptic world.

The predominance of the mask in Jennings's work brings together many of these tropes. Jennings describes these African masks as faulty circuits that promise but fail to link the consumer to whatever the mask symbolizes for them. For non-continental Africans, the mask, while appearing to link the consumer to a "homeland," actually disconnects him from the contemporary realities of African nations that increasingly exploit the disillusionment of First World/second-class citizens via heritage tourism that promises "home" through consumption. Any mask will do. It makes little difference where the mask originates and what purpose it was intended to fulfill. Through ownership, the consumer forges her own particular construct that the mask represents. Whether as an index of primitivism, or an exotic showpiece reflecting an anthropological investment in the accumulation of other cultures, or a balm to an exploited sense of disenfranchisement and homelessness, the mask is silenced. More often than not, the consumer cannot see and hear the mask as its vocalizations of its aesthetic and material value fall on deaf ears. As Jennings writes, "Late capitalism makes everything a potential extension of the commodity self" (e-mail, July 19, 2009). Our rituals are only ones of consumption.

However, Jennings reworks, remixes, and remakes the mask. Digitally scratching in the break, Jennings hides among African masks the startling image of MF Doom—a twenty-first-century alien par excellence. The hip-hop artist MF Doom (now known as Doom) was born in London, England, to a Trinidadian mother and Zimbabwean father and grew up in Long Island, New York. Legally named Daniel Dumile, MF (Metal Fingers) Doom's personas proliferate—his aliases include Viktor Vaughn, Zev Love X, King Geedorah, Metal Fingers, Danger Doom (when collaborating with Danger Mouse), and Supervillian. These names remix the names of popular cultural icons to create vibrant, edgy characters that express the rage and moan of black performance. King Geedorah, for example, is a three-headed space monster whose name alludes to the monster in *Godzilla* named King Ghidorah.

MF Doom's persona reappropriates the comic book supervillain, Doctor Doom or Victor von Doom (hence Victor Vaughn), the archenemy of the Fantastic Four. Victor von Doom's face was wounded during an experiment that his peers actively discouraged him from making where he attempted to communicate with the dead. Expelled, Dr. Doom wanders until a group of Tibetan monks take him in and teach him their way of life. To repay them, Dr. Doom becomes master of the monks, forges himself a suit of armor with a mask that only he can remove, and uses this suit to take revenge on the world. Jack Kirby, the artist who drew Dr. Doom, used the suit of armor and the mask to portray a deadly inhumanity, a disfigured metallic creature beyond humanity. This villain resonated with MF Doom, who adopted the name after a series of events: the death of his brother and fellow artist Subroc, who was struck and killed by a car, and the shelving of his second album, *Black Bastards*, due to controversy over the cover art, which depicted a graffiti-like Sambo hanging from the gallows. MF Doom spent the next couple years deeply depressed and homeless at times until he began performing again at open mike events, now as MF Doom. A disallowed sonic/visual experiment, years of exile in Manhattan, the need for revenge against a music industry "that so badly deformed him," all obviously parallel Dr. Doom's narrative progression (LeRoy, "MF Doom").

Through a sampling of one of the best crafted comic book villains, MF Doom positions himself as enemy, not only of the music industry but also of dominant constructions of identity that relegate him as a black man to second-class citizenship. An obvious trickster, MF Doom assumes the identity of a white comic book patriarch, blackening it in his quest for social justice. Through the interplay between comic book hero, flesh, and metal, MF Doom moves away from traditional liberal notions of him as human/black/artist. He rarely removes the mask in public for there is no real him underneath the armor. Like Sethe's mother in Toni Morrison's *Beloved*, who "had the bit so many times she smiled. When she wasn't smiling she smiled, and I never saw her own smile" (240), there is no authentic psychic interiority under MF Doom's mask. Rather, his identity is a complex interplay of flesh and machine, commodity and a voice that speaks for itself, outsider to the music industry society and an essential part of it. Jennings's piece enters into a conversation with MF Doom. The sepia tones of the image together with exquisite eyes that stare out at him represent a dialogue between two sonic/visual artists. Both exist in the break, using digital/metallic extensions of themselves to push against their commodification as black men even while knowing the limitations of liberal humanism and that the commodity can speak. In some senses, Jennings's image of MF Doom is a self-portrait of a digital artist who exists at the crossroads of 33⅓ (the standard format for vinyl albums), making new meanings out of a hypervisibility, speaking on lower registers.

The cybernetic tendrils that I argue represent an all-encompassing, disembodied power source that re-creates itself in the blackness of bodies assume new meaning when we consider MF Doom/Jennings's power to make meaning, specifically here regarding notions of framing and context. The borders of the image can function as cuts or breaks that sever the cords, disconnecting them from the external power source. Jennings himself thus resists the subjugation of the black body with his stylus, mixing and minimizing certain beats by wielding the cutting edge of the image's frame like a sword.

Cut . . . breathe . . . blink.

Postscript

Eshun writes that "sonically speaking, the posthuman era is not one of disembodiment but the exact reverse: it's a hyperembodiment, via the Technics SL1200" (Eshun, -002). Yet this hyperembodiment cannot exist without disembodiment—the two are not binary opposites but rather needle and prosthetic arm, silence that marks noise, absence that shapes the contours of presence. To misquote Avery Gordon, "hyper[embodiment] is a persistent alibi for the mechanisms that render one *un*-[embodied]. . . . The mediums of public image making and [hyperembodiment] are inextricably wedded to the co-joined mechanisms that systematically render certain groups of people apparently *privately* poor, uneducated, ill, and disenfranchised" (17).

I would like to end with Iké Udé's series of photographs in *Beyond Decorum* that dwells in the site of absence, of the trace, of the forgotten but not gone. The series consists of tightly framed photographs of pressed white shirts and ties, worn shoes, and ill-fitting coats on largely headless bodies. What prevents the series from too closely resembling a clothing catalogue is the wornness of the clothes and the pornographic labels that replace the designer labels. Consider the inside of a crisp white cotton shirt with black and brown tie whose label reads: "'BLOW JOB' Clean bi Asian male 41 & expert cocksucker, will suck & deep throat your clean, healthy cock as long as you like. No recep, No Asians, Hispanics & Fats Call: Lee Box #41077" (11). Udé shows us that transgressive economies of (sexual) pleasure and pornography underpin the flow of capital in so-called legitimate markets. The smuttiness of the ad is contradicted by the starched, stiff lines of the shirt that can only be accomplished by the absence of a messy body. Yet this disembodiment is intimately tied to the presence evoked by the label—the wearer haunts the photograph.

Sir John Tenniel's cartoon titled "The Haunted Lady," or "The Ghost in the Looking Glass," was published in *Punch* in 1863 after seamstress Mary Ann Walkley died from working without rest for twenty-six and a half hours (McClintock, 98). The cartoon depicts an English lady who starts to gaze admiringly at her exquisitely dressed image in the mirror. Instead of seeing a reflection of herself, the woman is startled and horrified to catch a glimpse of an exhausted and dying seamstress, slumped in a corner. The dead seamstress who lives in the corners of the room haunts the wearer. Through her, the commodity refuses its mute objecthood, morphing instead into an eloquent indictment of the conditions and methods of production. Just as Aunt Hester's screams index the production of the slave in Frederick Douglass's narrative, so, too, does the dress speak for the absent seamstress.

The wornness of the clothes and shoes in Udé's photographs speaks volumes—the leather of a silver pump folded by the absent wearer's gait, the wrinkle of the shirt where the wearer sat, stretched, perhaps walked. Like skin, the articles of clothing speak about their maker and about those who consume them, including us. Udé draws out attention specifically to the "voice or authorship" that the used quality of the fetish suggests. "The wornness is to account for the presence and absence of the wearers. . . . The shirts have a voice or authorship because of their used quality, which validates and authenticates the absence of the beloveds who once occupied those spaces" (Bessire, 8). The commodity holds on to the trace of the relations it obscures. Presence is evoked by absence; hyperembodiment is evoked by disembodiment. Udé's work exposes how the commodity, instead of replacing bodies, conjures them up via their absence. The white shirt, the tie, the ascot in his photographs, all speak through the trace, the index, the knot of seething, material gaps.

For both Jennings and Udé, the commodity speaks on many frequencies. Jennings depicts a sonic world where the black body is the twenty-first-century commodity—remixed, sampled, subjugated, and resistant. For Udé, the commodity has rendered the black body invisible, yet its absent presence speaks volumes that both reinforce and disrupt consumer capitalism. Thus both artists, located at seemingly opposite ends of the spectrum of hyperembodiment and disembodiment, are working in the break, striving to understand the specters that leak and erupt from its recesses and hoping to "fill in the content differently" (Gordon, 19). By making the commodity speak, whether as ghostly trace or post-human cyborg alien, both Jennings and Udé attempt to conjure up a different kind of world that through the sonic visual refocuses our attention on the intimate encounters between capitalism's violence, artistic world-making, and a nondeterministic universality.

Notes

1. Sylvia Wynter posits a new methodology (the "demonic") that challenges liberal Enlightenment man and posits her notion of the human. The "demonic" in physics is a process without a determinable outcome. Wynter's demonic frameworks highlight uncertainty, nonlinearity, and a radical re-temporalization. See Wynter.

2. Thomas Wiggins, a slave born in 1849, was also known as "Blind Tom." I will discuss the importance of his musical performances later in this chapter.

3. This riffs off Elizabeth Alexander's "'Can You Be BLACK and Look at This?': Reading the Rodney King Video(s)."

4. Recently, British law student Riam Dean has filed suit against Abercrombie and Fitch's infamous "look policy," saying she was discriminated against because of her prosthetic arm. She has worn a prosthetic arm since she was three years old. "It was part of me, not a cosmetic." "Abercrombie's 'Look Policy' under Fire," CBSNews.com.

5. The longer I stared at the image, the less certain I became about which profile represented which position.

HIP WORK

Undoing the Tragic *Mulata*

Prologue

I sit down to write and I cannot stop crying. I am hesitant to admit to these emotionally charged currents of tears as it is not my intention to coyly perform the tragic *mulata* of this chapter's title. But, in effect, the tears continue. I think about my recently deceased maternal grandmother, Elba Inés, a Colombian mulata, hailing from the Caribbean coast of the country and working long, nervous hours at the mayor's office of Barranquilla, fearing for her job every city election. As a single mother of two daughters, she could not have risked unemployment. I imagine my longtime deceased paternal grandmother, Carmen, a Cuban mulata, walking down the narrow streets of Ranchuelo, Cuba, on her way to work at the Popular cigarette factory. She had worked for the founders of the cigarette brand, los hermanos Trinidad, since she was fourteen, and when they opened up their factory, she remained there for another forty years. I try to piece together family narratives of my maternal great-grandmother also named Carmen (of black and Indian descent) who died of a hemorrhage after a miscarriage, orphaning six children, one only six months old. To make a living, she worked as a seamstress and would also make candies and other sweets that her eldest daughter sold. I wonder what it must have felt like for my paternal great-grandmother, yes, another mulata, to have her eldest daughter, María, be recognized as the only legitimate child from her long relationship with a Spaniard from Asturias that produced seven other children. If he had recognized the other children as legitimate, my last name would be García, not Blanco. These are several of the mulata histories that make up my own, histories that time, my search for family legacy, and my scholarly research have only made more necessary to revisit. My tears suddenly lead me to recall the Afro-Cuban/ Yoruba anthropomorphic energy force or deity Ochún/Òsun. What can "she" do? What does she represent? John Mason, a scholar and practitioner of Yoruba spirituality, writes about Òsun's association with tears. He states, "Tears are our first physicians; they carry away body poisons and signal that we are alive. They are a sign of deep feeling, pain, joy, sorrow, remorse, and remembrance. . . . Feelings . . . are the doorways to our ancestors" (Mason, *Orin Orisa*, 316). My crying is not in vain.

This performative turn to the self-reflexive echoes what D. Soyini Madison writes when she explains, "how you, me, the self, or, more precisely, 'the self-reference' can actually be *employed*, can actually *labor*, even be productively exploited, for the benefit of larger numbers than just ourselves" (Madison, "Labor of Reflexivity," 129). Thus, I bring these personal histories into the larger historical framework of the mulata experience in the circum-Caribbean. I refuse to accept my family history as one solely fraught with characteristics associated with tragic mulatas: unable to completely inhabit one side of the racial dichotomy, riddled with socioeconomic problems, entering into heterosexual relationships out of economic necessity, to name a few. I reject carrying the burden of this loaded literary trope on my skin, my physicality, my corporeality. I would rather undermine the problematically constructed representations of the mulata that are unable to acknowledge her agency, potentiality, and prowess. As such, I struggle with the familiar moniker of the "tragic" mulata when I think about these corporealities' roles in the making of both everyday and "official" histories of the circum-Caribbean. I become baffled at the disjunction between the tragic narrative associated with the mulata, and the visceral, vivacious corporeality moving through the rooms of a salon or ballroom, sitting at a desk and working long hours to support her family, using her hands to roll tobacco, or to make and sell confections, or even dancing today on the cabaret stages of the Havana Tropicana. Instead of admitting to the tragedy implied by discursive renderings of the mulata's inability to fully inhabit the either/or of constructed racial categorization, I propose to insert a radical shift in the thinking of the mulata as tragic.[1] By radical shift, I mean to corpo-realize this figure through her active mobilization of her own body. To corpo-realize means to make the body a real, living, meaning-making entity; a focus on the material body in the social sphere enables an understanding of how subjects find and assert their agency. Drawing from histories, hagiographies, and hysteria about the transnational, circum-Atlantic body witnessed as mulata, particularly her choreographies of race and gender, I shall enable a reconsideration of her historical significance, her access to citizenship, and her body. A focus on the body, or more specifically corporeality, adds a new dimension to an ongoing discourse about the mulata's role and significance within the greater African diaspora.

By comparing and contrasting several spaces where the mulaticized body prevailed, such as quadroon balls in New Orleans, or *bailes de cuna* in Havana, the idea of a tragic mulata dissipates as the visceral, active body takes its place. The act of turning the noun "mulata" into a verb, "mulaticize," reflects my theoretical postulation that bodies are interpellated as raced and gendered not just by visible economies, but by the actual corporeal herself. As such, choreographies of mulata were in fact one of the few opportunities available to these corporealities where they could acquire some form of self-determination regarding their gendered, racial, and social status. Moving through different locales in the Caribbean allows me to draw certain examples of mulata economies to elucidate, first, how the European cultural imaginary's predilection for almost-other flesh established a libidinal economy where mulaticized bodies had particular spaces, labors, and value; and, second, how these bodies engaged in self-sufficient means of employment specific to the intersection of the political economy and libidinal economy where they circulated.

My analysis of mulatas depends heavily on her hips, as they not only become sexualized, deified, and vilified, but—as I argue—emerge as the signifying characteristic of mulata bodies.[2] One need only to read a comment written by Cuban social hygienist Benjamin de Céspedes in 1888 to see what I mean: "No existe tal cortesanía, ni cultura, ni belleza ni halagos en ese tipo semi-salvaje de la mulata ordinaria que solo posee el arte de voltear las caderas acrobáticamente" (There is no such civility, nor culture, nor beauty nor flattery in that semi-savage type of the ordinary mulata who only possesses the art of turning her hips acrobatically) (Céspedes quoted in Lane, 180). Rude dismissals aside, the mulata's hips serve as a rich site from where to consider her powerful potentiality. The use of those hips for acts of sex, labor, mobilization, pleasure, and dance provides a way to re-historicize the mulata's lived presence and significance in the circum-Altantic, or, as I prefer to call it, the hip-notic torrid zone.[3]

Informed by a background in critical dance studies where the body and its corporeality emerge as sites for investigation and of power, the mulata exists as a sentience that is always present and visible, staking out space, territory, and meaning with the same body that has been used against her. As a visceral body with embodied knowledge, manifesting, circulating, and re-membering memories, and transmitting and producing knowledge, the mulata body inhabits a space outside yet is as valuable as logos. By positing the notion of voice outside of the structuralist presupposition that voice and logos are concatenated, the idea of "voice" can insert itself onto the mulata's hips and turn them into a communication device and, more important, a theoretical tool for dismantling the tragedy that discursive practices have constructed.

The mulata body is a form of performative labor, a racialized choreography. That is, her body develops and goes through the process of becoming and being read as mulata by and through the cultural work that precedes her. This is not to say that her body does not have the capacity to learn, manipulate, and mobilize itself in ways that either encapsulate or resist preexisting constructions of said body. She has gestures, texts, and utterances that emanate from the hip, since what she says has already been discursively and socially pre-scripted. Thus, the power of the mulata comes from her ability to improvise and to choreograph her hip from undelineated texts. This then leads to the focus on the hips as tools for communication. Although the hips have been racialized and gendered, the mobilization of this body part serves as a means to address the sociohistorical situation where these mulaticized bodies came to be, multiplied, and were valorized for their mere phenotypical and epidermal realities: their mulata-ness. They populate the hip-notic torrid zone, making declarative statements with their bodies, both past and present.[4]

By focusing on the body of the mulata as a site and source of power and potentiality, her corporeality sets up a space betwixt and beyond mere locality. She in-sinew-ates a transnational body politic and epistemology through her body that speaks in tongues: not just English, French, Spanish, Portuguese, Creole, or other languages from the circum-Caribbean, but also a bodily rhetoric by and about women that sets out to historicize a space, a place, and reconfigure and deconstruct notions of "race" as they correspond to gender.[5] In this chapter, I also draw from the genealogy of racialized religiosity in the Americas, specifically tying the mulata to the Yoruba cosmology and the energetic force deified as Ochún in Cuba. My use of Ochún as a trope, and "her" relationship/association with mulata bodies, attempts to show alternative means for understanding how women who can inhabit this colonial sign of the unmoored, independent woman with the ever-moving hip of varying brown skin tones might negotiate an active sociohistorical role. The practice of Ochún will manifest through the many corporeal activities of the mulatas moving herein. Ocassionally, Ochún will "speak" through these pages, offering insights of "her" own.

Act I: The Market for Mulatas

Histories of colonialism in the circum-Caribbean have set up and main-tained racialized exchanges of power and desire. To this day, Cuba continues to exist as a libidinous site for sex tourism, with mulata and black female bodies often used as advertisements to lure foreign capital in the form of lustful men, yet ultimately becoming the targets of national discrimination against them.[6] Perhaps a genealogy of the mulata, namely the ways in which she moves through a changing yet still extant marketplace of desire coupled with race, might offer a way to think about its legacies, but also, more impor-tant, how history might engage with the bodies making, doing, or simply just making do. I introduce this mulata genealogy of the Americas by briefly con-textualizing a history of concubinage beginning in the eighteenth century. Jenny Sharpe, a scholar of Anglo-Caribbean literature, has explained that for many black and/or mulatto women in the eighteenth century, concubinage existed as a means for them to extract certain favors from their white master (husband, lover, or patron). How did these women function within these constraints and utilize their mulaticized flesh and its value as capital as a bar-gaining tool? Although these hypergamous affairs were indeed exploitative, the kinds of exploitations and power struggles within them were nuanced depending on the ideological system in place.[7] It is from these complex re-lationships and negotiations of power, a New World libidinal economy if you will, that the role of the mulata as an exchangeable (but powerful) com-modity solidified itself within the social spaces of the nineteenth-century quadroon balls in New Orleans and the bailes de cuna in Cuba. By the nine-teenth century, the market for mulaticized flesh that emerged from these competing narratives of desire—the mulata's to have greater significance as a citizen, the white man's to be coupled—formulated certain economic opportunities for women of color working as shopkeepers, landlords, and servants of the sacred. In Cuba, for example, the nineteenth-century elite sought to replicate the social order so many of them had witnessed and ad-mired in France and Spain, attempting to import the separate-sphere para-digm as a cult of domesticity. This cult of domesticity primarily assigned specific bodies to either private or public space. Despite Cuban elite desire to control and enforce the separate-spheres paradigm, it was difficult to adhere to given the radical mobility of the mulata. "The strategies, maneuvers, or means [free women of color] deployed" and how these women were "moti-vated by a desire to place themselves beyond slavery" with "economic and occupational resourcefulness" stand out as remarkable given the various le-gal, political, and power struggles that filled their everyday.[8]

A seeming disassociation from "blackness" occurs in how these women negotiated their spaces of identity given the fact that blackness was synonymous with slave, and slave status did not offer any form of choice, mobility, or freedom. Since certain mulaticized bodies (depending on their phenotype and how closely it approximated whiteness) could move through varying spaces of (ambiguous) racial identity and domesticity, one might position the mulata as a woman with a certain degree of access. As a house servant or washerwoman carrying soiled clothes to wash by the river, she partook and maintained the flow of domestic activities in the private sphere. As a concubine or *placée* (the term widely used in New Orleans to identify a mulata mistress), she was the public mistress of white masculine domesticity, a female body visibly sexualized and racialized by the men who, in some cases, paid extraordinary amounts of money to conquer, buy, and keep her. Finally, as a public businesswoman (artisan, confectioner, seamstress, among others) one of her more notable roles was as a lodge keeper, maintaining inns for European male travelers in cities like Havana, Kingston, and New Orleans.[9]

One of the more sensationalist spaces featuring moving mulatas were the quadroon balls of New Orleans, where concubinage, or *plaçage*, played a significant role in the everyday reality for many mulatas. These balls occupy the focus of several scholarly works that highlight the construction of these quadroon balls as nothing more than a dressed-up, fancy version of the auction block.[10] Caramel-skinned, honey-colored, tawny, and/or tanned, the *mûlatresse* populated these social-dance events set up as erotic entertainments for their display and exchange among imperial men with capital. The incentives and goals were the same: to parade mulaticized flesh for plaçage in a more relaxed and less socially constricted environment than the exclusively white balls. Ritualized codes, behaviors, and choreographies of exchange between mûlatresses and their would-be patrons cemented certain socioeconomic conveniences for these women, who sought to support and maintain their lifestyles and to secure the future of their offspring from such liaisons. Thus, the libidinal imperial economy created pre-scripted choreographies of racialized and gendered performances that mûlatresses adopted, learned, and exchanged as a way to gain greater access to citizenship and personhood.

Not surprisingly, legal measures and laws often attempted to control mulata "freedom" of access or expression. If, as Lady Nugent (a British traveler to Jamaica from 1802 to 1807) wrote in her journal, imperial men were "almost entirely under the dominion of their mulatto favourites," then something had to be done to contain the problem (quoted in Sharpe, 45). In 1786, Spanish New Orleans's governor, Esteban Miró, instituted the Tignon Law forbidding all women of color from wearing jewels, fine fabrics, elaborate headdresses, or feathers; it required "negras, mulatas, y quarteronas" to wear their hair flat or, if styled, with a modest scarf wrapped around their head, hair hidden, as a signifier of their lower status (Cocuzza, 82). Sure enough, *tignons* began to be made out of expensive cloths, and many free women of color made fashion statements with their tignons as subtle defiance of the law. This issue of mulata beauty bears mentioning for hair (color and type) represented part of the eroticism linked to the mulata body. Although they had to keep their hair "invisible," mulatas found other ways to demonstrate their allure (especially if their economic position depended on it) through the fabrics chosen for the tignon, or simply by playing up the face "unperturbed" by the hair. Jewelry made of "coral, gold or carnelian" further adorned and embellished her, with or without the tignon (Cocuzza, 82). The issue of how their epidermal reality contrasted with the tignon and other accoutrements, and/or whether or not some of the ones with a lighter epidermal reality created a disconnect with the "race marker" of the tignon, surely added to the mystique and further eroticized the mulata and her "absent" hair.[11]

The nineteenth-century circum-Caribbean trafficked in women of color potential, yet female power and agency were constrained under a series of codified juridical and corporeal practices. The dynamic social participation of mulatas in the public sphere led to the contradictory development of the mulata as a social threat, a femme fatale and signifier of nation and religiosity, primarily in Cuba. Luz Mena's "Stretching the Limits of Gendered Spaces: Black and Mulatto Women in 1830's Havana" argues that because of the important social contributions made by free women of color in Havana, the white Cuban elite felt it necessary to denigrate her socially productive status to one of moral transgression and degeneration. In this way, her power and autonomy would be compromised. Although the mulata-as-sign (i.e., the culturally coded signifier of a racialized identity recognized/agreed upon as "mulata," a stereotype) operated as a public commodity, the visible corporeal examples in the public sphere challenged these stereotypical circulations, seeking "liberation" by whatever resources were available to them. Writing in his travel journal of Cuba, which was published in 1871, Samuel Hazard describes a mulata confectioner as such:

> Now we meet a "dulce" [sweet] seller. As a general thing they are neat-looking mulatto women, rather better attired than most of the colored women one meets in the streets. They carry a basket on the arm, or perhaps on the head, while in their hands they have a waiter, with all sorts of

FIGURE 4.1. Rumba Dancers, circa 1942. From the collection of Mayda Limonta. Limonta rescued this picture (among others) from being thrown in the fire at the Tropicana.

sweetmeats,—mostly, however, the preserved fruits of the country, and which are very delicious, indeed,—much affected by ladies. We need not have any hesitation in buying from these women, as they usually are sent out by private families, the female members of which make these *dulces* for their living, the saleswoman often being the only property they own, and having no other way (or perhaps, too proud, if they have,) of gaining a livelihood. (167)

It appears as if he assumes the mulata is "property" of another family, perhaps even a white one, as the use of the word "private" would indicate. Additionally, for Hazard the mulata's racialized body automatically renders her labor as "property," as work done for another's benefit. Fortunately, Mena's research enables a different interpretation as many mulatas were their own employers, participating in a self-sufficient economy. Furthermore, they also had a reasonable variety of occupations to choose from, given the woman-centered economy in which they operated; they were nurses, teachers, businesswomen, midwives, artisans, peddlers, to name a few. Other than being astute businesswomen, mulatas were often moneylenders themselves and, given their daily activities involving money exchange, many were skilled in mathematics and business proceedings, often to the chagrin of the white patriarchal elite.

Interlude I

Singing begins to be heard in the distance . . .

> *Òsun se're kété mi, owó*
> *Òsun se're kété mi, owó*
> *Omi dára o dára oge o*
> *Òsun Wére kété mi, owó*

> Ochún make blessings without delay for me, money.
> Ochún make blessings without delay for me, money.
> Beautiful water, you are beautiful and ostentatious.
> Ochún quickly without delay for me, money. (Mason, *Orin Orisa*, 375)

Òsun speaks:

> Tears . . . crocodile tears that come as prayers of supplication awaken me . . . asking me for money. Yes, you will keep your possessions. No one can take what you earned away from you. It belongs to you and your sisters. My daughters, all of you, be firm, keep to your work. Strive, be tenacious. Use your charm if you must, enchant them on my behalf. Let them see your beauty that needs not eyes to be appreciated. Go, keep to your work.

Act II: Òsun/Ochún as Trope

Òsun/Ochún has arrived. She has responded to one of her praise songs.[12] Òsun is known as the "Occidental Venus" in the Yoruba pantheon. Allotted love, luxury, beauty, and the sweet waters, Òsun represents those things that make life a sensual experience: money, love, sex, and family. Adorned in yellow vestments with wrists encircled by gold bracelets, her delicate hands carry a fan usually made of peacock feathers, her favorite bird due to its flagrant display of arrogance and beauty. In his canonical work on African and Afro-American art and spirituality, Robert Farris Thompson's *Flash of the Spirit* describes Òsun (or as he spells it, Oshun) this way: "[She has a] reputation for great beauty. . . . She was romantically transmuted into the 'love goddess' of many Yoruba-influenced blacks in the western hemisphere. But there are dark aspects to her love . . . her masculine prowess in war; her skill in the art of mixing deadly potions, of using knives as she flies through the night. . . . But Oshun's darker side is ultimately protective of her people" (80). Additionally, Òsun "has a deep relationship with witchcraft, powders, charms, amulets, and malevolent forces" (Mason, *Black Gods*, 101). Renowned for her beauty and charm, she is both sensual (hip) movement and an unmoored woman with a capacity to love, cure, enchant, punish, excel, and please as she sees fit. In the Yoruba community, she is bestowed with the title of Ìyálóde, a title given to the most popular and powerful woman, in terms of women's affairs (99).

The circum-Atlantic voyages of the slave and tobacco trade brought Òsun to Cuba, where her name slightly altered to Ochún and her myths, fables, and magic were interpolated by representations of miscegenated female bodies; the concept of Ochún materialized as the beautiful mulata within the Cuban national imaginary by the nineteenth century.[13] Although Òsun has fifteen avatars or spiritual roads, each assigned a different aspect or personality associated with the deified energetic force, the avatar most widely accepted and circulated in Cuba is that of Ochún Yeyé Kari (mother who is sufficient) and/or Yeyé Moro (mother who builds wealth). This avatar is described as "the happiest, most extravagant, most flirtatious of all the Òsun. She is constantly on the stroll, wears make-up and perfume, and constantly gazes at herself in the mirror" (Mason, *Orin Orisa*, 317; see Cabrera). Some of her practitioners that I consulted with claim that these avatars developed from praise names, that is, names pronounced during the rituals to invite her to manifest. They state that these names are not part of the original fifteen. The avatar Òsun Pasanga (the stream that is a prostitute) would then stand out as the avatar from where Yeyé Kari and Yeyé Moro may have developed. This Ochún loves to dance, revels in coquetry, and represents salacious behavior. It was this Ochún that coalesced onto the (late) nineteenth-century mulata, further elaborated through textual, visual, and theatrical representations of this hybridized body as one that, despite its seductive appeal, was both a social and a sexual threat.[14] These discursive practices served to cement the mulata-as-sign in the Cuban cultural imaginary; a palatable, corporeal representative of a colonized country searching for some form of national identity. The mulata sign reverberated as an apparently neat representation of not-so-neat and vastly different criteria. As a result, the mulata did not have to labor to become; rather, that body's meaning was fully inscribed and interpellated by the forces of colonial history, myths (both African and Creole/Cuban), and widely circulated and widely held ideas about racial categorization. The mulata's laborless body as mere sign enables a country to represent itself to itself, all the while denying/avoiding the subject status of the corpo-real who occupies the space of mulata.

In contrast, Òsun/Ochún-as-practice becomes useful as a way to in-sinew-ate "her" onto the hip movements and somatic activity of the mulata and her explosive sign, and to mobilize her body through spiritual and cor-poreal labor. For example, devotion to Òsun, as reenacted in yearly festi-vals at Osogbo, Nigeria, celebrates her power, charm, wealth, beauty, and wisdom. Dierdre Badejo's *Oshun Sèègèsi* documents one of these festivals. While in Osogbo, Badejo witnessed how the festival drama and its produc-tion (in the Marxist sense) display the intricacies of these Nigerian women's daily activities—particularly how adroitly they conceive and materialize the festival. These renderings of Òsun's significations in the context of these Ni-gerian women laboring and producing a festival in her honor demonstrate how women's work not only materializes the principles of Òsun, but adds value to the social. Badejo explains, "The annual Òsun Festival and oral literature [of Òsun] attest that even within the patriarchal Yorúbà system, women are central to the proper function and survival of humanity" (177). Indeed, Badejo's concept of humanity erases the technologies of power and ideologies based on Enlightenment principles that separate human bodies based on their differences, yet it is the activities of these women—their la-bor, and their working, sweating bodies as they execute and demonstrate the multiplicity of factors involved in realizing an object of veneration—that best demonstrate how production of knowledge operates. Through this lens, the festival occurs not as a flawless, beautiful, or celebratory place where dancing, singing, and worshipping black bodies exist bucolically; rather, it is a site of social and political commentary, reverence, and female cultural production. Here, women negotiate in the market; they both acknowledge and challenge patriarchy and male authoritarianism; and they demonstrate why one of the praise names for Òsun, that of Ìyáloja (mother of the mar-ket), speaks to the social organization, business acumen, and skills of the marketplace that these "daughters" of Òsun demonstrate. Although Òsun/Ochún reifies gendered ideas of being, she (as she is understood and prac-ticed among her devotees) nevertheless enables an understanding of women as knowledge bearers and producers. By tying the deified energetic force Òsun/Ochún into the corpo-mulata, the person engaged in this amalgam results as a potent force.

Òsun/Ochún exists variously as the beautiful sensual dancer, the astute market woman, and the ornery "old woman spitting curses at the world because of the loss of her beauty" (Mason, *Black Gods*, 98). Ornery and ornate, bedecked and bedazzling, the mulata as Ochún (re)appears as a re-membered, performed corporeal iteration of the complex histories in the circum-(black) Atlantic, or more precisely, the hip-notic torrid zone. Named the circum-Atlantic by Joseph Roach and the black Atlantic by Paul Gilroy, the bodies and histories of the figure of the mulata and her enunciating hip transform this particular territory into a hip-notic torrid zone. It becomes a space for and about women of color—black, brown—mulatas with their bodily labors, practices, histories, and defiances. The mulata as producer of Ochún becomes a participatory body in the socioeconomic networks of the colonies, unable to extricate herself from the political economy of desire. Thus, when mulatas "in pursuit of their rights as women and free persons, [flaunt] gold jewelry, headdresses, and clothes that only whites were sup-posed to wear" and continue to produce beauty with accoutrements that Ochún favors (gold, coral, feathers), it is a practice of Ochún, of Ochún hav-ing her way, ensuring not only the presence and vitality of these women, but their historicity (Hanger, "'Desiring Total Tranquility,'" 546).

Interlude II

(Singing heard in the distance)
Ìyá mi ilé odò. Ìyá mi ilé odò
Gbogbo àse
Obí ni sálà máā wò e
Ìyá mi ilé odò

My mother's house is the River.
My mother's house is the River.
All powerful
Women that flee for safety habitually visit her.
My mother's house is the River. (Mason, *Orin Orisa*, 361)

Òsun interrupts:

I am the River. My sister is the sea. I dance with her. I lie next to her. I spill forth into her. I lead you from her to me aboard ships with mermaids on the prow. She leads the way. She rocks you. I lead you from my River

Osogbo to the (Atlantic) ocean, to the sea (Caribbean) to another River (Mississippi). All waters are mine and my sister. We flow to, from, in and through each other. I swerve this way and that. I undulate through and to a new place. My daughters, come to me. I am here for you whenever you need me. I have never left you.

Act III: Choreographing Mulata Bodies

How, then, does a mulata choreograph her gender and her body, specifically through her hips, in order to make insertions into the visual, theatrical, and libidinal economies where her sign is most frequented? Might sexuality, acts of sex, be ways of choreographing gender? How might these women of color's choreographies become cultural productions produced, exchanged, and commodified as mulaticized bodies? Such cultural choreographies of identity manifested quite literally in bailes de cuna and in quadroon balls, social-dance(d) spaces for re-presentations and performances of mulata-ness, operating as local hip-notic torrid zones. Driving my analyses of the quadroon balls and bailes de cuna is my goal to intervene in the modernist opposition between the corporeal and the linguistic. By locating knowledge outside of its historically normative space of language and text, even disturbing pat assertions of "embodied textuality," the lived materiality of an acting body mobilizes the historical and cultural codes where it sits and, in this case, dances. At the quadroon balls and/or bailes de cuna, for example, the mulata made choices as to how to represent herself given her everyday surroundings, demonstrating how gender coupled with race operates as a seductive choreography, so seductive in fact that articles, research, travel journals, novels, and films continue to submit to their allure.[15] These balls/dances, whether they took place in Havana or New Orleans, both burgeoning cities of the Spanish empire, provided the dancing mulatas a space to choreograph the complexities of race and gender that defined them to their male provocateurs and created codes of behavior for themselves to choreograph and (un)successfully perform. A possible performance might be a woman who refuses to co-opt mulata, choosing to establish another form of corporeality with different sets of options. Henriette DeLille, for example, the founder of the Sisters of the Holy Family Catholic order in New Orleans, was in fact a quadroon with a family history of plaçage. She was expected to follow the "tradition," yet she, in effect, chose to still her hips and render her body inexchangeable. Her corporeality, through its religiosity, purposefully choreographed a mulata outside the libidinal economy (see Guillory, "Under One Roof"). Others may have specifically mastered the codes of mulata, for it provided them with a comfortable and recognizable space from which to act. Rosette Rochon, one such placée, made a considerable fortune in New Orleans real estate and apparently left a property valued at the equivalent of $1 million today.[16] It is important to note here how the mulata firmly situated herself into an economy of exchange and made an attempt at self-produced economic agency, essentially managing her body as (her) capital for some access, and/or social mobility.

BAILES DE CUNA

A brief critical examination of Cuban cultural scholar Reynaldo González's analysis of the mulatas hosting and attending the bailes de cuna in the nineteenth-century Cuban *costumbrista* novel *Cecilia Valdés* by Cirilo Villaverde positions the mulata as a discursive site where ideas of race, gender, and class choreograph themselves. *Cecilia Valdés, o la Loma de Ángel* serves as one of the foundational texts in the trope of the tragic mulata in Cuba. Cecilia, the mulata of the title, falls in love with Leonardo Gamboa, a white, wealthy criollo (Cuban-born Spaniard), who unknown to them both is her half brother. Their illicit affair—along with Cecilia's relentless desire for higher social and racial status—contributes to her tragic demise. A baile de cuna hosted by a mulata named Mercedes introduces the reader to their social interactions. Said reader, through Villaverde's exquisitely detailed accounts, experiences the bailes where wealthy criollos attended for the pleasure of being among the most beautiful mulatas in Havana. These danced spaces served as spectacles of the pairings between race, class, and gender as performed by the *canela* (cinnamon) bodies of the mulatas and their white suitors. They danced *la contradanza cubana*, or *danza* (Cuban contredanse which eventually led to the development of the *danzón*), a syncopated version of European country dance described by Villaverde as follows: "The feet moved incessantly as they were softly dragged to the rhythm of the music, the dancers mixed and pressed in the midst of a packed crowd of onlookers, as they moved up and down the dance floor without break or pause. Even above the deafening noise of the kettledrums, in perfect rhythm with the music, the monotonous and continuous swish sound made by the feet could be heard. Colored people believe this to be a requirement for keeping perfect rhythm to the danza criolla" (Villaverde quoted in Gevara, 124). Villaverde's focus on the feet fails to articulate other movements of the danza dancing body. For example, the syncopation led to "more lateral movement [of the] hips," these movements called either *escobilleo* or *sopimpa* (Chasteen, 63). Villaverde's account differs from that of María de las Mercedes Santa Cruz y Montalvo, or the Countess of Merlin. In her journal from 1840, she wrote that the dancers moved "more with the body than the feet. . . . Some seem to glide as if on wheels, [others use] quick turns and backsteps, now to the right or to the left [but] all keep up the same graceful movement of the body" (Merlin quoted in Chasteen, 63). Considered transgressive to the elites because of the Africanist element in its rhythm, the close proximity required of the dancing couple, and its popularity, the danza's mystique only heightened if it could be danced in the arms of a mulata at a racially mixed dance event, such as a baile de cuna. The allure of the mulata's hips moving beneath cumbersome layers of fabric, and more specifically what lay between those hips, marked the bailes de cuna as spaces rife with meanings and negotiations in terms of courtship, arrangement for concubinage, pleasure, and economic stability for the mulata. *Cecilia Valdés* features three incidents of danced drama, but it is the baile de cuna toward the beginning of the novel where the material for analysis is rich.[17] González summarizes:

Los bailes de cuna representaban el crisol del acriollamiento: el amulatamiento cultural. Los jóvenes blancos ricos que en ellos se sumergían, salían amulatados en su ánimo. Contribuían a este embrujo tanto la música que se escuchaba y bailaba como la seducción de las mujeres. Eran bailes dado por mujeres, por eso se les llamaba "la cuna de Fulana o de Mengana"; en ellos predominaba la regencia femenina, sus designios, sus juegos de tácticas y estrategias. Más que en el baile "de etiqueta o de corte," también dado por negros y mulatos, estas cunas, por su sencilla promiscuidad, propiciaban el entrecruzamiento cultural y racial. (206)

(The "cradle dances" represented the melting pot of creoleness: cultural mulaticization. The young white rich men who submerged themselves in them left mulaticized in their mood. The music that was danced [in these bailes] contributed to their bewitching as much as the seduction of the women. The dances were held by women, that is why they were called "the crib of so-and-so"; feminine regency dominated these places, their purposes, their games of tactics and strategies. More so than in the black tie dances or the court dances, also held by blacks and mulattos, these "cribs," for their simple promiscuity, propitiated the racial and cultural exchange.)

In this rendering of the baile de cuna, González uses the positivist language of the nineteenth century to mark these cunas organized by women as feminized spaces of sin, seduction, and cultural intermixing. It is important to note that González writes from a privileged scholarly position in revolutionary Cuba, where part of its dogma asserts a specific, essentialized Cuban identity. In so doing, many scholarly texts endorse a stable, universal idea of *cubanía, cubanidad, mestizaje,* mulato-ness, transculturation: critically discursive neologisms used to describe the Cuban cultural condition and its cultural production. At the same time, González's description of these bailes de cuna highlights how the literary imagination adds to the complicated web of race, class, and gender negotiations critical to this study. For González, the mere act of integrating these nuanced terms led to simple promiscuity, thereby acknowledging the widely held nineteenth-century Cuban belief that intermixing led to moral and sexual degeneration. He also proclaims, using words usually associated with Michel de Certeau, that the mulata-actions within the bailes de cuna operated as "games of tactics and strategies."[18] (Un)Knowingly, González affords some kind of power to these mulatas. For my purposes, I want to transport strategies and tactics to the bailes de cuna and quadroon balls, where the mobilizers of strategies and tactics dispute simple categorization. Granted, these bailes de cuna and quadroon balls existed within the place of colonialism and its insidious ideological ramifications. Yet the particular space of the baile de cuna as controlled by women and their negotiations for some kind of economic agency confirm how these mulatas shifted between what Gonzalez calls "games of tactics and strategies." I contend that mulata corporeality, specifically the hips of the mulata, existed as the primary tactic operating in these spaces. The desire for the mulata body (in the many ways that that might possibly manifest) set up the mulata as an active agent in situations that, given the complexities of power, might render her mute, passive, and merely objectified.

QUADROON BALLS

In contradistinction to the bailes de cuna of Havana, which were held at a woman's—usually a well-established or respected mulata's—house and orchestrated by her alone, the New Orleans quadroon balls or *bals en masque* were white male capitalist productions conceived, controlled, and attended by them for their own material and sexual enjoyment. The prize or thing to be consumed, enjoyed, and exchanged, the capital, was the mûlatresse (quadroon). These balls "would emerge as the unique formula of Auguste Tessier, an actor and dancer with a local opera company" (Guillory, "Some Enchanted Evening," 27). His formula was quite simple: advertise it as a twice-weekly affair held exclusively for free colored women and white men. Offer some surplus value, or "perks," by way of carriages at the door and private room rental at the end of the evening. Many other entrepreneurial men followed suit. They even respected each others' dates and avoided scheduling conflicting balls on the same night. "A man so inclined could still spend three days a week with his family," one man observed (Guillory, "Some Enchanted Evening," 28). These balls were highly popular during the era of Spanish rule in New Orleans (1763–1803), tying these productions of gendered performance and power to those of Havana, another major Spanish colonial enclave.

Just as the bailes de cuna had (white) witnesses who waxed poetic in their journals or letters about the skill of the dancing bodies, the quadroon balls also enjoyed a fair share of discursive accounts. One such visitor, an Edward Sullivan, wrote about the quadroons' movements at these balls as "the most easy and graceful that I have ever seen. They danced one figure, somewhat resembling the Spanish fandango, without castanets, and I never saw more perfect dancing on any stage. I wonder if some of the opera lessees in Europe do not import them for their corps de ballet" (Sullivan quoted in Li, 94). His admiration of the mulatas' dancing skill suggests an association between their apparent talent and their race. Another observer, an H. Didimus, states the following about a particular quadroon who caught his eye: "She is above the ordinary height, and moves with a free, unrestrained air, distinguished for grace and dignity" (Didimus quoted in Li, 94). Again, movement renders her body noticeable and notable. I realize most of these accounts stem from a white, patriarchal perspective, desire mitigated by a supposed objectivity, and rather than accept them as careful, factual accounts of what may have occurred, I read them as discourses that show how the corporeality of the mulata was something to witness and subsequently write about. These documents serve to memorialize the swaying, preening, turning, curtseying, danza-ing corporeality that so fascinated at these social events. There, the mulata could only rely on other mulatas and their acquired knowledge about their situation for the kind of protection necessary for optimum benefits. Therefore, when negotiations for plaçage took place, it was a mother, an aunt, or another close, trusted, older woman who took charge of the young mulata and made the arrangements with the white man. A matrilineal, matri-focal, or woman-centered production of knowledge circulated the mulata-product in these libidinal market economies. These women learned how to mulaticize themselves and then used the value that their bodies had to wield it as capital and market themselves. Although the New Orleans quadroon balls lie in a mythological space somewhere between romanticism, nostalgia, and sexual exploitation, the lived presence of the mulata there serves to undo the myths and discursively rendered tragedy, offering a way to remake the space into one of negotiation and power exchanges. Herein is where the significance of the body, or more precisely the hip, lies.

Interlude III

Yèyé yèyé mā wò'kun; mā yíyan yòrò
The Mother of mothers always visits the sea;
Always walking with a slow swagger to melt away.
(Mason, *Orin Orisa*, 372)

Ochún interrupts:

My daughters walk, they map out space. They take up space. They use their bodies, bodies I need to exist, bodies I bestow with grace, health, vibrancy . . . bodies that work for me, venerating me. Their eyes sometimes are filled with tears, and they cry. Their tears call me. Their tears connect many of us. They also work, they sweat, they breathe, they move, they dance. Theirs are bodies that both feel, and make you feel, make you sensate . . . experience . . . express, re-dress. Use your bodies, think with it, feel with it. That is me. Keep to your work, my daughters.

Epilogue

My Cuban grandmother, Carmen, did not like to dance. She preferred to watch my grandfather sway to the danzón in their kitchen on Sunday afternoons during the weekly danzón radio shows. She was demure in her appearance, wearing almost no makeup, faint perfumes, and a gold necklace with a round Virgen de la Caridad del Cobre charm. Ochún (re)appears here as La Virgen as they operate coterminously in Cuba, syncretized versions of the same deified feminine force. Both are considered patron saints of Cuba, one Catholic, the other African. That both of my grandmothers did not dance strikes me as particularly ironic given the intrinsic social role that dance played in their respective cultures (Cuban, and Caribbean-Colombian). Nevertheless, I have laid out a genealogy of histories and situations that perhaps informed their understandings as to how their bodies could and should act. I often wonder what each would say if they saw me dancing for Ochún, dancing the danzón, or the *cumbia*—the heavy hip-laden dance of coastal Colombia. As I sit, think, and write about ideas, (dance) histories, and racialized gendered bodies, I realize just how far removed I am from the kinds of labors my grandmothers and great-grandmothers had to engage in. Part of me wants my intellectual labor to serve as a form of honor and veneration for my female ancestors, yet somehow I believe that my body, dancing, thinking, moving, and perhaps even hip-notizing, acts as the real *ebo*, or offering to them. I still think that my tears will get the best of me when I remember those that I knew and those that I (re)imagine. Yet, my act of crying is nothing compared to how *ellas seguirán*, how they will endure as I continue to sit and write, walk and dance for them.

Mbe mbe máa Yèyé
Mbe mbe l'órò.

Exist exist continually Mother.
Exist exist in the tradition.

I exist in many incarnations. When she decides to wear her gold bracelets and her brass rings, I am there. It's not allowed, they tell her. I don't care. I must be beautiful, I must be clean, clear, like the water. Look at her and you will remember me. When another one moves her body, shaking, shimmying, swaying her hips back and forth to transfixed and hip-notized eyes, I am there.

Go, my daughters, make them see you. Make them love you. That way, they will see me, they will acknowledge me. They will understand what they have done. My daughters are everywhere—black, brown, copper, brass, gold, wheat, honey—beautiful, embellished, beloved, ornery, ornate, and honored. Make beauty. Never let them forget the work involved.

Ochún begins to swirl away as the last of her praise songs echoes above the stream that is her.

Notes

1. I use the Spanish spelling of the term when I focus on the mulata in Cuba and Spanish New Orleans. When I write about French New Orleans, I use *mûlatresse*. When I mention said corporeal in Jamaica, I use the term "mulatta" or "mulatto woman."

2. See Kutzinski for numerous examples of mulata poetry that both exalts and demeans the mulata and her hips or buttocks.

3. The hip-notic torrid zone is my way of thinking through the transatlantic diaspora that Paul Gilroy's *The Black Atlantic* and Joseph Roach's *Cities of the Dead* establish. I highlight the feminized space of the diaspora through the hips of the mulata and the different labors women of color have had to do and endure given the histories of slavery, colonialism, and patriarchy in these locations.

4. Here I would like to address the work that Jayna Brown's *Babylon Girls* does in rethinking the concept of transatlantic modernity through the traveling, singing, and dancing bodies of black women performers in the early twentieth century. Brown's extensive research frames these women's bodies against literature and drama, European primitivism, and colonialism (2). By so doing, Brown troubles the epistemologies that situate the body and performance outside of history-making and demonstrates how the transatlantic movement of black expressive cultures undergirds any discussion of modernity. This type of analytical work is crucial to the study of transatlantic black

performance and influences my own thinking of the mulata as a transnational actor moving with and through her hip.

5. These languages are primarily spoken in the Caribbean and in North and South America.

6. Amalia L. Cabezas writes extensively on sex work in Cuba and the Dominican Republic in her monograph *Economies of Desire*. Other publications include "Discourses of Prostitution: The Case of Cuba," and "On the Border of Love and Money: Sex and Tourism in Cuba and the Dominican Republic." Her work specifically looks at the history, market, and participants of this phenomenon. Performance artist and activist Coco Fusco has also written on the *jineteras* in Cuba. See "Hustling for Dollars: Jineterismo in Cuba."

7. Anglo-Caribbean historian Trevor Burnard questions most American slavery scholarship that only examines sexual relationships between women of color and white men as merely exploitative: "The pronounced differences in the treatment of the Caribbean and North American experiences of enslaved women or free women of African descent are striking, given the existence of similar power relationships between white men and black women in both regions" (85). Some of these differences include the following: greater influence of feminist thought in North American slave historiography; greater historical and contemporary acceptance of interracial sexual relations in the Caribbean than in the United States; the absence in North America of the concept of an intermediate racial category of mulatto, since the existence of a mulatto class of "browns" with greater privileges and higher status than blacks is a distinctive feature of Caribbean society, both during and after slavery (101 footnote 17). Although not denying the violence and exploitation that occurred, Burnard comments that in the Caribbean, historians tend to view interracial relationships more positively. See Burnard's chapter on Thistlewood and his slave lover, Phibbah, in David Barry Gaspar and Darlene Clark Hine's *Beyond Bondage*, where he quotes from Edward Cox (1984) and Barbara Bush (1990), other historians of Caribbean women, to qualify his argument about the "less exploitative" relationships between Caribbean slaves, mulattos, and their white masters.

8. In Gaspar and Hine's edited volume *Beyond Bondage*, the various authors voyage throughout the Americas and situate these women in different economic positions (x).

9. In her chapter "Victims or Strategists? Female Lodging-House Keepers in Jamaica" featured in Verene Shepherd, Bridget Brereton, and Barbara Bailey's edited volume *Engendering History: Caribbean Women in Historical Perspective*, Paulette A. Kerr presents how the mulatto woman mobilized her identity within the political economy of colonization. For the Jamaican mulatto woman, the keeping of lodging houses and taverns was "one of the few means of economic and possibly social independence for women during and after slavery" (198).

10. Monique Guillory's dissertation, "Some Enchanted Evening on the Auction Block: The New Orleans Quadroon Balls," does comparative analysis between historical accounts, fictional representations, and ephemera from the era of the quadroon balls. She makes the claim that although the events were sumptuous in their produc-

tion, they were merely a fancier version of the auction block. Lisa Ze Winters's dissertation, "Specter, Spectacle and the Imaginative Space: Unfixing the Tragic Mulatta," examines both the quadroon balls of New Orleans and the *signare* balls in Senegal as a way to rethink the mulata as a relevant diasporic actor.

11. The term "epidermal reality" comes from Anna Beatrice Scott's work on blackness, race, and carnival in Brazil.

12. Òsun is the Yoruba spelling. Ochún is the Cuban spelling. I differentiate between the two to demonstrate how this deified energy force is understood in these cultural contexts, and how Cuban Ochún developed differently.

13. During the nineteenth century in Cuba, Yemayá (Ochun's sister, and another water goddess) came to represent dark beauty, while Òsun represents honey-colored beauty. Yoruba scholar John Mason states that Yemayá contains qualities of another African deity, Mamí Wàtá (pidgin English for "mother of the water") (*Olóòkun*, 56). Mamí Wàtá, similar to Òsun, procures gifts and wealth to her followers. The mulata, as a product of Africa and Europe, benefited from the mobility and access afforded to yellow bodies. Mason corroborates by writing that "in the Americas, this position [being mulata] allowed for greater facility of movement in the procuring of wealth and position. Òsun's traditional role as Ìyálóde (titled mother who deals with external affairs/strangers) sets the New World stage for the mulatta/Òsun/Màmí Wàtá/child of whites to step into the role" (55).

14. Kutzinski's *Sugar's Secrets* and Lane's *Blackface Cuba* trace the development of the mulata archetypes that circulated in Cuba by the end of the nineteenth century.

15. Dance scholar Susan Leigh Foster's "Choreographies of Gender" aims to naughtily disturb, disrupt, and contribute to the fields of feminism, dance, and performance studies. For her, a dissection of choreographic strategies in dance enables a clearer understanding of the intention behind the dance. Her adamant suggestion to examine gender as a form of choreography stresses the significance of how bodies both create and resist culturally specific coded meanings. She writes: "To analyze gender as choreography is to acknowledge as systems of representation the deeply embedded, slowly changing rules that guide our actions and that make those actions meaningful. Not biologically fixed but rather historically specific, these rules are redolent with social, political, economic and aesthetic values . . . connect[ing] that body to other cultural orchestrations of identity" (29) .

16. See the Musée Rosette Rochon website, http://www.rosetterochon.com, for details on how one of her homes is being renovated to become a museum. Wikipedia also features a long biography of her under the heading of plaçage, notable placées.

17. The other two danced events in *Cecilia Valdés* are a black tie dance and a dance for the Spanish peninsular aristocrats, respectively. These two were homogeneous dance environments where minimal, if not nonexistent, contact between races and different social classes predominated.

18. De Certeau explains that "strategies are actions, which, thanks to the establishment of a place of power, elaborate theoretical places" while "tactics are procedures that gain validity in relation to the pertinence they lend to time" (38). He contends that

strategies and tactics volley between the roles that space and time afford one or the other. Strategies depend on having an established location as the locus of power, while tactics find moments within the historical progression of power and time to insert their "guileful ruses." Theoretically, strategies and tactics operate as distinctly separate spheres of influence. That is, one emerges, the strategy, as more triumphant than the other, thereby establishing what we come to understand as the ideological status quo: patriarchy, logos, transnational capitalism.

PART II / Black-en-Scène

BLACK-AUTHORED LYNCHING DRAMA'S
CHALLENGE TO THEATER HISTORY

Of what use is fiction to the colored race at the present crisis in its history? . . . . Fiction is of great value to any people as a preserver of manners
and customs—religious, political, and social. It is a record of growth and
development from generation to generation. No one will do this for us: we
must ourselves develop the men and women who will faithfully portray the
inmost thoughts and feelings of the Negro with all the fire and romance
which lie dormant in our history, and, as yet, unrecognized by writers of the
Anglo-Saxon race.
—Pauline Hopkins, September 1900, prospectus and preface to her novel
Contending Forces

Drama more than any other art form except the novel embodies the whole
spiritual life of a people; their aspirations and manners, their ideas and
ideals, their fantasies and philosophies, the music and dignity of their
speech—in a word, their essential character and culture and it carries this
likeness of a people down the centuries for the enlightenment of remote
times and places.
—Theophilus Lewis, theater critic for the black newspaper *Messenger*,
October 1926

Lynching, as an antiblack form of political terrorism, was a distinctly post-emancipation phenomenon. Whites suffered financial losses whenever a slave died, but once blacks were no longer
chattels, there was no incentive to avoid killing them. The Reconstruction era saw an increase in racial violence that only intensified in post-Reconstruction, when federal troops left the South in
1877, inaugurating what historian Rayford Logan later famously
termed the "Nadir" of U.S. race relations. The number of lynch-

ings rose throughout the 1880s, reaching its first apex in 1892, but the post-Reconstruction decades were also punctuated by race riots. Indeed, violence helped turn the century, with the massacre in Wilmington, North Carolina, during the elections in 1898, the Atlanta Riot in 1906, and the mayhem that overtook Springfield, Illinois, President Lincoln's birthplace, in 1908. Thus, the period known as the Progressive Era was also one of racial terrorism against blacks; understanding turn-of-the-century U.S. culture is therefore impossible when historians bracket bloodshed.

Yet, unfortunately, when scholars attend to racial violence, artistic output can be easily overlooked. Following Rayford Logan's lead in seeing these years as a "low point" for African Americans, many assume that the struggle to survive left blacks little energy for other endeavors. Despite this assumption, black political activism cannot be denied. The records of organizations like the National Association for the Advancement of Colored People (NAACP) certify that blacks more than survived; they worked for equality for themselves and for future generations.

As my epigraphs make clear, however, there remained an awareness that traditional political activism must be accompanied by artistic expression. African American novelist Pauline Hopkins argued in 1900 for the value of writing fiction even in times of crisis. While her novel *Contending Forces* presented "both sides of the dark picture—lynching and concubinage," it also preserved the race's religious, political, and social customs by depicting its "inmost thoughts and feelings" (15, 14). Hopkins's work thereby asserts the value of African American culture. If the race's traditions must be maintained and recorded, then blacks' self-conceptions were worth reaffirming. After all, their customs reflected their view of themselves, not what mainstream discourse said about them. Thus, even creative work produced during adversity is not solely a response to outside forces; it is an attempt to safeguard community perspectives.

If adversity intensified the need for self-affirmation, and black-authored novels helped fill that need, the same can be said for the increasing value placed on serious, nonmusical black drama at the turn into the twentieth century. Following theater critic Theophilus Lewis, I contend that drama was perhaps even more responsive than fiction to the historical moment because it directly addressed the fact that theater and lynching were working together to strengthen the assault on African Americans' self-conceptions. In the early 1900s, blacks were acknowledged on the mainstream American stage in the most stereotypical ways. At worst, the images were denigrating and dehumanizing; at best, comical. At the same time, mob violence became increasingly theatrical. Indeed, shortly after the NAACP came into existence, an incident in Livermore, Kentucky, epitomized the degree to which lynching and U.S. theater were infinitely compatible. In 1911, Will Porter was tied to an opera house stage, where "his body [was] riddled with one hundred bullets by mob members who purchased tickets to participate" (Zangrando, 26). As historian Philip Dray reports, fifty men paid to occupy either orchestra or balcony seats; the more expensive seats came with the freedom to fire one's gun six times, while those in the balcony were asked to limit themselves to one shot (178).

It is no coincidence that the American stage would prove as suitable for killing African Americans as for portraying them in dehumanizing ways. Stereotypical depictions of blacks as submissive uncles, vacuous buffoons, or uncivilized brutes helped create an atmosphere conducive to racial violence—and vice versa. If such violence seems out of place in an opera house, that may say more about false distinctions that have emerged in scholarship than about the historical moment under consideration. Generally, U.S. theater history does not reflect an understanding of how compatible theater and lynching were, yet African Americans who lived during this period very consistently identified connections between these cultural forces. In fact, they developed the unique genre of lynching drama during this time. Their doing so suggests that African American communities recognized the extent to which theater and lynching *worked together* to make blacks' conceptions of themselves as modern citizens irrelevant.

While theater and lynching joined forces in order to erase blacks' "record of growth and development," some African American poets and fiction writers turned to drama "as a preserver of manners and customs." As pioneering theater scholars Kathy Perkins and Judith Stephens established in 1998, "a lynching drama is *a play in which the threat or occurrence of a lynching, past or present, has major impact on the dramatic action*" (3). American writers had always addressed racial violence, but the mode developed "when playwrights moved beyond brief references and focused on a specific lynching incident" (Perkins and Stephens, 4). What is most striking about the earliest plays in this tradition is their focus on the black home. Black-authored lynching plays present mob violence more as a crime against households than against bodies. They take the audience indoors, where widows and children suffer, and the scripts barely describe—never mind portray—physical violence. As the survivors' grief overwhelms the scripts, the genre suggests that the brutality continues long after a corpse would have deteriorated. Thus, the plays direct the gaze away from what the song made famous by Billie Holiday called "strange fruit." Readers and viewers are made to focus on, not the body, but the household from which it was taken. These plays present the black home as the lynched body. A body is recognizable because it coheres and has integrity, and the same is true for a home. By presenting intact households marked by their harmony and happiness, the scripts can detail their mutilation. In these plays, the home is mutilated just as a body can be. When an honorable father, brother, or son is taken from the family, the household is metaphorically castrated and its head removed.

It was particularly important to place in the archive evidence of devastated households and the pain experienced by lynch victims' loved ones because society denied that these stable households ever existed. In fact, the mob was continuing the work that slavery had done to destroy black families. Under slavery, romantic bonds among blacks were disregarded, and those who had children often saw them sold. After emancipation, many worked to reestablish familial ties, searching for lost wives and husbands, daughters and sons, sisters and brothers. However, African Americans' efforts to establish and maintain stable homes, and to reassemble broken families, often made them targets of lynching. After all, mob violence was a way of denying "black people public recognition of their identities as husbands and wives, parents and children" (Rosen, *Terror in the Heart*, 225).

As a number of black authors became lynching dramatists, they seem to have resolved that, even if some families did not remain intact to pass down stories from generation to generation, a broader racial family could do so—through intimate, performance-centered rituals. As I discuss elsewhere, the majority of lynching plays written in the midst of mob violence were one acts, which were not attractive to theater practitioners but were conducive to publication in periodicals, including the NAACP's *Crisis*. Magazines already cherished by African Americans, and routinely read communally, now contained scripts that prompted performances or dramatic readings about the injustices of lynching. Because these one-act scripts capture the "ideas and ideals," "fantasies and philosophies," of African Americans living in the midst of mob violence, they remind scholars that this historical moment was the nadir, but it was also the postbellum/pre-Harlem era. Thus, the genre offers guidance for assessing the accuracy of patterns that have emerged in historical accounts of the period.

At a time when lynching photographs circulated in newspapers and as picture postcards, depicting mob victims as isolated brute rapists who cared nothing for stable domesticity, these plays focused on the families and communities devastated by black male absence. The genre suggests that mourning is the proper response to lynching because the mob's victims are not isolated brutes but often family men targeted after they had reached a level of success that enraged the mob because it bespoke black progress and citizenship rather than subordination. Ultimately, lynching drama survives in the archive as not only a record preserving truths that the mob sought to erase but also as a challenge to American theater history more generally. Namely, it demands a reassessment of the tendency to separate U.S. theater history from the nation's record of racial violence.

Rethinking Mainstream American Theater History: The Theater/Lynching Alliance

Blacks living and writing at the height of mob violence interpreted their surroundings critically and equipped their communities to do the same. While lynching rituals and photographs sent a powerful message that African Americans were not citizens, black writers, philosophers, and activists questioned mainstream assertions. Lynching plays emerged from this effort; they stand as evidence of blacks' critical readings of the nation's discourses and practices. African Americans understood theater and lynching to be more interdependent than separate. After all, when lynchings became spectacular by the 1890s, their ability to terrorize relied increasingly on theatricality. Especially between 1890 and 1930, lynchings were frequently theatrical productions. The violence began to follow a predictable script, and "white participants would often bring food and drink to the place of execution" (Harris, *Exorcising Blackness*, 6). Furthermore, "to insure that an audience was available for really special lynchings, announcements of time and place were sometimes advertised in newspapers." Once in attendance, "white men, women, and children would hang or burn (frequently both), shoot, and castrate the [alleged] offender, then divide the body into trophies" (Harris, *Exorcising Blackness*, 6). In other words, newspapers often announced the time and location so that crowds could gather, and spectators knew that they would see familiar characters (so-called black "rapists" and white "avengers") perform a predictable script of forced confession and mutilation. Souvenir hunting would complete the drama with audience participation, but because the most coveted keepsakes (such as the victim's bones and burnt flesh) were in limited supply, pictures became souvenirs. These pictures now survive to verify lynching's theatrical qualities and the variety of stages that mobs claimed, for their victims dangle not just from trees, but also light posts, telephone poles, and bridges.

Because African Americans were attuned to the power that theatricality lent to the mob, when black authors began writing lynching plays, they continued the tradition of exposing the ways in which theater and lynching worked together to conceal evidence of black humanity and achievement. At least since the 1890s, African American activists addressed what I term "the theater/lynching alliance"—the way that mobs relied on theatricality, and the mainstream stage relied on the mob's themes, characters, and symbols.

African American leaders often insisted upon addressing theater and lynching simultaneously. For instance, Ida B. Wells spoke of lynchings whose conveners functioned as emcees, or masters of ceremonies, and she noted when the "programme . . . was carried out to the letter" (52). Similarly, when a lynching took place on the campus of the University of Missouri in 1923, W. E. B. DuBois declared, "Many of our American universities have long defended the institution, but they have not been frank or brave enough actually to arrange a mob murder so that the students might see it in detail" (*Crisis*, June 1923, 55). As the student body became the mob's audience, the university could be said to have provided a demonstration of the practices that constitute a "good" lynching. That is, pupils had an opportunity to observe what many called "lynchcraft"—which was a sort of art appreciation, not unlike the ability to recognize excellent "stagecraft." In all instances, the genius of the craft was that it left little doubt that blacks were anything but the brutes or buffoons that the mob or mainstream stage said they were. For the average observer, the mob depicts those with black faces as rapists only because they are, and blacks appear onstage as buffoons simply as a matter of truth. Recognizing the effectiveness of these cultural institutions, African Americans often worked to expose the alliance that constantly tried to destroy black dignity.

Writing about lynching in dramatic form was therefore simply the next logical step for those vulnerable to this powerful partnership. Still, by even more directly addressing theater and lynching simultaneously, the playwrights demonstrated their immediate recognition of what scholars are rediscovering: theater and lynching were not discrete entities that sometimes cooperated; they were interdependent. Like those at the last turn of the century who recognized "lynchcraft," scholars such as Jacquelyn Dowd Hall, Trudier Harris, and Robyn Wiegman have shown that race-based lynching was explicitly theatrical. Hall asserts that lynching relied on spectacle and spectators beginning in the 1890s: "Even as outbreaks of mob violence declined in frequency, they were increasingly accompanied by torture and sexual mutilation" (330). Partaking in such a production gave whites the satisfaction of seeing the accused tortured, not just killed. Hall also argues that reports of the incidents became increasingly graphic. The victim's agony was described in detail, and so was the crime that supposedly precipitated it: the alleged rape of a white woman by a black man. Therefore, Hall dubs the discourse surrounding lynching "folk pornography," thereby indicating that it was a shared, voyeuristic discourse that expanded the number of audience members. Even those who did not attend the lynching "viewed" it with their mind's eye by consuming the story and taking pleasure in its details (Hall, 335).

Trudier Harris's *Exorcising Blackness* and Robyn Wiegman's *American Anatomies* build on Hall's work and similarly note the importance of spectacle. Harris emphasizes the ritualized nature of the violence and argues that crowds soon counted on a familiar ceremony (2). Thus, the obligatory accusation, forced confession, mutilation, and souvenir hunting became a sort of script. Wiegman focuses on why castration became the mutilation of choice and asserts: "Lynching figures its victims as the culturally abject—monstrosities of excess whose limp and hanging bodies function as the specular assurance that the racial threat has not simply been averted but rendered incapable of return" (81). The assurance was specular because the crowd was comforted by the sight of subdued black manhood.

I would add, though, that because it was a theatrical ritual, there were many signs of the white participants' dominance. The "sign system" through which they created and conveyed meaning included much more than words and static images. Surely, it mattered that they heard the victim's screams and moans and smelled his burning flesh. Accordingly, newspaper reports noted the crowd's cheers in addition to describing the victim's howls and contortions and the unmistakable odor of a burning human body. Like good theater reviewers, journalists tried to capture the dramatic moments and sensual pleasures of theatrical production.

Thus, both the intention of mob violence (to cast lynching as a community-wide response to a black threat) and its ability to convey its message ("know your place") resided in its theatricality. However, the work that has illuminated these truths has said little about stage performance at the turn of the century. Few have analyzed how the mainstream stage lent credence to *and benefited from* racial violence.

Yet African Americans living in the midst of lynching recognized both sides of the theater/lynching partnership. The earliest black lynching playwrights left a unique archive recording their awareness of the practices that defined their historical moment. Their works offer insights that scholars have not gleaned from other documents. When this archive is placed on par with other cultural artifacts of the same period, one finds that U.S. theater cooperated with the mob in two major ways: (1) it sometimes explicitly legitimated racial violence; (2) more often, it established its own relevancy to the nation by translating lynching's tropes, themes, and symbols.

The American stage was most explicitly used to define lynching as a patriotic duty by Baptist minister Thomas Dixon Jr., whose white supremacist novels *The Leopard's Spots* (1902) and *The Clansman* (1905) were best sellers. After the extraordinary success of *The Clansman* in 1905, Dixon wrote a play version of the novel and formed two acting troupes to tour the country simultaneously and bring his work to life (Gunning, 29; Cripps, 52). Dixon's novels had already cast black men as rapists, but putting this image onstage intensified the effect by exploiting the range of meaning-making possibilities that accompany performance. Dixon's violent dramatic vision found favorable conditions. Up to that point, the images of blacks that reigned onstage were that of the feminized Uncle Tom and the laughable buffoon—both of whom confirmed that African Americans were unfit for citizenship. The beast rapist was relatively new but seemed the next logical step in blacks' descent, which had been foretold in (for example) newspaper editorials, political tracts, "scientific" studies, and fiction. Dixon simply dramatized the presumed realization of white suspicions and fears. There was already mainstream agreement that blacks were not citizens; indeed, they were labeled uncivilized, but their presence could be tolerated as long as they were considered harmless. Once deemed a threat, however, the "beast" must be killed. With these ideas circulating, the stage could easily communicate that, because black skin signifies degeneracy, lynching is a necessary evil. Used in this fashion, theater both excused past lynchings and touted the need for future mob activity. By disseminating images of blacks that put fear into white hearts, American theater defined racial violence as the answer for outrages against white women, white families, and the nation. In short, the mainstream stage helped give lynching its accepted meaning.

U.S. theater historians have not claimed Dixon as a founding father, but black-authored lynching drama's inaugural text, Angelina Weld Grimké's *Rachel*, helps remind us of his importance as an American playwright. Grimké's determination to use drama to address lynching did not begin after the release of the film *Birth of a Nation* in February 1915, as some histories suggest. She was circulating her manuscript at least by January of that year, so Grimké's interest in writing a play targeting a white audience predated *Birth*. Also, as Grimké's rationale for the play made clear, she was very much attuned to the damage done by stage images. If the impact of *Birth* is to be credited at all in connection to Grimké's *Rachel*, it can only be in its earlier incarnation as Dixon's play.

In other words, Grimké recognized theater's contributions to its partnership with the mob; the popularity of Tom Shows and the success of stage versions of Dixon's novels suggested that theater was helping legitimate racial violence. Grimké's dramatic work was shaped by this awareness, and it helped to set several people and processes in motion that fueled the development of black drama. Given the many ways in which Grimké's text, and the performance of it, influenced her contemporaries, it should not be overlooked today as we work toward an understanding of this period.

Considering the awareness that inspired Grimké, I contend that though theater scholars have been silent on this point, when one takes a closer look at Dixon as dramatist, it seems significant that his plays emerged at the same time that critics were insisting that the American stage should instruct, not just entertain. In other words, it was time to use theater to shape national identity, to stop mounting European plays and use "native" drama. Critics felt that American writers of fiction and poetry had reached a literary standard that represented the nation well and distinguished it from England; it was now time to *dramatize* American exceptionalism. That is, as William Dean Howells and others promoted the development of a uniquely American stage realism, Dixon's work did not exist in a separate realm but was very much helping to define realism's conventions and the ways in which audiences were encouraged to interpret physical features as indicative of an inner truth.

Indeed, I contend that U.S. theater benefited from lynching by taking from it a grand set of themes, characters, and symbols. The brutal scenes acted out on the nation's trees, telephone poles, and bridges used readily recognized characters ("rapists" and "avengers"), and the discourse surrounding these events made for excellent drama. Real-life lynching incidents provided the perfect mixture of danger, passion, and triumph with which to elaborate the uniquely American narrative of white bravery versus black barbarity. In examining American distinctiveness, Toni Morrison's *Playing in the Dark* suggests that those fleeing to the New World believed themselves to be exceptional men who branched out on their own; faced a wide, dark expanse; and tamed it. I would add that, by the 1890s—precisely because it worked within this master narrative—the lynching narrative became as powerful as the flag itself. The predictable lynching story built on existing American mythology but took it to new heights, by infusing it with a black sexual threat.

Building serious American drama upon such a mythic narrative was necessary because the United States did not have a long line of texts from a figure like Shakespeare providing the foundation for its national theater. It therefore chose to build its tradition on grand themes, and lynching helped create the identity that white men preferred at this time—that of masculine avenger, loyal brother, and protective father. Given these circumstances, Morrison's ideas extend to this transitional period in American drama history. Her examination of fiction writers ranging from Edgar Allan Poe to

William Faulkner reveals "the ways that Americans chose to talk about *themselves* through a sometimes allegorical, sometimes metaphorical, but always *choked* representation of an Africanist presence" (17, my emphasis). White writers frequently conceived of their identities, and those of their white characters, in opposition to an often unacknowledged Africanist presence, and this is no less the case for the nation's early mainstream dramatists.

While lynchers attracted audiences and their violence followed familiar scripts, mainstream playwrights dramatized American identity as one of heroic self-determination, and as they did so, they marked "true Americans" most often by denying black citizenship and black humanity, producing scenarios, images, and discourses not unlike those disseminated by the mob. This is not to suggest that "black equals evil" was a new formulation. But it is significant that, as American theater was marked in the 1890s through the 1910s by the push and pull of melodrama and realism, and the struggle to guide audiences away from farce and comedy to an appreciation of serious drama and problem plays, it built its new identity around dark difference. As more and more critics made claims about theater's potential to galvanize citizens and distinguish the nation from England, many of American theater's modes relied on the mainstream audience's aversion to blackness—which was intensified as photographs of lynch victims circulated.

As Morrison would predict, even when black characters do not figure prominently, theater's strategies for providing entertainment, and encouraging audiences to identify with characters, centered on differentiating "whites" from "others." For example, in 1895, William Gillette's drama *Secret Service* created the cool, understated hero who still dominates American action adventures. Captain Thorne is in total control of himself and of every situation he encounters. He stands in "natural" opposition to Jonas, a black servant. The very first time that Captain Thorne appears, he is escorted into the scene by Jonas—who bows submissively, speaks dialect, is humbly dressed, and is, in every way, clearly *not* in command. To similar effect, dramatist William Moody makes distinctions among the men who invade the heroine's home on the western frontier in *The Great Divide* (1906). Ruth is afraid of all of these criminals, but she soon realizes that she can survive by choosing one of them as a lover. It is no accident that, according to the stage directions, one is a "Mexican half-breed [and] the others are Americans." For the audience and for Ruth, the Mexican makes the white scoundrel that she chooses seem like a prize.

Initially performed in 1895 and 1906, respectively, these American realist dramas emerged alongside the spectacle of lynching. Because photographs of mob victims were distributed as picture postcards, circulated in newspapers, and were sometimes used by advertisers as attention-getting devices, lynching was as much a backdrop for these playwrights' imaginations as was the recent slave past, western expansionism, and U.S. imperialism. Thus, extending Morrison's ideas to early mainstream drama allows us to appreciate what blacks understood at the century's turn, that lynching had infused *black* and *white*, *dark* and *light*, with unparalleled metaphorical intensity. Arguably, behind every characterization of a good, pure, or brave white person was the belief that blacks were brutes, whores, and buffoons. Because blackness was understood in an unfavorable way in virtually every sector of American society, it repeatedly reaffirmed positive assumptions about whiteness. Put another way, "nothing highlighted freedom—if it did not in fact create it—like slavery"; nothing elevated virgins like the existence of whores; and nothing produced (white) innocence like the consistent assumption of (black) guilt.

Acknowledging the interdependence of theater and lynching is particularly important because mainstream theater resided on America's stages and on its trees-turned-stages. American drama therefore cannot be excluded from Morrison's analysis of the uses of an Africanist presence: "Africanism is the vehicle by which the American self knows itself as . . . not repulsive, but desirable; not helpless, but licensed and powerful; . . . not damned, but innocent" (52). Lynching helped to determine the affective responses stirred by the bodies that audiences saw on stage. Perhaps more important, as Morrison would hasten to add, mob violence *helped to determine what the dramatists could imagine in the first place.* Therefore, American theater at the turn of the century—as it increasingly abandoned European scripts for "native" ones—perhaps could not have developed and become a respected, citizen-shaping institution without maximizing the dramatic power of lynching, lynching narratives, and lynching photography.

Recognizing that theater and lynching were kin forms of knowledge production and cultural expression led many African Americans to engage theatricality, but they did so critically, intervening in its discourses and rejecting many of its tendencies. African Americans living at the turn of the century knew that black bodies were central to lynching's theatrical power and to theater's signifying power, with both hinging on negative interpretations of the black body. I mean this in the most basic and most radical sense possible. At this time, a mutilated black body hanging from a tree was theatrical. This is why newspapers announced the time and location of lynchings, crowds gathered to see them, and then journalists reviewed the performances. Just as consistently, a black man, woman, or child grinning and shuffling was theatrical.

In this climate, black dramatists offered scripts that emphasized the dignified presence of the black body. The earliest black-authored lynching plays do not focus on physical violence because the authors refused to replicate the dramas acted out on the nation's trees. Likewise, they would not put dancing, grinning characters on display at a time when those were the uses for black bodies in minstrelsy and musical comedy. Instead, lynching playwrights created characters who often quietly sit and read, debate the issues of the day, and show each other affection, activities that mainstream "realist" scripts rarely demanded of black bodies. African American domestic novels had already begun this work of defining black characters through activities that connoted sophistication and familial stability. It was time to create dramas that offered similar portraits, to be animated by amateurs, by the African American citizens whose real lives served as the black artist's inspiration and the mob's murderous motivation.

These scripts' survival certifies that African Americans understood the extent to which the workings of the theater/lynching alliance exceeded the mob's use of theatricality and had permeated the dynamics of mainstream stage performance. Lynching dramatists thus continued the work that activists such as Ida B. Wells had undertaken earlier. That is, they assured African Americans that they were witnessing a multifaceted attempt to deny the race's accomplishments; they were witnessing lynchcraft and stagecraft at their best.

READING "SPIRIT" AND THE DANCING BODY IN THE
CHOREOGRAPHY OF RONALD K. BROWN AND REGGIE WILSON

Clearly, it is impossible to reduce "spirit" to a single meaning or context. As dance scholar Gerald Myers writes, "Calling something 'spiritual' carries meanings that transcend pinned-down connotations, so its vagueness is not regrettable but essential; its vagueness reflects the only partially understood and thus somewhat mysterious nature of the spiritual itself" (4). As an African American who grew up in a black Pentecostal church, I have a particular notion of and experience with spirit that has played an important role in my life, including as a divine presence or force that has influenced how I understand religion, the way I react to music, the way I interact with people, the way I feel things, and especially the way I dance. Myers's eloquently ecumenical articulation and my own lived understanding serve as a departure point for theorizing a black religious/spiritual and culturally inflected spirit, which can be "read" in the dances of New York–based choreographers Ronald K. Brown and Reggie Wilson.[1]

My selection of these choreographers is based on the contention that Brown and Wilson are among late twentieth-century Africanist modern dance choreographers whose use of the dancing body explicitly foregrounds black/African aesthetics, culture, iconography, and movement in ways that privilege spirit in the meaning-making processes of their dances.[2] So my central question for this chapter is, how does this spirit manifest itself through the body and dances of these two choreographers?

As I take up this question, I draw from diverse sources that help elucidate linkages between spirit, concert dance, and cultural representation (Chatterjea; Gottschild, *Black Dancing Body*; Myers).

Additionally, I draw on various writings in anthropology and black theology that establish a discursive theoretical grounding for interrogating spirit across black religious and secular realms (Bridges; Daniel, *Dancing Wisdom*).

Spirit and the Body—Sacred and Secular

In the African diaspora view, spirit is understood variously as an unseen power, such as God, a divinity, a generative life force, a soul force, and a cultural ethos of a people, all of which have distinctive interpretations across different cultures (Fielding-Stewart; Lincoln and Mamiya; Murphy). This view also holds that spirit (and spirituality) suffuses all aspects of black life and courses through the way blacks understand and express themselves (Bridges; Fielding-Stewart; Mbiti). Adding to these ideas, African scholar Babatunde Lawal maintains that it is through the body that this spirit or life force manifests itself, acting as a threshold between the secular and the sacred, enabling the human being to interact directly with the super-human (41). Furthermore, Africanist theorists place specific emphasis on the expressive/dancing black body—and its relationship with music and orality—as the site of spiritual survival and expression (Daniel, *Dancing Wisdom*; Pasteur and Toldson; Thompson, *Flash of the Spirit*).

It follows, then, that in African diaspora religion, culture, and performance, spirit functions as embodied knowledge and contributes to and underlies meaning on deeply metaphysical, cognitive, and somatic planes (Daniel, *Dancing Wisdom*). Thus, undergirding performance, spirit stirs creative, psychic, and liberative energies, which can manifest themselves through communal lived experiences as well as through spontaneous, ec-static, and kinetic "mounting" of the body and soul (e.g., possession), as in "getting the spirit," or "getting happy" (Gottschild, *Black Dancing Body*).

Sterling Stuckey helps illuminate these connections in his discussion of the shouting body in the black church. He begins with James Baldwin's fa-mous passage from *Go Tell It on the Mountain*. "[Elisha] struck on the piano one last, wild note, and threw up his hands, palms upward, stretched wide apart. The tambourines raced to fill the vacuum left by his silent piano. Then he was on his feet . . . the muscles leaping and swelling in his long, dark neck. . . . His hands, rigid to the very fingertips, moved outward and back against his hips, his sightless eyes looked upward, and he began to dance" (Baldwin quoted in Stuckey, 56).

Stuckey's intention here is first to explicate what he calls the "language of the body in time and space," where, in the moment of possession, spirit transforms and bears witness to one's beliefs (41). Yet, as he continues his de-scription, Stuckey also proclaims that this language, this "bearing witness," is not confined to the church setting. He theorizes a relationship between the preacher and the blues singer that realizes communal spiritual and artistic interplay. He sees this as "a reciprocal back-and-forth of music and motion between sacred and secular realms" (56). I propose that this notion is useful for interrogating the lived (cultural) as well as the ecstatic (spontaneous) linkage between the shouting black body and the black/Africanist concert dance body.

Contextualizing Spirit in the Africanist Concert Dance Body

Thus far I have talked broadly about spirit in the black religious and cultural sense. However, I believe it is also important to flesh out its dimensions within the theatrical concert dance framework. This is somewhat problematic, because, as Thomas DeFrantz cautions, concert dance is a public space, a white modernist, European space of production and consumption (De-Frantz, "Foreword: Black Bodies," 13). DeFrantz argues that reading "African cultural residues" is complicated by the Western structures of art (including matters of audience response, technique, intent, and aesthetic value) and by the fact that "concert dance is never vernacular" (16). We do well, therefore, to stipulate that culturally based ecstatic and antiphonal expressions are, by definition, greatly neutralized or rare in the concert dance performance. But, surely, cultural residues are not universally elided either. So how can we claim a black spirit or spiritual trope within the concert dance?

I turn first to Gerald Myers's insights on spirit in modern theatrical dance: "Calling a dance spiritual orients us to its tone or atmosphere, and acute observers can use that orientation for more specific identifications—of the choreographer's intentions, the choice of steps and gestures, the use of music, words, and other media" (Myers, 4). Here, Myers identifies an inherent spirituality in modern dance, which has been predicated on profoundly explored artistic and philosophical impulses since its beginnings. Consider his example from Isadora Duncan: "I spent long days and nights seeking the dance, which might be the divine expression of the human spirit through the medium of the body's movement" (Duncan quoted in Myers, 4).

Yet at the same time, Myers's reference to "the observer's identifications" invites us to further particularize the spirit, according to our own experiences. It is at this juncture that culture becomes relevant and DeFrantz's admonition to fully examine the notion of cultural residues in the black concert dancing body becomes crucial (DeFrantz, "Foreword: Black Bodies," 13). Invoking Frantz Fanon's notion of "the circle that permits and protects" from *Wretched of the Earth*, DeFrantz situates the black (vernacular) dancing body, sense of self, and cultural identity within that circle. But he also avers that the black body can step out of the circle into the realm of consumption; and that it is, in large part, though not completely, the black dancer's choices that determine how far away from cultural grounding that is (DeFrantz, "Foreword: Black Bodies," 13).[3]

I take from this that, even as we appropriately acknowledge the implications of Western production and consumption, black concert dance can indeed embody substantial cultural residue, including ecstatic qualities. Gottschild supports this by writing that, in its intertwining with black social, religious, and folk forms, black concert dance is a potential conduit of spirit (Gottschild, *Black Dancing Body*, 225). Therefore, similar to Gottschild, I want to claim, for the Africanist concert dance body, a space for what I might call the "imminent potentiality" of spirit, the imaginable interplay of artistic intention and enlivened spiritual expression. To put it another way, I claim a space for the Africanist concert dancer to strive for the transformational power of the religious and culturally based spirit; and also for the spectator to experience it. For examples of this, we only need to point to the black concert modern dance tradition with pioneers like Katherine Dunham, Pearl Primus, and Alvin Ailey, who infused their theatrical modern dance with explicit black spiritual/religious and cultural forms. I turn now to reading this imminent potentiality through the works of Ronald K. Brown and Reggie Wilson.

Brown and Wilson emerged as choreographers in a mid- to late 1980s postmodern pluralism that saw individualistic, often autobiographical, approaches to performing identity and sociocultural representation. Like some African Americans who looked to Africa at the time, they pursued a dualistic integration of black aesthetic and cultural values with postmodern dance strategies (see Osumare, "New Moderns," 27). For my purposes, locating spirit in this historical moment is crucial for exploring individual psychic and creative processes within the postmodern context (see Chatterjea, 56).[4] These concerns, as I shall demonstrate, can shed significant light on ways in which spirit interacts with representations of racial, gendered, and sexual identity in Brown's and Wilson's Africanist/modern dance approaches. To explore these areas, I first look at selected biographical data about the choreographers, and then I examine Brown's *Dirt Road: Morticia Supreme's Revue* and Wilson's *Black Burlesque (Revisited)*. However, it is also necessary, at this juncture, to clarify that I do not claim that these works are *about* spirit or that spirit is the main theme. Rather, my reading of spirit through these works is grounded in the choreographers' stated philosophies about spirit as integral to their creative and meaning-making processes.

Ronald K. Brown: Spiritual Journey and Identity

Born and raised in Brooklyn, New York, Brown projects a powerful and sensuous presence both on- and offstage. He talks openly about his emotional and spiritual struggles while growing up in Brooklyn and his relations with his family as an important part of becoming a dancer. Significantly, he states that his initial emergence as a choreographer marked a period of "spiritual warfare" where he sought ways to "tell stories about [his] identity as an African American male, and also testify to the evidence of the ancestors that came before [him]" ([ergo, the name, the Ron Brown / Evidence Dance Company], Brown, pers. comm., December 11, 2002). Immersing himself in the modern dance and disco scenes, he mixed freestyle and house dance styles with African movement. Also an aspiring writer, Brown sought moral and artistic support with a group of black gay male poets who created lyrical works that dealt with issues around black gay male identity (cited in White-Dixon, 7). During that time, he created *Cooties Don't Bug Me* (1984), which was about the AIDS crisis. He recalls that, although he was serious about the subject, the piece was a rather "sophomoric" attempt at dealing it: "You know, complete with masks and don't touch me gestures" (Brown, pers. comm., December 11, 2002). But Brown would go on to create more serious pieces on this topic.

By 1994, after studying with several West Africans in the United States and in Ivory Coast, Brown decided that contemporary African dance made the most sense to his body. "I connected with the worldly contemporariness and sensuality of Sabar [Senegal], the showing off in the club part of it" (Brown quoted in Roberts, 89).[5] As a result, Brown developed a technically demanding modern dance style that is inspirational not only because of its spectacular aesthetic and kinesthetic power, but also because it draws on and conveys a deep spiritual ethos rooted in his black church upbringing. Brown states: "It feels so good to give yourself over to the dance, to just let your spirit go on the journey, being connected to the divine in the way that you're connected to that when you shout, when you praise in church" (quoted in Gottschild, 241).

We might note that Brown's words recall the shouting black body in Baldwin's description (see Stuckey), and thus demonstrates the spirit's imminent potential. But the passage also speaks to "spiritual journey" and "exploration of self." These themes almost always play out in the narratives and structures of Brown's dances. For example, he likes to choreograph bodies moving in procession, which, as he describes it, "portray people going somewhere"

(Brown, pers. comm., December 11, 2002). Other times he uses the circle, focusing energies inward in antiphonal relationships in which the individual interacts with the group. And he typically sets this movement to uplifting compilations of gospel, new age, jazz, and black popular music and spoken text, often in the form of poems or lyrical phrases, which tell emotional and spiritual stories.

Dirt Road: Morticia Supreme's Revue is an evening-length work (seventy-three minutes) that premiered in 1995 at Dance Theater Workshop Performance Space (PS122) in New York. For analysis, I used a video recording of the performance at Dance Theater Workshop's Bessie Schonberg Theater in New York on October 29, 1995. Performers include Harmonica Sunbeam as Morticia Supreme (the host/emcee), Renée Redding-Jones (Mother), Niles Ford (Father), Cynthia Oliver (Sister/Sister), Ronald K. Brown (Junior), Earl Mosley (Buddy), and vocalist Tamara Allen. Costumes are by Patricio Sarmiento. The work's eleven sections include "Cocktail Party," "Overture," "When My Brother Fell / The Rescue," "Introduction of Characters," "My Brother, Jr.," "Heavy Breathing," "Father and Mother," "Waiting, Strange Fruit / The Car Trip Home," "Mighty Real/Church," and "Heaven Home." The musical score consists of excerpts from recordings of Rolls Royce, Aretha Franklin, Sylvester, Billie Holiday, and various disco/house selections, as well as Mahalia Jackson and contemporary music.

A program entry states that "*Dirt Road* is a dance story about a black family on an intergenerational journey: 'going home'" (Brown, New York Public Library Archives, 2007). From this central theme, several subthemes intertwine in ways that, according to Brown, are not necessarily autobiographical, but that I submit nevertheless seem to create a platform for him to work through various issues that concerned him at the time. Among them are identity, rage, sexuality, social injustice, and personal and collective healing.

As the title of the work suggests, the action alternates between two motifs: (1) Morticia Supreme's gay club scene, where Brown provides entertaining and ironic dance theater that combines racial, familiar, and sexual identity with social commentary; and (2) the "Dirt Road," representing the path to the South for the funeral of a dead Brother who has been shot by a white sheriff for some "unknown transgression." Here the brother doubles as a member of this imagined family and also as the metaphorical, "any black brother" (Brown, pers. comm., February 13, 2007). Among the many striking images are people in mourning with veils over their heads as others dance along diagonal paths. Also, several changes of clothes, from black to off-white or beige dresses and pants, all relatively simple in design, suggest

FIGURE 6.1. Ronald K. Brown and Evidence, A Dance Company in *Dirt Road: Morticia Supreme's Revue*, 1995. Photo by Tom Brazil. Courtesy of Ronald K. Brown, Evidence, A Dance Company.

corresponding changes in emotional and spiritual states, although they are not explicitly defined as such.

The piece begins with an intricate interplay between Junior's (danced by Brown) relationship with his family and his relationship with Buddy (Junior's friend/lover, danced by Earl Mosley). The opening cabaret scene introduces the characters, starting with Harmonica Sunbeam (a tall and lanky, cream-colored drag queen) as Morticia Supreme. As the hostess, Morticia enters as if actually opening a show in a club. She is wearing high heels, a woman's black-and-white print pants and jacket suit, a huge pocketbook, and a big Afro wig (the joke perhaps being that, by this time, the Afro was a bit out of style). Morticia announces: "We have a fabulous show for you tonight. So many people . . . so little time. In fact [*she begins to sing from a Pointer Sisters song*] I am so excited. I just can't hide it, I'm about to lose control and I think I like it" [*The audience laughs loudly*].[6]

On the surface, Morticia is entertaining, but as with all the characters, Brown attempts to show a deeper side. In one section, while the drag queen dances and poses, Brown's taped voice recites a passage inspired by the gay activist poet Essex Hemphill: "Honey chile, when I die, my angels will be tall black drag queens. I will eat their stockings as they fling them into the blue shadows of dawn. I will suck their purple lips and anoint my mouth with the utterance of prayer." This passage seems to claim a spiritual place for the drag queen on her terms.

Next comes a scene featuring jazz dance movements (set to jazz standards sung by Tamara Allen) where Mother meets Father, Sister/Sister appears rebellious and willful, and Junior and Buddy establish a relationship. At one point, the two men approach each other cautiously, first sizing each other up with hypermasculine body attitudes that seem to say *"what's up . . . what's up with you?"* But slowly they reveal their attraction for each other and walk off together. Developing throughout the piece, this relationship appears to be a means for Brown to explore ways in which gay identity navigates within normative social situations. This is evidenced more overtly when Junior and Buddy perform a second duet while other members of the family are present onstage, but not reacting to the duet. This suggests that they are in another place, or that they are present in Junior's mind. The duet begins with Junior and Buddy stripping to tight-fitting shorts. They perform physically daring and poignant partnering and floor work where they slide fleetingly and suggestively over each other. As the two men dance, we hear Brown's voice on tape say, "A grown man loving me like he wanted to. I know that I want to love him. Thanks for being my buddy. I want to love you." Note Brown's use of the words "a grown man" and "friend" and his avoidance of the word "lover." I suggest that, in portraying Junior's trepidation about this relationship, both on the matter of its social and familiar acceptability and in relation to Junior's sense of masculine identity, Brown brings to the fore Junior's spiritual dilemma: how does his sense of self align with his sexuality? We see Junior resolve this through movement that is at first tender and tentative and becomes increasingly athletic and determined. In other moments as well, Brown uses this relationship to talk about different types of love and also explore Junior's fears and prejudices about AIDS. At one point, Junior worries over the potential loss of Buddy.

As they prepare to travel to the South to bury Brother, strong bonds among the family members become apparent with the aid of spoken text and beautifully danced sequences. Here, we see Mother and Father as caring figures and Sister/Sister and Junior as close friends. A major high point comes during an emotionally wrenching duet between Junior and Sister/Sister (Cynthia Oliver) as the family arrives at the funeral. We see the two crying, screaming, running, and consoling each other in full-out modern dance movements, accentuated with ferociously expressive gestures that suggest praying, protesting, and cajoling. Meanwhile, a taped voice praises the bravery of Brother and protests his loss to the racist white sheriff's bullet. (It is worth noting that, at one point in rehearsal, Oliver expressed concern to Brown that he often seemed possessed in this part because of his intense emotional and physical involvement; Brown, pers. comm., February 13, 2007).

After this duet, the piece shifts sharply in mood, from rage and anger to a quest for healing. This is indicated in the spoken text and by reversing the direction of the movement, which previously went away from the bench and now moves back toward the bench. This represents returning to church or "home," which the program states. This section is set to Aretha Franklin's uplifting "Holy Holy" and Mahalia Jackson's "Precious Lord," as well as various disco mixes. Alternating between disco moves and praise gestures, the dancers seem to invest their entire emotional and physical beings. The shouting and whooping calls of the audience (on the video) seem to reflect a viscerally engaged reaction to this portrayed and felt emotional/spiritual journey.

In sum, Brown's *Dirt Road* explores spiritual journey, identity, and social commentary where dancers reveal dimensions of self, gender, and sexuality through their characters, their passionate interactions with the music, and their embodiment of love, rage, and healing. In its kinesthetic and emotional unfolding, the spirit empowers, affirms, and subverts. We see this, for example, in the role of the drag queen and in the relationship between Junior and Buddy.

We also see the Africanist dancing body as inspired and inspiring in this unfolding. Its culturally inflected virtuosity and powerful communicative qualities "bear witness" to the psychic and sensual connections between the spiritual individual and the well-being of the community. Consequently, it creates a vitally dialogic space for performer and audience in which the spirit can emerge as ecstatic feeling and emotion, and promote understanding and transformation.

Reggie Wilson: Spirit, Culture, and Community

Reggie Wilson, a native of Milwaukee, Wisconsin, is a personable, lean-built man with thick dreadlocks (at the time of this interview, July 1, 2006) and a perceptible southern/midwestern accent. He possesses an inquisitive and mischievous wit, which becomes evident in his provocative and characteristically conceptual choreography. Anthropological in his approach, Wilson formed the Reggie Wilson / Fist and Heel Performance Group in 1989 in New York, incorporating black traditional religious and cultural practices (like the ring shout). The term "fist and heel" refers to the worshipping style in which enslaved Africans, who had been denied the drum, made music with stomps, claps, and vocal sounds. This is powerfully exemplified in Wilson's unique use of live a cappella arrangements of field hollers, blues, gospel, and folk songs from the black southern culture of the United States, the Caribbean, and Africa. This combination imbues much of his works with a religious, mystical quality.

In developing his approach, Wilson began researching his family roots (which are in Mississippi and Tennessee). He then went to New Orleans to study the religious and cultural practices of black Catholics and then to Trinidad and Tobago, where he worked with Noble Douglas to study the religious practices of the Spiritual Baptists. Finally, in the mid-1990s he began a series of trips to Zimbabwe, where he studied, taught, and performed.

Wilson's movement style combines his training in Martha Graham, José Limon, and Merce Cunningham, with some contact improvisation-like partnering, and African and African American social-dance forms. In talking about themes that inspire him, Wilson states: "I was always intrigued by the way black people worshipped. . . . I was interested in exploring untold stories. . . . I wanted to know why Mother So and So cried and testified every Sunday, and why Mr. So and So shouted up and down the aisles" (Wilson, interview, July 1, 2006). Yet in talking about how emotion plays into this, Wilson is somewhat ambivalent. He insists that individual manifestations of feeling, even though they come through, are not as important to him as the dancers embodying the cultural integrity of the movement.

In explaining this philosophy, Wilson describes himself as a postmodern choreographer "who draws from black cultural heritage" (Wilson, interview, July 1, 2006). For him, "postmodern" means that he associates with the conceptual and experimental choreographic strategies of downtown dance. For example, he combines task-like structuring, juxtaposition, and fragmented imagery with spoken text and open-ended or nonliteral approaches to meaning. He cites Merce Cunningham as a big influence in this regard (Wilson, interview, July 1, 2006).

But Wilson's "postmodernism" is relevant here more specifically because it presents an interesting challenge in terms of how we might read his work within the context of black dance and the spirit. Alluding to this, dance critic Julinda Lewis writes: "Wilson imbues familiar themes with a sense of mystery that is at once as exhilarating as it is unsettling" ("A Black Burlesque," in *Dance Magazine*, July 1995, 67). Lewis's critique exposes a tension between the expectations that Wilson's use of black cultural material engenders and how he chooses to frame this material in his choreography.

To illustrate this point, I offer an example: Wilson's *Rise Sally Rise* (2001) is a trio for three women in voluminous tattered dresses, suggesting women who toil in the fields. According to Wilson, they represent "the essence of women rising to adversity" (Wilson, pers. comm., March 23, 2009). Here, Wilson juxtaposes highly abstract African/modern dance structures against mournful field hollers. However, as Lewis suggests, the way in which Wilson deploys the music, movement, and theme can "unsettle" our expectations in terms of what things mean, since he does not give us traditional syntactical or contextual reference points. For his part, Wilson is keenly aware that he unsettles our expectations. But he insists that he is interested in exploring new ways of interpreting the cultural material and rejects what he calls "traditional interpretations of blackness" (Wilson, pers. comm., March 23, 2009).

So how can we reconcile these aspects of Wilson's work with the notions of spirit I have been talking about in this chapter? Or is it the case that these aspects simply crowd out the potentiality of spirit? To address these questions, I cite reviewer Michael Wade Simpson: "Those who came expecting Alvin Ailey–style theatrics probably went away perplexed and disappointed. This was an evening where theory and representation were explored. . . . This approach has its merits" (review of Wilson's company in the Yerba Buena Performing Arts Center, California—program: *Introduction, Jumping the Broom, [untitled]*, April 30, 2007, 2). As I am attempting to show here, Simpson recognizes both Wilson's approach and also the theoretical problem of situating it within traditional frameworks. Simpson's article continues: "The ritualism communicates. Wilson offers depth instead of flash, a kind of cumulative spiritualism rather than any 'wow' moments."

Simpson's term "cumulative spiritualism" is helpful here. Therefore, I appropriate it and combine it with Kariamu Welsh-Asante's notion of "holism" in her writings about African dances. She argues, in essence, that parts of a creation are not necessarily emphasized, but that the gathering of parts within a multiple experience can engender spirituality (150). And as if to concur with this, Wilson himself states: "When I think about spirit and spirituality, I think of community. . . . My upbringing is in the [black] church. It is an important part of me, it feeds my work, it inspires what I do" (Wilson, pers. comm., March 23, 2009). Considering this, then, although Wilson's conceptual trope might challenge conventional ideas about spirit and cultural meaning, his holistic use of elements (texts, music, and movement) and, especially, his personal investment in his work constitute a cumulative and imminently potential embodiment of spirit in the performance event. Let us now explore this.

Wilson's *Black Burlesque (Revisited)* premiered in 2003, eight years after the original evening-length *Black Burlesque* (1995). The first version, which is set in an imaginary New Orleans brothel/nightclub, has a concrete narrative,

FIGURE 6.2. Fist and Heel Performance Group in *Black Burlesque (Revisited)*, 2003. Photo by Julieta Cervantes. Courtesy of Reggie Wilson, Fist and Heel Performance Group.

which offers an ironic take on "the traumatized, sexualized, and racialized black body" (Wilson's Press Kit, 2003). *Black Burlesque (Revisited)*, however, is more abstract, evincing very little reference to burlesque and trauma, although he does not completely eliminate the display-like focus on the racialized black body. According to Wilson, this newer version "explores the intense involvement, which people of the African diaspora generally have with religious and/or ritual life and the historic arch from spiritual practice to popular entertainment in the participating artists' homelands" (Wilson's Press Kit, 2003).

The performance of the work I used for analysis was video recorded on January 22, 2004, by Wonderland Productions, lasting fifty-five minutes and twenty-six seconds. The cast is a combination of dancers, singers, and actors, consisting of five women and seven men. The performers are Rhetta Aleong (Wilson's longtime artistic collaborator), Paul Hamilton, Penelope Kalloo, Pene McCourty, and Reggie Wilson (from Fist and Heel); Charlene Harris, Richard Lessey, Louanna Martin (from Noble Douglas Dance Company); and Thomeki Dube, Dumisani Ndlovu, Brian Sibanda, and Clemence Sibanda (from Black Umfolosi). Tyler Micoleau created the lighting, and Thomeki Dube created a huge leatherlike backdrop that resembles a patchwork of various skins sewn together, which, when lit across the various scenes, takes on beautiful visual textures. The costumes, which are cut in smart contemporary patterns, comprise a mixture of African garb and versions of what poor black sharecroppers might have worn in bygone days. In the opening scene, two turning disco mirror balls project lights into the space and on the backdrop at various points. Wilson's use of the mirror ball is his way of inserting elements that "deliteralize" [my word] and fragment time and place (Wilson, pers. comm., July 1, 2006).

Consisting of two acts, the piece begins with the lights focused on the dancers' feet as they perform a ring shout in complicated rhythmic arm movements and shuffling foot patterns. The music has a driving Afro-disco beat with overlaid sounds that resemble factory sirens and human grunts, which convey a work-like drive as the dancing builds in emotional and kinesthetic intensity. The mood changes abruptly as a scratchy recording of a female blues singer with a high-pitched voice interacts with a male voice, singing about the virtues of "a proud pretty mama." During this song, the dancers walk sideways across the stage in single file as if they are being displayed for sale. Expressions on their faces range from defiance, bemusement, pride, and fear to indifference. This seems designed to imbue the bodies with individual subjective agency, suggesting a sense of power over one's own situation. This is enriched by the fact that the performers are from different countries and, therefore, provide evidence of their subjectivity through their interpretation of the movement.

The somber parade then dissolves into a bright and boisterous community of people who greet each other, talk, dance, sing, and play games in a circle, as they speak in various languages (English, Trinidadian patois, and Ndebele [Zimbabwe]). After the greeting, the group forms couples, including one male-to-male couple, which appears to have no particular significance. The scene is like a call to prayer. At first, the performers sing softly together in harmony, then dance around each other in close spatial relationships. They finish, standing together with arms reaching toward the sky while Wilson sings a solemn field holler about "going to glory" and Rhetta Aleong follows with a Trinidadian song about "Adam hiding from the Lord." The motif of couples remains prominent throughout the rest of the piece.

In one of the most powerfully danced scenes, the entire group sings various South African songs with rhythmic grunts while performing explosive repetitive rocking, leaping, and stomping movements, reminiscent of the Dinhe dance (Zimbabwe). This dance traditionally calls on spirits and reflects on agricultural traditions of the community. As they move, the dancers seem to gather strength and courage from each other, which allows for tiny moments of improvisation. Another lively moment occurs when four of the male members from the Umfolosi group perform the intricate foot-stomping, hand-clapping Ingquzu (gum-boot dance) and improvise competitive interactions with each other while the other dancers perform in slow modern dance movements around them. This section is met with enthusiastic applause at the end (audible on the video).

The final scene of Act I features the entire cast dancing to an up-tempo percussion score in an elegant procession, which follows a serpentine path throughout the space. With hands on hips and syncopated heel and toe movements, the couples smile at each other as they sway side to side and move forward. Although not the end of the piece, this scene solidifies the community energy through a celebratory offering of song, dance, and theater.

Act II reprises several themes from the first act. It begins with the entire cast seated in a semicircle, intoning a solemn Ndebele hymn sung in three-part harmony. An intimate amber glow pervades, suggesting a new day, once again highlighting the huge cloth backdrop. Ensuing vignettes shift rapidly through dances from different cultures, culminating with the entire company taking up the intricate boot dance again in a rousing crescendo.

But the spiritual climax of Act II comes when Wilson channels this energy into one body. Here, Aleong performs a solo where she is seated on the floor, with legs forward, body upright, and arms folded in front of her. This dance consists of inching forward on her behind along a diagonal path while she is urged on by the drummers and other dancers. She becomes increasingly possessed (portrayed and felt), fighting off the spirit and then embracing it, as if afraid of it, yet consoled by it. It is worth noting that Wilson has used this powerful image in other works. When the solo ends, the audience applauds loudly, as Aleong seems genuinely moved; and the dancers take up a final farewell dance.

In sum, in *Black Burlesque (Revisited)* the dancing body conveys spirit and meaning through community and cultural representation. In Act I, bodies enact invocation, play, ritual, and communal prayer. In Act II, the group performs together in various ways and then channels the energy back to one body. For me, a particularly memorable feature of the work is that in bringing together the three companies, from three different cultures, and with different backgrounds in training, Wilson succeeds in invoking and celebrating a unified sense of spiritual and community practice. This is also expressed in the video documentary of the piece, where several of the performers talked about discovering a sense of community that derived not only from wanting the work to succeed, but also from learning about the commonalities of their cultures (*Black Burlesque [Revisited]*, Dance Theater Workshop, 2003).

In Conclusion

In this chapter I have attempted to show that spirit courses through the dances of Ronald K. Brown and Reggie Wilson as an imminent potentiality. Since coming of age as dance makers in the 1980s and 1990s, Brown and Wilson are among those choreographers who have created works not merely for theatrical consumption but also to convey transformational spiritual experiences, which explicitly link their individual identities as human beings to their sense of an Africanist cosmic and cultural family (Daniel, *Dancing Wisdom*, 64). In this context, the Africanist dancing body is the threshold (Lawal), the performance site where spirit can emerge in both familiar and new ways. As such, it bears witness to psychic and performative dimensions that, even within the structures of concert performance, allow for a heightened black religious/spiritual and culturally inflected expression.

For me, as an audience member, experiencing spirit in this type of dance brings to mind the Yoruba concept of *àshe*, as articulated by Robert Farris Thompson: "the power to make things happen, a key to futurity and self-realization" (Thompson, *Flash of the Spirit*, xv). This power to make things happen resides in that antiphonal spiritual-artistic relationship—expressed through the praising, shouting, dancing body—which inspires, informs, and transforms, and is, therefore, essential to the ongoing spiritual agency of faith, healing, survival, and empowerment of black people.

Notes

1. In *Resurrection Song: African-American Spirituality*, Flora Wilson Bridges talks about the importance of understanding the convergence of the sacred and secular in black/African culture. Her central point is that "the African American community, with its unified worldview, does not confine spirituality to religion . . . that African American religion is not the same as African American spirituality, though the latter certainly includes the former" (3).

With regard to the concept of "reading dance," I draw on Susan L. Foster's notion of "reading" as an interactive interpretation of "dance as a system of meaning" (Foster, *Reading Dancing*, xvii). Hence, my methodology will integrate what I understand to be the choreographers' intended meanings and use of the body with my understanding of spirit in relation to these meanings.

2. In *Digging the Africanist Presence in American Performance: Dance and Other Contexts*, Gottschild uses the term "Africanist" to indicate the presence of black African cultural retentions in the black diaspora (xiii). Although this term may not fully address the complexity of African and African diaspora cultures, it has taken on a ge-

neric currency in dance studies that refers to emphasis on African and African American diaspora cultural and aesthetic forms. I use the term in this sense, and in addition, I place emphasis on the suffix "ist" to underscore Brown's and Wilson's artistic choice to explicitly foreground African-derived dance.

At the same time, I note that Brown and Wilson do not describe themselves as "Africanist modern dancers," although they also do not reject the concept. Brown prefers the term "contemporary African dance" and Wilson uses the term "neo Afro hoodoo postmodern dance" (Brown, pers. comm., February 13, 2007; Wilson, pers. comm., March 23, 2008).

3. DeFrantz deploys Frantz Fanon's conceptualization of "the circle that protects and permits . . . as a space of black expressive culture" (DeFrantz, "Foreword: Black Bodies," 10). DeFrantz focuses on ways in which we might understand dancing black bodies and cultural meaning in and out of the protective circle and relates this concept to the black dancing body in concert dance.

4. In her book *Butting Out: Reading Resistive Choreographies through Works by Jawole Willa Jo Zollar and Chandralekha*, Chatterjea talks about two female choreographers "of color" (one African American, the other Indian) who infuse in their work aesthetic and spiritual elements from their cultures in ways that reflect specific dimensions of self and levels of meaning.

5. In a discussion of Ron Brown in *The Black Dancing Body: A Geography from Coon to Cool*, Gottschild provides an instructive description of Sabar technique: "fast footwork, turned-in knee and hip positions, and flying or wind milling arms, ending with flexed wrists" (287). Brown told me that, for him, "the rhythm is in the feet and the arms are decoration, they express what you want to say" (pers. comm., December 11, 2006).

6. Sunbeam uses this tableau to break the ice. The Pointer Sisters were very popular among black gay drag queens in part because they were fun to imitate.

UNCOVERED: A PAGEANT OF HIP HOP MASTERS

A PERFORMANCE CONCEIVED AND DIRECTED BY RICKERBY HINDS
This text is adapted from an interview conducted by Richard C. Green.

> [Record covers] . . . should be understood as complex cultural artifacts—
> objects—in their own right.
> **—Paul Gilroy, "Wearing Your Art on Your Sleeve"**

Uncovered: A Pageant of Hip Hop Masters re-creates life-size versions of classic hip-hop album covers from artists considered to be pioneers in this musical genre through the use of the *tableau vivant* theatrical technique. The artists included are Run-DMC, Queen Latifah, LL Cool J, Salt-N-Pepa, A Tribe Called Quest, Wu-Tang Clan, MC Lyte, Notorious BIG (Biggie), Tupac, Jay-Z, and Nas. This re-creation is accompanied by a live DJ mix of songs from each artist and complemented by the performers embodying the movement of the artists as well as dance styles that were popular during the album's release.

The name of this project, *Uncovered: A Pageant of Hip Hop Masters*, comprises three individual components. "Uncovered" references the act of exposing what exists behind the album covers: the music, movement, or dance associated with the particular artist, as well as the messages embedded in the music. One level of uncovering occurs in the exploration and positioning of these narratives in front of an audience, giving them the opportunity to discover or rediscover the music and artists through the live performance. Un/covered simultaneously alludes to the artists coming off the two-dimensional cover to become three-dimensional beings in performance.

"A Pageant" refers to both the style of the performance as a pageant—a show or exhibition, especially one consisting of a succession of participants or events—as well as the performance that inspired this piece, the *Pageant of the Masters*, an annual performance in Laguna, California, in which life-size versions of paintings by the "masters" are re-created through the use of tableaux vivants (see http://www.foapom.com/).

"Hip Hop Masters" refers to the moniker originally given to rappers, "master of ceremonies," but is also intended to subvert the idea of those portraying "masters" as a group that will never include anyone who looks like any of the masters of ceremonies included in *Uncovered*.

The albums were selected based on artists that were part of the beginning of hip-hop's recorded history and who were transcendent figures (Run-DMC, LL Cool J, Salt-N-Pepa, Queen Latifah, A Tribe Called Quest), as well as artists who had a tremendous impact on hip-hop and American popular culture (Wu-Tang, Tupac, Biggie, Nas, Jay-Z). As part of the production's process, the performers were asked to do their own research, not only on the visuals and movements associated with their artists, but on their historical impact and significance. Rehearsals included discussions between old and new hip-hop heads, and information considered common knowledge by some was discovered not to be so common. One memorable moment was a conversation about the significance of Queen Latifah as a strong female rap artist when she came on the scene and an attempt to contextualize and explain the importance of her songs "Wrath of My Madness" and "Ladies First" for those who only know her as an actress and a singer.

Although rehearsal conversations often focused on artists from the past, romanticizing the "good old days" was never the goal, since more often than not the idealization of the past as "so much better than now" recycles flawed reasoning based on an idealized reimagining of said past. And unfortunately sometimes we let the nostalgia for the "good old days" distort our view of the greatness of the present. Are records better than CDs, better than MP3s, better than . . . whatever the next technological breakthrough will be? I guess this would be like saying that canvas Chuck Taylor sneakers are better than the latest version of leather Adidas. In either case it probably boils down to who is wearing them and what they can do in them. A while back there was a commercial with the tagline "It's gotta be the shoes," as Michael Jordan performed amazing feats wearing Air Jordans, but the clear implication was that it really wasn't the shoes, it was the wearer.

The shift from records to the digital realm definitely precludes certain forms of sharing by this generation. Clearly, there aren't a bunch of teenagers sitting around listening to a record player and passing the album covers around anymore. But isn't there a community formed whenever music is shared? Clearly, it's a different type of community, but the Facebook community shares photos, articles, videos, thoughts, and even music artwork— digitally.

With its artists spinning on their heads; spraying vibrant, rebellious colors on subways; participating in battles that stretched from individuals to crews, to neighborhoods, to states, to regions from coast to coast, the much-maligned art form of hip-hop has withstood thirty years of misogynistic lyrics, gangster bravado, homophobia, and violent deaths. When Nas proclaimed "Hip-hop is dead," perhaps he was referring to the spirit of hip-hop, the essence of the pioneers of the culture. Although hip-hop culture was not perfect, in its original form it was not solely a multimillion-dollar enterprise as it is in many cases now. It was about the act of reclaiming one's environment and reimaging it in creative, dynamic ways. That is also the act of *Uncovered*, revealed in these photographs.

On Framing *Uncovered: A Pageant of Hip Hop Masters*

In conceptualizing *Uncovered* my intention was to simultaneously salute and disturb a traditional form of artistic expression—the tableau vivant defined as a representation of a scene, painting, sculpture, and so forth, by a person or group posed silently and motionlessly. Anyone even vaguely familiar with hip-hop culture understands that it is anything but silent and motionless, but instead could be more accurately described as just the opposite—often loud and in perpetual motion. My goal then in melding these two forms of artistic creation was to discover that place where their intersection would produce a performance that would elevate both forms and together create a unique and compelling theatrical experience. By taking what I perceived as the strongest element of the tableau vivant (the three-dimensional, life-size re-creation of images) and the strongest element of hip-hop culture's performance (dance, emceeing, and DJ-ing) and combining them, I believed that this would create a dynamic and memorable performance.

I additionally wanted to decrease the distance between the audience and performers. To that end, instead of staging the performance on a traditional proscenium stage far away from the audience and having the performers come "onstage" as the audience sits and watches, I set up the stage as an art gallery (University of California, Riverside's Sweeney Art Gallery) where the audience did not sit and wait but moved from exhibit to exhibit, from album cover to album cover, to find either the tableau already formed, in which case it would then "come to life" triggered by the DJ's mix, or the performers would enter and complete the picture by adding their body to the incomplete tableau set pieces. This performance technique not only kept the audience engaged by providing them with a variety of beginnings and endings, but it also put them in the middle of the performance as unwitting and sometimes unwilling participants.

This performance style references another legacy of hip-hop's tradition of audience inclusion. From its constant use of call-and-response as well as the cipher as space of creation, audience members are expected to be more than spectators. You are, as a part of the circle, expected to participate in the event taking place, thereby enhancing the "community" through your own performance skills no matter what they are.

Salt-N-Pepa

Salt-N-Pepa were included in *Uncovered* because of their pioneering status as female emcees. They came up during a period when not only was the dominance of male emcees the norm, but hip-hop had not produced a female emcee who could go up against her male counterparts in spittin' rhymes or in bringing fans to their concerts and selling records. Salt-N-Pepa did that. Their sound, as well as their look—from their hairstyles to their leather and spandex outfits—became ubiquitous, transcending the hip-hop community and becoming a part of American popular culture. The album cover for *A Salt with a Deadly Pepa* succinctly demonstrates the dichotomous relationship between hip-hop and women, who are required to be at once sexy, tough, and flexible, hence the spandex, leather, and hair.

The Salt-N-Pepa cast culminated *Uncovered* with a performance of "Push It," taking the audience back to the first hip-hop women emcees to combine sexuality with strength. The three members of the group were introduced to the routine that was imprinted on the bodies of most teenage girls into hip-hop at the time.

Run-DMC

Run-DMC's *Tougher than Leather* was included in *Uncovered* for many reasons, the first being the stature of Run-DMC in the hip-hop world as arguably the most important musical group to come out of hip-hop culture. As pioneers in an art form that was maligned and vilified as much at its inception as it is presently—but without the critical acclaim, financial track record, and cultural impact to fall back on—Run-DMC stand head and shoulders above any artists laying claim to being the fathers/founders/

FIGURE 7.1. Salt-N-Pepa Rehearsal (Maiah Wesson, Rhaechyl Walker, Errin Johnson, Jonathan Droualt). Copyright © 2009 The Regents of the University of California. Photo by Nick DiFilippo, UC Regents. Courtesy of Sweeney Art Gallery.

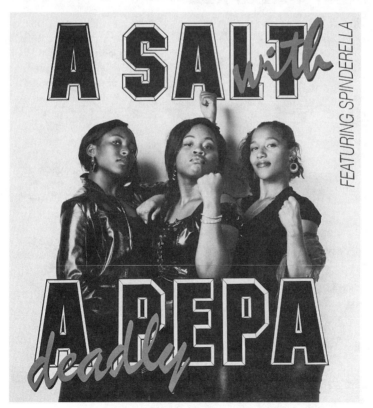

FIGURE 7.2. Salt-N-Pepa (Maiah Wesson, Rhaechyl Walker, Errin Johnson). © 2009 The Regents of the University of California. Photo by Nick DiFilippo, UC Regents. Courtesy of Sweeney Art Gallery.

FIGURE 7.3. Run-DMC Rehearsal (Alex Avila, Jonathan Droualt). © 2009 The Regents of the University of California. Photo by Nick DiFilippo, UC Regents, courtesy of Sweeney Art Gallery.

FIGURE 7.4. Run-DMC Rehearsal 2 (Jonathan Droualt, Alex Avila). © 2009 The Regents of the University of California. Photo by Nick DiFilippo, UC Regents. Courtesy of Sweeney Art Gallery.

FIGURE 7.5. Run-DMC (Alex Avila, Alexander Brown-Hinds, Jonathan Droualt). © 2009 The Regents of the University of California. Photo by Nick DiFilippo, UC Regents. Courtesy of Sweeney Art Gallery.

creators of hip-hop culture's masters of ceremonies. I felt that a performance entitled *Uncovered: A Pageant of Hip Hop Masters* would be blasphemous without their inclusion.

The album cover for *Tougher than Leather* was selected for several reasons: the iconic "fashion" on display; the Kangol, "dookie" gold chains, Gazelle glasses, shoes with no shoe strings, and especially the Adidas, which represent the beginning of the connection between hip-hop and name brands, sports, and popular-culture fashion. This cover was also visually compelling, featuring the black outfits against a plain backdrop (in performance the backdrop was white, while on the album cover the backdrop is blue). Finally, this was one of the few Run-DMC covers prominently featuring Jam Master Jay—especially important to me since his passing in 2002. The performance aspect of this tableau invited each performer to embody Run-DMC and Jam Master Jay through the use of movement/dance and slow motion.

FIGURE 7.6. Wu-Tang Clan Rehearsal 1 (Alexander Brown-Hinds, Timothy Dupree, Errin Johnson, Tyron Sutton). © 2009 The Regents of the University of California. Photo by Nick DiFilippo, UC Regents. Courtesy of Sweeney Art Gallery.

FIGURE 7.7. Wu-Tang Clan Rehearsal 2 (Alexander Brown-Hinds, Timothy Dupree, Errin Johnson, Tyron Sutton). © 2009 The Regents of the University of California. Photo by Nick DiFilippo, UC Regents. Courtesy of Sweeney Art Gallery.

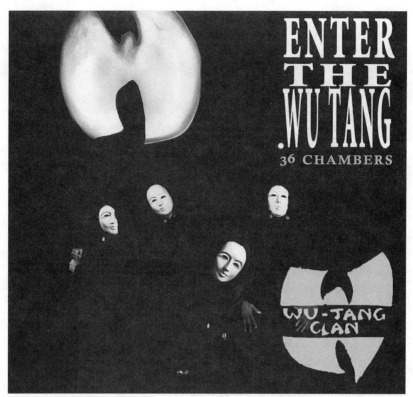

FIGURE 7.8. Wu-Tang Clan (Alexander Brown-Hinds, Timothy Dupree, Errin Johnson, Tyron Sutton). © 2009 The Regents of the University of California. Photo by Nick DiFilippo, UC Regents. Courtesy of Sweeney Art Gallery.

Wu-Tang Clan

Enter the 36 Chambers represented a seismic shift in hip-hop music, not only because of the sound and look of the Wu, but, as was later discovered, because it changed the relationship between rap groups—and what defined a group—and their record labels. The Wu managed to be simultaneously signed as a group to one label and as solo artists to another. But the Wu sound was what placed *36 Chambers* in its own class, from the distinct production style to the gutter rhyming style to the almost horrific images conjured by the lyrics as well as the videos, when the Wu was a different animal. This album cover was selected for the visual dynamics that it offered: there are no human faces on the cover, but rather mostly blackness, letters, and the Wu logo.

This cover also afforded the opportunity to incorporate Krump dance into the production. (Krump is a dance form physically characterized by

FIGURE 7.9. Queen Latifah Rehearsal (Selvana Elwardany). © 2009 The Regents of the University of California. Photo by Nick DiFilippo, UC Regents. Courtesy of Sweeney Art Gallery.

FIGURE 7.10. Queen Latifah (Selvana Elwardany). © 2009 The Regents of the University of California. Photo by Nick DiFilippo, UC Regents. Courtesy of Sweeney Art Gallery.

expressive, exaggerated, and highly energetic movement involving the arms, head, legs, chest, and feet.) As soon as I decided to include *36 Chambers* in this production, I knew that the only dance style that could do it justice was Krump. This segment of the show became one of the audience's favorites. The power of Krump coupled with masked dancers and the instrumental version of Cream created one of the most captivating performance moments in *Uncovered*.

Queen Latifah

The inclusion of Queen Latifah in *Uncovered* was unquestionable. Before becoming an award-winning actress and singer, Queen Latifah was a vital part of the "conscious era" of hip-hop music as the "Princess of the Posse," with the Native Tongues. She sought to bring dignity and pride to female emcees through her lyrics, her look, and her eventual evolution from emcee to actress, businesswoman, and legend.

PART III   /   Black Imaginary

BLACK MOVEMENTS

Flying Africans in Spaceships

In songs, stories, and literary representations, images of psychic, emotional, and physical flights permeate African American expressive culture. From narrations of the Flying Africans, by informants born in the late nineteenth century, to Toni Morrison's novel *Song of Solomon* (1977), flying represents one of the quintessential thrusts of African American aesthetics—the pursuit of freedom. However, unlike many early black emancipation narratives including those of Frederick Douglass, in the Flying Africans tale freedom is gained through death, not necessarily through literacy. The Flying Africans began as a tale circulated among enslaved black people in the Americas that depicted Africans who, tired of the oppressive conditions of chattel slavery, used metaphysical powers and flew back to Africa. Some theorists argue the myth communicates enslaved Africans' mass suicide. Through death, the Africans metaphorically flew from a state of oppression to freedom. Within this metaphysical context, the imagery of the Flying Africans demonstrates an ambiguity toward death.

In the twentieth century, *Song of Solomon* marks that ambivalence as it shifts the terms of the pursuit from physical and social death to a psychic one as well. In the final scene of *Song of Solomon*, the main character, Milkman, engages in a life-and-death battle with his friend Guitar. Depicting it as a flight, the novel omits the final location of the journey and therefore leaves ambiguous whether Milkman dies a physical or a psychic death. *Song of Solomon* leaves room for the possibility that Milkman cheats physical death, defeats Guitar, and as a result, dies a psychic death that enables the emergence of his newly freed self. Similar to *Song of*

Solomon, funk band Parliament's album *Mothership Connection* (1976) offers strategies to combat the psychic and social deaths experienced by black subjects in America. Drawing from technological innovations, Parliament recoups the imagery of the slave ship and transforms it into a spaceship that brings mother Africa to black Americans. The migration home, in this case, does not require black people to retrace the Middle Passage. Building on the imagery of Africans flying in spaceships, Grammy Award–winning hip-hop artist Kanye West posits acceptance of psychic death induced by racial recognition as a prerequisite to flight through the juxtaposition of "I'll Fly Away" and "Spaceship" on his debut album.

On West's album, hearing "I'll Fly Away," a familiar refrain in African American sacred and secular expressive culture, reminds the listener that oral performance has the potential to enact flights with a cost. While most theorists consider the visual imagery of the Flying Africans and the way flight acts as a signifier of freedom in general, I am also interested in the way each of the depictions of the Flying Africans I consider (the folktales, Morrison's novel, and musical interpretations) uses sound to signify on the embodied movement, the physical display—a display that, importantly, serves as a metaphor for death. Each performance of Flying Africans negotiates death, albeit different types, as a conduit to freedom. The nature of the death (physical, social, psychic, or some combination therein) correlates to the geographical movement imagined in the texts. This chapter considers the depictions of Flying Africans as black performances and more particularly black movements, paying particular attention to the way the depictions of flight enact a performance and imply other meanings of movement, including political and geographical. I argue flight is a paradigm of black performance precisely because it communicates an ongoing life-and-death battle in black culture. Although the implications shift over time and across geographic locations, the negotiations with the freedom drive and the death drive persist in depictions of Flying Africans.

Black Performance in/through Black Migration

The Flying Africans, often referred to as a tale, exceeds the literary and calls for not only the interweaving of the literate and the oral but also the incorporation of performance. The expression of the Flying Africans tale falls under the broad category of performance; however, I further specify it as an archetype of orature and emblematic of black movement. Black movement identifies orature that includes migration. Orature is an aesthetic system coined by Ugandan literary theorist Pio Zirimu and developed by Kenyan novelist, playwright, and essayist Ngugi wa Thiong'o. According to wa Thiong'o,

Zirimu developed the term to distinguish between oral and visual narratives. Wa Thiong'o builds on Zirimu's theorization, describing orature as "a total aesthetic system" (117). He categorizes: "Orature transcends the narrow binaries of the written and the oral that condition so much of anthropological and literary thought today. It suggests a transcendence over both the purely oral, the purely literary, and the purely performed" (119). In black literary studies, theorists continually debate the relationship between oral and written narrative. For example, key figures in the debate, Madhu Dubey and Harryette Mullen, question Cornel West and Henry Louis Gates's tendency to privilege orality. West argues: "The ur-text of black culture is neither a word nor a book, not an architectural monument or a legal brief. Instead, it is a guttural cry and a wrenching moan" (*Black Spiritual Strivings*, 81). Mullen counters: "Any theory of African-American literature that privileges a speech based poetics, or the trope of orality, to the exclusion of more writerly text will cost us some impoverishment of the tradition" (670–71). Meta DuEwa Jones and Brent Hayes Edwards find some middle ground between orality and textuality, noting their mutuality. That mutuality enables a similar but significantly different move by wa Thiong'o, who deploys the term orature to account for orality, textuality, and performativity.

Wa Thiong'o's intervention has been useful to many scholars, including Joseph Roach. In *Cities of the Dead: Circum-Atlantic Performance*, Roach details the applicability of the term "orature" across time (from an interpretation of the Declaration of Independence to late twentieth-century celebrations of Mardi Gras in New Orleans) and space (the relationship between the Declaration of Independence and the Haitian Revolution). He explains that the flexibility of the concept comes from the way in which "orature comprises a range of forms" and "goes beyond a schematized opposition of literary and orality as transcendent categories; rather, it acknowledges that these modes of communication have produced one another interactively over time and that their historic operations may be usefully examined under the rubric of performance" (12).

Roach strategically foregrounds performance in his interpretation to clarify how orature moves beyond the literary/orality divide. Dwight Conquergood explains wa Thiongo's concept of orature as "that liminal space between speech and writing, performance and print, where these channels of communication constantly overlap, penetrate, and mutually produce one another" ("Rethinking Elocution," 147). Therefore, I hold on to wa Thiong'o's claim that orature, as an aesthetic, recognizes performance, orality, and literacy as mutually constitutive. At the same time, orature allows me to consider how the Flying Africans function, in part, as a mode of black performance and more specifically black movement. By categorizing the circulation and transformation of the Flying Africans tale as black movement, I extend their theorization, which has been primarily from a literary perspective, beyond the literary/orality divide, and I am also able to intervene in the discourse of black performance.

The category of black movement brings together studies of migration and performance in order to decipher the implications of an embodied action across time and space. The Flying Africans tale draws attention to the connection between modes of resistance informed by life in the nineteenth century on the Gold Coast of Africa and in the twentieth century on the Georgia coast. I define performance, to borrow and intertwine Richard Schechner's and wa Thiong'o's theories, as restored or twice-behaved behavior (Schechner, 36) that "assumes an audience during its actualization" (wa Thiong'o, 5). The explicit inclusion of audience helps explain the political dimension of Flying Africans tale in that the audience becomes interpellated and therefore implicated by the performance. The political aspect constitutive of black movement exists alongside the other meanings of movement, for example, geographic. What might performance studies learn from studies of migration, and how might a turn to performance shed light on theoretical blind spots in theories of geographic movement? Although the focus of much of migration studies is not performance, a few studies have considered the intersection of performance and migration studies. In *The Black Atlantic: Modernity and Double Consciousness*, Paul Gilroy theorizes the circulation of black culture as a process that shapes the black Atlantic. Similarly, in the introduction to *Black Cultural Traffic*, Kennell Jackson describes "the movement of cultural matter" in terms of cultural traffic (14). Jackson details: "Performance is a key element in such traffic" (4). Within these studies, *Cities of the Dead* stands out as an exemplar of how to engage both fields. Roach's argument is singular in its call for the centrality of performance in the constitution of circum-Atlantic culture. He contends: "The scope of the circum-Atlantic interculture may be discerned most vividly by means of the performances, performance traditions, and the representations of performance that it engendered. This is true, I think, because performances so often carry within them the memory of otherwise forgotten substitutions—those that were rejected and, even more invisibly, those that have succeeded" (5). Roach's insertion of the role of memory transforms much of performance studies and plays an important role in my analysis of the Flying Africans. The idea of embodied practice having the capacity to function as a reservoir that remembers centralizes performance as a field that makes important contributions to other modes of inquiry, including literary and historical studies.

The Flying Africans inspire cultural memory through sound—"I'll Fly Away"—and sight, as they draw attention to a "'singing' impulse in black literature" (Edwards, "Introduction," 6). Emphasizing the way sound echoes in the ear, on the page, and in different spaces, some of the earliest depictions of Flying Africans resound in literary representations of the black diaspora and hip-hop lyrics.[1] Iterations of the Flying Africans tale skate along the edge of orality and textuality creating formal qualities that mark life-and-death struggles. In its earliest renditions in the United States, the Flying Africans offered hope for freedom and transcendence, even though that flight might mean physical death. In its most recent articulations, the narrative provides temporary relief to struggle as it continues to invoke death as a mode of deliverance. Although the modern permutations contain problematic aspects, they offer a model of aesthetics deeply rooted in political and social choices. Toni Morrison describes the options of her flying male characters thus: "Unlike most mythical flights, which clearly imply triumph, in the attempt if not the success, Solomon's escape, the insurance man's jump, and Milkman's leap are ambiguous, disturbing" (*Song of Solomon*, xiv). Similarly, the iterations of the Flying Africans and their reincarnation in rap music depict difficult choices made under physically and psychologically trying circumstances.

First Iterations: Folktales

The fluidity of life and death expressed often in *Drums and Shadows: Survival Studies among the Georgia Coastal Negroes* (published by the Savannah Unit of the Georgia Writers' Project, Works Projects Administration), the earliest literary representation of Flying Africans, points to "the underlying logic found throughout traditional African systems of thought: that the sacred and the secular, the physical and the metaphysical were not separate spheres but rather integrally together and manifest in the material world," to quote Stephanie Smallwood (130).[2] The theme of death in life or life after death haunts the Flying Africans narrative, which usually contains four pivotal moments: (1) a depiction of exhausting labor, (2) a confrontation with a brutal figure expressing coercive power, (3) an enunciation on the part of an African gifted with supernatural powers, and (4) a vision of an African or a mass of Africans flying away. This structure applies to depictions of Flying Africans by Africans or black people in the United States. Another version exists in which Africans arrive in the Americas and fly back almost immediately. Since I am primarily concerned with how black artists in the United States have utilized flight, I focus on the former rendition. In 1940 the WPA compiled a collection of folklore in *Drums and Shadows* that contains several versions of the Flying Africans, including the ones that influenced *Song of Solomon*.[3] In one version, narrator Tonie Houston describes an African, Solomon Jones, who departed "for his native land, some five or six years ago" and has not been heard from since (67). *Drums and Shadows* juxtaposes Houston's description of the disappearance of Solomon with a depiction of ritual, including a circle dance and the beating of the drums of death to summon "the 'settin-up' or wake" (67). The circle dance served to create a communion among the living and the dead. Although not explicit in Houston's recalling, *Drums and Shadows* categorizes narrator Jack Wilson's depiction of ghosts and his knowledge of Flying Africans within the rubric of the supernatural. Wilson does make the distinction between his spiritual knowledge, which allows him to see and communicate with ghosts, and the magic power of the Flying Africans. Nevertheless, these types of juxtapositions persist and point to a connection the editors and perhaps narrators gleaned between the pursuit of freedom and physical death.

The storytellers in *Drums and Shadows* embody that dichotomy through their act of narration. The syntax and spelling throughout *Drums and Shadows* draw attention to the narration as a speech act; however, one of the storytellers, Paul Singleton, foregrounds sound in his recounting. I distinguish between a speech, which produces sound, and the sound depicted in Singleton's text to foreground the way the narrative calls for sensory engagement. While the reader may overlook Singleton's narration as a performance, paying attention primarily to the narrative and not the form, the depiction of sound insists on such multifaceted attention. Singleton, who claimed to have been brought to Savannah in 1869, recalls two stories told to him by his father, the first of people who could fly back to Africa and the second of enslaved Africans drowned in a creek: "Dey say yuh kin heah um moanin an groanin in duh creek ef yuh goes neah deah tuh-day" (17). The coupling of flight and acoustic production, moaning and groaning, follows a structure similar to Morrison's novel even though Singleton's narrative implies that the Africans who flew away and the ones producing the sound may be the same. In contrast, *Song of Solomon* clarifies that the flight of Solomon, Morrison's Flying African, creates the condition for his wife Ryna's screaming that later becomes associated with the acoustic production of Ryna's Gulch. In Morrison's novel, the sonic materiality of death becomes displaced onto the female character. The novel attributes her heartrending screams to the loss of her husband and the corresponding burden of raising their twenty-one children.

I will return to *Song of Solomon* but would first like to establish another mode of acoustic intervention associated with death in Langston Hughes and Arna Bontemps's recounting of the Flying Africans folktale.

Drawing on the geographic and extending the formal distinctions of *Drums and Shadows*, "All God's Chillen Had Wings," anthologized by Hughes and Bontemps, places the Flying Africans tale in "the sea islands and out-of-the-way places in the low country" as it produces traces of the oral and the acoustic in the text (62). "All God's Chillen Had Wings," which takes place on a plantation, depicts, early in the story, an overseer who uses his lash to strike a young mother for falling down from exhaustion. The young woman seeks counsel from an old man, but "the driver could not understand what they said" (63). The inability of the narrator to translate the conversation between the young woman and the old man places the reader in the position of the overseer; Hughes and Bontemps's story does not give us access to the words they said, limiting our information and calling our attention to the acoustic difference produced by the old man and the young woman. In this case the narrative marks the sound by complete absence, differing from the phonetic approximations offered in *Drums and Shadows*. At the same time, the structure of the narrative varies from *Drums and Shadows*, by including artistic interpretation. In Hughes and Bontemps's story, the acoustic dissonance results from the overseer's linguistic difference, which is analogous to the reader's alienation. The text includes this productive alienation to limit the impulse to claim mastery of the Flying Africans by codifying the occurrence in narrative.[4] Instead of allowing the reader to assume a comfortable place of dominance, the text creates disruptions that point to the reader's inability to access the words fully, to hear what was said or even gain a translation that approximates literary and acoustic fullness.

After establishing the limited, yet still influential, power of the reader/listener, "All God's Chillen Had Wings" creates another moment for improvisation. Anticipating that the young woman will fall again, "the driver came running with his lash to drive her on with her work, she turned to the old man and asked: 'Is it time yet, daddy?' He answered: 'Yes, daughter; the time has come. Go; and peace be with you!' . . . and stretch out his arms toward her . . . so. With that she leaped straight up into the air and was gone like a bird, flying over field and wood" (63, ellipses in the original). The ellipses invite speculation, or, as Jennifer DeVere Brody says, the addition of "supplements to the printed matter in/of the text" (*Punctuation*, 680). The shift in the voice—from the old man to the narrator—suggests that he or she describes the old man's and young woman's actions. What does the old man do or say to prepare her for flight? Does the language in between the ellipses indicate instruction or a demonstration? The text leaves ambiguous the old man's words and the possible motion of the two bodies as it codifies these possibilities. According to Brody, "the ellipsis can be read as a site that invites improvisation: one might say that the ellipsis as a present figure of absence is paradoxically more meaningful, rather than meaningless . . . as the marks that hail the reader as a participant, inviting the audience into imaginative engagement with the text" (*Punctuation*, 687–88). The absence presents the reader with a challenge to listen to the echoes that linger and continue to produce improvisation in African American cultural productions. The punctuation enriches "our understanding of how the vocal and the visual are performed across the geographic space of the page" (Jones, "Jazz Prosodies," 66). Through the use of ellipses, "All God's Chillen Had Wings" demonstrates black movements, inserting an absence that requires readers, from their points of geographic specificity, to translate the action and fill in the gaps. Moreover, the ellipses hail the reader and therefore implicate him or her in a politics of transcendence through death, whether physical or social.

In "If You Surrender to the Air: Folk Legends of Flight and Resistance in African American Literature," Gay Wilentz establishes a central tension among theorists and writers concerning whether the Africans actually flew away or committed suicide. Michael Gomez's historical study *Exchanging Our Country Marks: The Transformation of African Identities in the Colonial and Antebellum South* argues that the Flying Africans serve as evidence that Igbos, enslaved Africans from the Bight of Biafra and West Central Africa, committed suicide in larger percentages than other slave populations. Gomez references the narratives collected in *Drums and Shadows*, which indicates that early populations of enslaved Africans along the Georgia coast came from "the Gambia River and Niger sections; later the coast from the Congo River to the southern end of Portuguese West Africa" (*Drums and Shadows*, xlii). He asserts that these later populations were known to commit mass suicide by drowning and individual acts of disappearance—so much so, he argues, that South Carolina planters refused to purchase Igbo captives. Wilentz turns to Gomez's analysis to establish the different belief systems at work in the analysis of the Flying Africans tale. Although Wilentz raises important questions about the underlying theories that drive different modes of interpretation, I am less interested in whether the Africans actually flew away, which according to Gomez they did not, and more concerned with the impact the Flying Africans had and continue to have on black cultural production. Even as Gomez argues that contemporaries knew the Flying Africans committed suicide, he maintains that the act reflected a will to resist and "contained within it the seed for regeneration and renewal" (120). The choice, then, to tell the story in the contexts recounted in *Drums and Shadows* suggests a commitment to freedom underpinned by a particular metaphysical point of view. The shifting contexts contemporary artists choose imply alternative perspectives.

"Can't Nobody Fly with All That Shit": *Song of Solomon*

Toni Morrison's *Song of Solomon* serves as a touchstone for the theorization of the Flying Africans as black movement precisely because it depicts geographic and psychic migration, emphasizes performance by calling the reader to hear the text, and shifts the politics of flight by introducing a protagonist, Macon Dead III, also known as Milkman, who shows ambivalence to death. Arguably Morrison's most male-centered novel, *Song of Solomon* demonstrates that the maturation of Milkman requires him to go on a journey that the novel associates, from his childhood, with flight. In fact, at age four, when Milkman discovered "that only birds and airplanes could fly—he lost interest in himself" (9). His attempt to regain that interest sparks a quest that occupies the remainder of the novel and results in Milkman claiming his ability to ride the air.

Despite its departure from earlier representations of flight, the novel intertwines the oral, textual, and performance practices constantly at play in revisions of the Flying Africans tale. Much of the critical analysis of *Song of Solomon* considers Morrison's text, to borrow Henry Louis Gates Jr.'s configuration, as a speakerly text.[5] Equal attention has also been paid to Morrison's use of myth, from traditional Western to African American ones.[6] Awareness of the constitution of content through form allows me to move from literary studies of *Song of Solomon* focused on Morrison's negotiation of orality or the function of myth to the way the novel demonstrates orature. In my interpretation I utilize what Brent Hayes Edwards calls the ability to mine "the fertile edge between 'orality' and 'literacy'" and frame that edge with performance (Introduction, 5). From the opening scene to the final one, the novel evokes embodied action. In the opening pages of *Song of Solomon*, Pilate, Milkman's aunt, sings, "O Sugarman done fly away / Sugarman done gone / Sugarman cut across the sky / Sugarman gone home" in front of the hospital in which Milkman is born (6). Hearing the song, Milkman's mother, Ruth, goes into labor. Pilate's refrain serves to usher Milkman into the world and echo through the novel, as "I'll Fly Away" attempts to resonate through this essay. In an interview with Claudia Tate, Morrison explains her desire to "rewrite, discard, and remove the print-quality of the language to put back the oral quality, where intonation, volume and gesture are all there" (126).

Morrison makes explicit a concern with performance—intonation, volume, and gesture—that critics have not given sufficient attention.

Pilate's singing in the beginning of the novel establishes a critical acoustic theme reinforced by the visual display that simultaneously takes place. In the opening scene of the novel, Mr. Smith commits suicide by flying from the cupola of Mercy Hospital. The physical mutilation resulting from Mr. Smith's untimely death introduces the material consequences of flight as it draws into focus characters that will test the strength of their wings. Although Mr. Smith's action does not garner much attention ("not more than forty or fifty people showed up"), Morrison contends, "He [Mr. Smith] hopes his flight . . . is interpreted as a radical gesture demanding change, an alternative way, a cessation of things as they are. He does not want it understood as a simple desperate act, the end of a fruitless life, a life without examination, but as a deep commitment to his people" (*Song of Solomon*, xiii). Morrison's analysis draws attention to the wording of the first line of the novel, and in particular, the use of the word "promised." "The North Carolina Mutual Life Insurance agent promised to fly from Mercy to the other side of Lake Superior at three o'clock" (3). Pointing out "promised" implies a contract "being executed between himself and others" (xiii). The others throughout the novel (family members, friends, and members of the community) hold Smith accountable and determine the implications of the flight. Morrison's choice of word also creates a clear indication of the way form implicates politics through the negotiation with and of others in the performance. All of the performances of flight depicted in *Song of Solomon* imply a type of death. Mr. Smith (a secondary character), Solomon (Milkman's ancestor), Pilate (Milkman's aunt), and Milkman must give up themselves, or what Morrison eloquently describes as "that shit that weighs you down," in order to fly (179).

The second half of the novel further clarifies the meaning of flight when Milkman begins a journey in search of his family treasure—gold—first to Danville, Pennsylvania, and then Shalimar, Virginia, the former home of his ancestors Solomon and Ryna. He believes discovering the gold will grant him financial autonomy and therefore freedom. Throughout the novel, Milkman financially depends on his father, Macon Dead II. Before Milkman leaves on his journey he complains to his friend Guitar, "I don't want to be my old man's office boy no more. And as long as I'm in this place I will be. Unless I have my own money" (222). Milkman's focus on material gains limits his plan to undercut the regulatory conditions that produce him. His journey sets in motion a series of events that further solidify his "mortiferous self-knowledge," to borrow a phrase from Gayatri Chakravorty Spivak.

Yet Milkman's tendency to concentrate on the past instead of plan for the future creates the condition that allows him to cultivate a different system of values and embrace his ability to confront what encumbers him even if that is his physicality. His quest transforms him through an orientation to his family history. Milkman's self-interested individualism dies as a result of the cultural primal scenes he faces in the South.

His southern migration does not provide the material rewards he thinks will allow him to live his own life, yet it establishes the need to look to the past in order to embrace the future. During his journey, Milkman discovers famed, flying great-granddaddy's self-interested pursuits had devastating consequences. According to the myth Milkman learns during his journey, Solomon, Milkman's great-granddaddy, took off and left his family behind. Michael Awkward explains: "The failure of Solomon's efforts to transport Jake [his son] along with him, in fact, serves to emphasize the ultimately individualistic nature of the mythic figure's flight" (484). Although Solomon attempts to take one son along with him, Awkward contends Morrison emphasizes the individual nature of Solomon's flight and its legacy by not only having Solomon fly off and leave Ryna, his wife, and their children but also intertwining Milkman's journey with the abandonment of his female cousin/sister, Hagar. By the end of the novel Hagar dies. However, when Milkman learns of her death he, unlike Solomon, recognizes his culpability because he sees the parallels between his and his ancestors' pursuits. Awkward's focus on the gender dynamic created by Morrison's representation of male flight prompts an investigation of the implications of visual versus acoustic performance in the novel since gender stratifies each type of performance.

Analogously, the positions of Ryna, Hagar, and Pilate resonate with Echo. In terms of Morrison's novel, Milkman learns to decipher the meaning of Solomon's flight by listening to children singing a song that describes it, the same song Pilate sings at the beginning of the novel. In order to obtain the information he desires, he must listen, since he lacks any device to record the song. Milkman's appreciation of the implications of the lyrics marks a turning point and establishes "the movement from visuality to orality" (172), an attempt "to supplant reading by listening," to quote Madhu Dubey (146). The alignment of Solomon with flight, primarily a visual event, and Ryna with sound seems to establish a gender dichotomy further solidified by Pilate acting as the foil to Milkman's father. Pilate, a bootlegger, blues singer, conjure woman, and historical archive, exists on the outskirts of the community. Macon, conversely, who perceives himself as the embodiment of the American dream, a self-made man, establishes his centrality to the community as a literate property owner who denies the past and focuses, almost exclusively, on the future. Although Macon finds solace secretly in Pilate's singing, he publicly disavows her and her practices.

Solomon leaves a visual legacy while Ryna produces an acoustic one, yet the two are mutually constitutive and destructive. Solomon, according to the myth presented in the novel, "left Ryna behind and twenty children. Twenty-one, since he dropped the one [Jake] he tried to take with him. And Ryna had thrown herself all over the ground, lost her mind, and was still crying in a ditch" (332). As walkers pass by the Gulch named for Ryna, an eerie sound can be heard that locals profess is the echo of her cries. The echo produced by Ryna's Gulch marks an absent presence; it reminds the listener of a sound (Ryna's voice) and a sight (Solomon's flight) no longer accessible. The conjunction of flying and dying establishes the political implications of Pilate's and Milkman's final flights. In the last sequence of the novel, Pilate returns with Milkman to Shalimar to bury her father's remains. An unexpected guest awaits Milkman in Shalimar. Coaxed by betrayal and necessity, Guitar, Milkman's friend, follows Milkman to the South thinking the protagonist has found the gold but is not willing to share it. Firing a bullet intended for Milkman, Guitar shoots Pilate, causing her death. Guitar places the protagonist in the position of a spiritual steward; he must now tend to his aunt's and his grandfather's remains.

Milkman sings, "Sugargirl don't leave me here / Cotton balls to choke me / Sugargirl don't leave me here / Buckra's arms to yoke me" (Pilate's song), as he caresses his dying aunt, bringing the acoustic arc of the novel full circle and indicating his ability to put into practice the lessons he learned. The ambiguous quality of the novel, however, disrupts this utopian moment. Milkman rises and calls out, "'Guitar!'" "*Tar tar tar*, said the hills," again resonating the deconstructive power of echo (337). His former friend steps forward as Milkman leaps toward him. "As fleet and bright as a lodestar he wheeled toward Guitar and it did not matter which one of them would give up his ghost in the killing arms of his brother. For now he knew what Shalimar [Solomon] knew: If you surrendered to the air, you could *ride* it" (337). The final lines shift the implications of the Flying Africans once again. In the tales told in *Drums and Shadows*, the narrators represent those who flew away as transcendent; here, the novel indicates surrender. Milkman, who throughout the novel sarcastically quips he's already "Dead," indicates the limited possibility made available by his ancestor Solomon, which sounds like, and is enunciated by some, as Shalimar. His final performance depends on a literal difference covered over by acoustic similarity that reads a dissonance, if ever so slight, into his flying.

The sound of echoing from Ryna's Gulch and Milkman and Guitar's battlefield works alongside the reverberations coming from the radio in the local barbershop depicted in *Song of Solomon* to establish the political and ethical implications of Milkman's flight specifically and black death generally. In an often cited, although brief, scene in *Song of Solomon*, Morrison recounts how some of the men in Milkman's community learn of the murder of Emmett Till. In 1955 a young black boy named Emmett Till was murdered in Money, Mississippi, after being accused of whistling at a white woman. Morrison impregnates the disembodied voice that spews into the barbershop from the radio with muttering patrons and a whistle, a whistle from the lips of a boy known to stutter and reside in the North. As I argue elsewhere, "Historically, the sound of lynching, to borrow from Fred Moten, could be best categorized as mo'nin,' a sound that registers and communicates mourning and pain. Cries of 'have mercy,' the dead silence of shock, and the gesticulations and heaving thrust of sounds that often accompany weeping all qualify. In art, Billie Holiday's weathered and sophisticated voice, a voice that sounds like it has 'been through something,' heard in her rendition of Lewis Allen's 'Strange Fruit,' is the sound most readily associated with lynching. These sounds are the mo'nin' produced by lynching" (162).[7] Morrison's novel disrupts and distorts the sound of mo'nin by filtering the news of the story through the radio heard in a barbershop whose announcer "had only a few speculations and even fewer facts. The minute he went on to another topic of news, the barbershop broke into loud conversation" (80). In many black neighborhoods the barbershop serves as a center of political and social debate, hence the comedic critique of cultural affairs in the film *Barbershop* (2002). While many critics have noted the way the voices in Morrison's barbershop serve to create knowledge, I highlight, in addition, the way *Song of Solomon* utilizes the technology of the radio to draw attention to the process of filtering disembodied sound. The "muttering" heard alongside the radio alters the sound, producing critique. The muttering registers anger and pain as it foreshadows the sound of the black power movement heard in the Afro-futurist funk music of George Clinton and his bands Parliament and Funkadelic.

Spaceships

George Clinton developed two bands, the Parliaments (1952; eventually renamed Parliament) and Funkadelic (1968), that reflected a new musical direction. George Clinton, known as one of the key innovators of the genre funk music—an outgrowth of rhythm and blues (R&B)—shifted the visual and acoustic landscape in the late 1960s. Abandoning the suits associated with

Motown performers, Parliament, most of whose members were also part of Funkadelic, wore trash bags, diapers, and space-age, metallic costumes. Musical scholar Ken McLeod's description of Parliament-Funkadelic's distinctive sound jives with their image: "The Afro-nauts of Parliament-Funkadelic combined synthesizers, acoustic piano, brass, heavy funk bass and wah wah effects to create their highly layered, otherworldly grooves" (343). The layer of sound allowed the band's music to resonate with R&B audiences while transforming the acoustic landscape.

In Parliament's performances the choice of costume and use of the mother ship made material the notion of past as present-future. Parliament deploys the imagery of the mother ship in their album *Mothership Connection* (1976), which *Rolling Stone* named one of the five hundred best albums of all time. Hip-hop audiences most readily associate the sound of *Mothership Connection* with samples used in Dr. Dre's multiplatinum album, *The Chronic*. The focus on drug culture in Dr. Dre's album, however, minimizes the powerful imagery of *Mothership Connection*. Discussing the use of space and alien imagery in the work of George Clinton, Lee Perry, and Sun Ra, musician and radio host John Corbett explains, "What Ra, Clinton, and Perry do is crazily reappropriate this image and retool it—transforming the sea-ship into a space-ship" (17). The sea ship, Gilroy notes, serves as one of the key images of the black Atlantic because it "immediately focus[es] attention on the middle passage, on the various projects for redemptive return to an African homeland, on the circulation of ideas and activists as well as the movement of key cultural and political artefacts" (*Black Atlantic*, 4). Similarly, the imagery of the mother ship attempted to recoup Africa by returning the continent to black Americans through the air, therefore avoiding the brutal Middle Passage. The sound of *Mothership Connection* allowed for the circulation of ideas detached from the ideological restrictions on earth. Clinton's group claimed liberation by technological innovation and manipulation of space.

The rebirthing of black politics staged in performances of the *Mothership Connection*—Clinton would emerge from a space pod as Starchild—were supported by Funkadelic's rendering of black nationalism. As Corbett describes, "With Funkadelic he [Clinton] established 'One Nation under a Groove,' an earthly, politically grounded type of dancing-populism or a funky form of black nationalism" (17–18). Corbett draws attention to one of the tendencies of artists during the Black Arts Movement to idealize Africa. The conflation of Africa and space associated the continent with a region free from the alienating effects of being a black person in the United States. Space represented an idealized, political alternative to life on earth. The desire to land the spaceship and incorporate the sound it produces into black culture in the United States distinguishes Parliament's politics from some other artists of the Black Arts Movement.

The notion of using the spaceship and technology as mechanisms to fly away would not only filter into the samples that distinguish the sound of some hip-hop artists but also embodied movements and their critique. In an interview with Mark Dery, Tricia Rose discusses hip-hop artists' deployment of the dance called the Robot. She argues for "an understanding of themselves as *already having been robots*. Adopting 'the robot' reflected a response to an existing condition: namely, that they were labor for capitalism, that they had very little value as people in this society" (769–70). Kanye West's debut album, *College Dropout*, contains a similar cry against alienated labor and incorporates bitter irony with notions of transcendence. West's album achieves the qualified investment in and critique of transcendence by flight through juxtaposition. One hears a troubled call-and-response in the placement of "I'll Fly Away" and "Spaceship," the fifth and sixth songs on *College Dropout*. As the title of the album indicates, West questions the expectation of benefits associated with the attainment of a college degree and by extension the Protestant work ethic. Similarly "Spaceship" casts doubt on the possibility of any form of transcendence in the absence of material gains. Although West makes no explicit references to Morrison, the imagery of freedom as a commodity remerges, but in this case the Flying African boards a spaceship. Nevertheless, *Song of Solomon* and "Spaceship" do not present total disillusionment but instead ambiguity by inserting acoustic disturbances that brush against the action.

West fills *College Dropout* with contradictions that lend to its appeal; his debut album went multiplatinum. Josh Tyrangiel of *Time* magazine claims, "It was immaculately produced, but what made it compelling was the contradictions" (para. 5). Some critics were less generous with their praise. Known for throwing tantrums, West demonstrated his ire when *Rolling Stone* gave his first album a rating of three-and-a-half stars out of five. Rob Sheffield of *Rolling Stone* explains, "For some, *Dropout* proves hip-hop is in a rut, as an example of what everybody else isn't doing; for others, it proves hip-hop is still evolving, as music nobody outside hip-hop could make. Whatever your pet theory on the state of hip-hop, Dropout gave a challenge, flaws and all" (para. 2). In another *Rolling Stone* article on *College Dropout*, Touré, a contributing editor and hip-hop aficionado, writes, "It confirms his place as one of the great modern hip-hop producers as well as a witty, neobackpack rapper" (para. 1). Most critics would agree that West's albums have gotten progressively better. *Graduation* (2007) shows marked improvement in his lyricism and is a tighter and more finely edited package as a whole. Never-theless, *College Dropout* has moments of brilliance and innovation worthy of note.

Tracks four through seven, "All Falls Down," "I'll Fly Away," "Spaceship," and "Jesus Walks," encapsulate the ideological and acoustic arc of the album. Those offering high praise for the album often note West's innovation in "Jesus Walks" (track seven). The song interweaves "spirituality with skepticism and rap with gospel," highlighting West's vulnerability and bravado (Tyrangiel, para. 5). The final line of the chorus, "I wanna talk to God but I'm afraid cause we ain't spoke in so long" fades into extended enunciations of "Jesus Walks with me" and serves as the transition into the second verse: "To the hustlers, killers, murderers, drug dealers even the strippers (Jesus walks for them)." The doubt and fear he proclaims does not impede his at-tempts to empower *even* the strippers. Leaving aside the sexism implicitly inscribed by creating a hierarchy of criminals and putting strippers at the top, West's music proves less message-based and more reflexive, or what he describes as self-conscious. I do not mean to downplay the impact of sexism in West's lyrics or in hip-hop in general. In fact, I find the representation immensely problematic. However, as Mark Anthony Neal explains, I believe "radical and progressive possibilities can and should be teased out of images that common logic suggests are problematic" (12–13). The constant divide between committing action (dealing drugs) and judging those acts (feeling the drug dealer cannot call on God) bolsters the paradoxical nature of his music and points to the progressive possibility Neal notes. West depicts him-self as a subject in a world plagued by ideology that keeps him trapped in a loop of unsatisfying actions that he has limited ability to manipulate. Within the psychic state of despair, he offers encouragement even as he notes the way hope works against the very matrices that induce the murderers, drug dealers, and strippers to believe they cannot talk to God. Another sign of the way the album confronts disempowering ideology occurs in "All Falls Down" when he ironically quips, "We rappers are role models we rap we don't think." West makes a joke of his simultaneous roles as hip-hop artist/pop star worthy of praise and emulation and as ignorant rapper spouting violent and sexist lyrics.

Using sarcasm and biting humor, *College Dropout* challenges the rela-tionship between the signifier and the signified. West's rendition of "I'll Fly Away" establishes the instability of the Flying Africans tale even as he transforms it into a new millennial, technologically empowered pursuit in "Spaceship." With the simple accompaniment of a pianist, two vocalists, Tony

William and Deray, sing Albert E. Brumley's "I'll Fly Away." In the rendition on *College Dropout*, the voices begin in unison and then break off, creating an echoing effect. The choice to have the solo piano intensifies the datedness of the song and draws attention to the innovativeness in "Spaceship," exemplified by the mixing of a sample of Marvin Gaye's "Distant Lover," the doo-wop style of the chorus, the gospel-influenced refrain "heaven knows," the heavy drum beat, and the suggestion that consumer culture creates a form of modern-day slavery. As Andrew Bartlett notes, "This expansive idea of musical composition and performance is the center around which contemporary hip hop constellates. Possibilities for simultaneous contrast are enhanced—if not revolutionized—by the art of digital sampling so prevalent in hip hop" (640). The sampling draws attention to what is lost and what has the possibility to emerge. The negotiation of past and present, according to Ken McLeod, "allows for a type of aural time travel" (345). McLeod continues, "With sampling technologies, black artists can juxtapose decades-old speeches by Martin Luther King or loops from James Brown against contemporary tracks. Thus such technology has allowed these artists to intertextually signify a collective notion of African-American historical memory" (345). West's choice to include the traditional gospel sounding of "I'll Fly Away" on the album suggests an effort to fit his work within a particular genealogy that serves as a meeting ground of the secular and the sacred. Such a move draws attention to the spiritual component at the heart of the Flying Africans tale and the way it functions as black movement, even in its most recent renditions, and requires contending with multiple configurations of black death and dying.

Performed with the artists Gangsta Legendary Crisis (GLC) and Consequence, "Spaceship" bemoans what it qualifies as the low-wage exploitation of working at the Gap. The album as a whole questions the benefits of playing by the rules, suggesting doing so results in psychic death. The song begins with West crooning, "I've been workin' this graveshift and I ain't made shit / I wish I could buy me a spaceship and fly past the sky." West intensifies the imagery of death conjured by truncating graveyard shift into "graveshift" in the gap between tracks four, "All Falls Down," and five, "I'll Fly Away." As the outro to track four fuses into the intro to track five, a voice says, "This graveshift is like a slave ship." Likening the labor West performs at the Gap, which presumably does not take place at night and into the early hours of the morning since he cites his interaction with customers, to the floating casket that many slave ships became as they traveled through the Middle Passage also strengthens the connection of the spaceship as appropriated slave ship present in Parliament's imagery. Importantly, West depicts psychic and social death as a result of alienated labor and not the additional physical death many enslaved Africans experienced. Nonetheless, even if hyperbolic, West's simile points to the continual necessity for flight. GLC acts as West's amen corner or hype-man, affirming his disdain and longing for liberation.

West's first verse, tonally infused with anger, interrupts the sense of pain communicated by interweaving his and Gaye's singing. The sound of West's music differs from the gospel and R&B it borrows from by incorporating the angry drum beats and lyrics with comforting, slightly mournful, melodic samples. The contradiction in his music exists at the level of narrative and sound. In addition, the use of "I'll Fly Away" and Gaye's song creates "a sense of familiarity," to quote Neal, "that heightens the sense of fracture and difference. . . . Something that was so familiar is rendered 'vulgar' and unintelligible" (15). Neal analyzes the music of R. Kelly to theorize post-soul aesthetic, which he argues emerges out of a politics exemplified by the *Regents of the University of California v. Bakke* (1978). The *Bakke* case limited the scope of affirmative action and brought the gains of the civil rights movement into question; over the next decade the federal government continued to erode those victories. I am less concerned with how "Spaceship" fits into a post-soul aesthetic, which I think it does, and more with West's mobilization and deconstruction of sound associated with hope.

The layers of sound heard in "Spaceship" echo the effect of *Drums and Shadows* and *Song of Solomon*. Heard alone, West's lyrics seem fatalistic, a simplistic investment in consumer culture as a mechanism of escape. He seems willing to commit social and psychic death in order to commodify and profit from his performance. However, if you listen to the track as a whole, you hear a genealogy of sound that does not end in a return to Africa or the reclamation of a southern past. It offers instead a temporary hiatus made possible by highlighting the contradictions inherent in depicting America as a meritocracy. "Spaceship" embraces the misalliance of effort and reward even as it desires that system. West explains, "Contradiction is part of who everybody is I am a real person. . . . One song is, I love God, and the next song is, Can you come over? That's how I feel. Sometimes you're in church, and you're looking at the girl's dress right next to you" (*College Dropout*, para. 3). The song ends with GLC singing, "I wanna fly, I wanna fly / I said I want my chariot to pick me up / And take me brother for a ride." Therefore, in its latest enunciation the Flying Africans move from the Gap to the studio, pointing out the limits and possibilities of new millennial black movements when Flying Africans board spaceships.

"Spaceship" depicts the hip-hop generation's sense of limited power and further circumscribes the possibilities for movement depicted in *Song of Solomon*. West's use of humor, bravado, and cynicism to reflect the reality that hip-hop is a global commodity yielding certain modicums of power to the lyricist even as he notes in "All Falls Down": "We shine because they hate us, floss cause they degrade us / We trying to buy back our 40 acres / And for that paper, look how low we a'stoop / Even if you in a Benz, you still a nigga in a coupe." For West the constructed nature of race does not offer much comfort to the experience he describes. The cultural landscape boasts of being postrace and still pre-reparations. The cynicism and humor emerge in defense of what West realizes is the bitter irony of trying to *buy back* our forty acres. The unfulfilled promise of reparations to black people in the Americas for the trauma suffered due to trans-Atlantic slavery meets consumer culture. And it demands a sense of entitlement, signaled by the word "back," that covers over the persistent longing for acknowledgment of and concession for wrongdoing. Moreover, the use of a spaceship instead of embodied flight critiques the idea of self-propelled action (i.e., Milkman being able to fly by his own volition) and provides a sense of the way technological intervention drives consumption. West's lyrics call for him to *buy* a spaceship and fly, making the spaceship a means for him to achieve his desired end.

Flying Africans being depicted in spaceships provide a new millennial spin on an old problem. While they maintain a political connection, it is only across the difference produced by time and space. Understanding the expression of the Flying Africans tale as black movement offers a model that attends to how geographical and temporal difference constitute black performance and participates in creating those times and places. If, as Brent Hayes Edwards argues, "the use of the term *diaspora* . . . forces us to consider discourses of cultural and political linkage only through and across difference," it seems such a definition could apply to embodied expression and their histories (Uses, 64). Thinking through the genealogy of the Flying Africans tale creates a linkage in the practice of diaspora.

Notes

1. Some works that have used the imagery of the Flying Africans include Ralph Ellison's "Flying Home" (1944), Ishmael Reed's *Flight to Canada* (1976), Paule Marshall's *Praisesong for the Widow* (1983), and Michelle Cliff's *Abeng* (1984).

2. Smallwood's book focuses on the Gold Coast of Africa, the origin of many of the first enslaved Africans on the Georgia coast.

3. In "Folklore and Community in *Song of Solomon*," Susan L. Blake details the influence of *Drums and Shadows* on Morrison's novel. Olivia Smith Storey makes a corresponding argument in "Flying Words: Contests of Orality and Literacy in the Trope of the Flying Africans."

4. See Taylor, 16–21.

5. See Dubey; Jones, *Liberating Voices*; Skerrett Jr.; Smith, *Self-Discovery and Authority*; and Wall.

6. Awkward; Blake; Harris, "Myth as Structure"; Lee, "Song of Solomon"; Storey; Wall; and Wilentz, *Binding Cultures*.

7. In Gayl Jones's novel *Corregidora*, Cat, a secondary character, categorizes the voice of the main character, Ursa, as a voice that sounds like "you been through something" (44).

POST-LOGICAL NOTES ON SELF-ELECTION

The morning after Barack Obama was elected president of the United States, I stopped to chat with the security guard at the entrance to my school. He is from Côte d'Ivoire and said someday, maybe forty years from now, he will return home.[1] He imagines his grandchildren will ask him about that day, and he will say—*I was there. I saw it with my own eyes.* When we shook hands to signal my leaving, we held on to each other as if passing a message of gratitude between us.[2] He whispered—*He is strong. Everywhere in the world the black man is not welcome. Everywhere he is feared, despised. He has had to be on his own. Who better to lead than him?*

This was when we started to show up in the evidence as more of us than ourselves, so many that we did not know how to estimate the distance between points of singular experience and multiple consequences. Our project of abstract reasoning required a deeper commitment than quotations assembled to support an argument. The pieces did not fit together as planned so we all took up more space.

According to a survey conducted by the social networking site Cupid.com in 2009, black women received the fewest responses to online dating invitations even though they were most likely to respond to messages sent to them by a person of any race.[3] Curiosity about dwindling opportunities for black marriage inspired numerous commentaries in major newspapers questioning the usefulness of expected gender roles in matrimony. As word of this report filtered through mainstream news channels, discussions reflected certain regional anxieties. When the lack of response to overtures by black women was discussed in the Northeast, the problem was called a failure to present oneself in comparison with a black actress or singer widely regarded as "hot."

It could be argued that poor knowledge of geography is a clear mark of one's intention to stay put, especially in cities where the borders between neighborhoods are not visible to those without some intuitive sense of residency. Mapping is always an act of distortion, and the fact that some of us live off roads not yet written down means that we do not exist.[4] Alternatively, it means that we exist as placeholders for someone else.

The gentrification of Washington, DC, was already impacting its black community by the time Barack Obama hit the campaign trail in 2006. A few poets attempted to write about the city's most important sites before they disappeared from memory, but so few people read poetry that those places nearly vanished anyway.

An aerial drawing of the city from 1822 made by H. C. Carey notes only the following locations: the Capitol, the Maritime Hospital, the President's House, the Navy Yard, and Greenleaf Point. All spaces in between, where people would live, are marked by rows of little black rectangles, stacked atop each other.[5] The Potomac bends to accommodate the city's sharp edges.[6]

By the time Michael Jackson died in the summer of 2009, the word on the street was that times were getting tougher for everyone, especially for the black middle class.[7] The black middle class didn't have much to say in response since most of them had either fled to the suburbs or hid in the under or upper classes, trying to avoid looking conspicuous. It is not shocking now to report that many of us believed in the inevitability of a middle class too much, just as we believed in

concepts of inequity like "celebrity" and "minority," words used to confirm the diminishing value of our contributions.[8]

While advertisers and political pundits were in a hurry to name upcoming trends in popular culture as "the new black," the old black continued its attempts to gain control over its image. This project was complicated by the sudden acceptance of the idea that "multi" constituted the fastest-growing racial category to be counted on the census. Multi aroused suspicion in the orthodox, or those who believe categories of racial identification are doctrine, as conflicting accounts of one's point of origin inspired too many stories moving in opposite directions. The orthodox refused to think in ways that jeopardized their need to distance themselves from the rest of us.

Frantz Fanon wrote this about his transformation in consciousness in 1969 as if he anticipated what many of us would be seeking in a multicultural society: "I came into this world imbued with the will to find a meaning in things, my spirit filled with the desire to attain to the source of the world, and then I found that I was an object in the midst of other objects. Sealed into that crushing objecthood, I turned beseechingly to others. Their attention was a liberation, running over my body suddenly abraded into nonbeing, endowing me once more with an agility that I had thought lost, and by taking me out of the world, restoring me to it."[9] In other words, a kind of freedom existed in being out of place. In order to take up space one needed to keep moving.

Thank goodness the technological means by which we could justify and express our narcissism were available on handheld devices by the time most people recognized their needs outweighed everyone else's. Missives on social status and desire could be broadcast twenty-four hours a day with minimal censorship or editing. Through this process of inventing our public face, our name became our brand, and we showcased our belief system each time we broadcast our taste.

These are the names of the men who signed the Constitution on September 17, 1787: George Washington, Benjamin Franklin, James Madison, Alexander Hamilton, Gouverneur Morris, Robert Morris, James Wilson, Chas Pinckney, John Rutledge, Pierce Butler, Roger Sherman, William Samuel Johnson, James McHenry, George Read, Richard Bassett, Richard Dobbs Spaight, William Blount, Hugh Williamson, Daniel of St. Thomas Jenifer, Rufus King, Nathaniel Gorham, Jonathan Dayton, Daniel Carroll, William Few, Abraham Baldwin, John Langdon, Nicholas Gilman, William Livingston, William Paterson, Thomas Mifflin, George Clymer, Thomas Fitzsimons, Jared Ingersoll, Gunning Bedford Jr., David Brearley, John Dickinson, John Blair, Jacob Broom, William Jackson.[10]

According to federal data, 539 white and 851 black juveniles committed murder

in 2000. By 2007, the number of whites changed only slightly, while for blacks the number increased to 1,142. Though murder rates in general had been much lower than in recent years past, the number of younger blacks who became victims of murder also went up.[11]

During the weekend of April 18–20, 2008, at least twenty-nine shootings took place within the city of Chicago.[12] Five people died. A majority of those targeted were young African American and Latino males. So much violence in the land of Lincoln meant we were not done hashing out who still owes whom for work undervalued, especially in economies where wealth is earned by showing no fear of death. In the months that followed, one Chicago paper began printing maps indicating where murders occurred each week.[13]

In the impoverished community of Central Falls, Rhode Island, police officers arrested undocumented workers from local businesses to fill jail cells.[14] The more prisoners, the more subsidies the city received from the federal government. To sort out the criminals from the victims in this equation requires narrowing one's point of view to where two paths converge. It is more difficult to distinguish the criminals from the victims at the vanishing point.

Cartographers would often climb to great heights surrounding the city they were depicting in order to put the landscape in perspective. They also knew maps would sell better when cities appeared to be endlessly busy. Everyone hustled across a landscape of endless productivity. Thus a feature of the bird's-eye map was misrepresentation of scale.

Most maps don't make clear why the colors picked to represent the individual states, municipalities, and communities fail to bleed into each other.[15]

In California, Proposition 8, said to "protect marriage," was voted in favor of by a majority of citizens in 2008.[16] Early reports attributed the success of this measure to homophobia in the African American community, inspired by religion and parochialism. This analysis was another way, albeit subtle, that black people were characterized as a subset of humanity, content with negating the vastness of our own lived experience.

Some of the first states to legalize gay marriage included Vermont, New Jersey, Connecticut, New Hampshire, Massachusetts, Iowa, and Maine, despite the once-popular Defense of Marriage Act, passed in September 1996. It attempted to prevent individual states from assuming the right to define marriage as anything other than a "legal union between one man and one woman." This confounded those of us who have been through a marriage, since so much time was spent defining what marriage *wasn't*—though no one could prove for certain what it *was*.

From the first moments she came to the attention of the public, Barack Obama's wife, Michelle, appeared in several

places she was not expected to be seen: in the fashion houses, in the garden, at the VA hospital, and in the poetry section of the bookstore. For many Americans who still did not comprehend how many innovations they had already failed to take note of, her presence disrupted the tradition of ignoring black women. Up until this point the black woman had functioned, whether as cartoon, caretaker, chimera, or Oprah, as the empathetic presence in fictions of racial harmony and desire, capable of the kind of understanding and forgiveness too sentimental to be heroic.[17] For generations she played fulcrum in the evolution of whites with privilege to a liberal consciousness. After Michelle she had become oddly untenable, multiple, and divergent.

At the time when so many changes began to unravel the way we thought about America, these were some of the poorest cities: Gary, Indiana; Hartford, Connecticut; Camden, New Jersey; St. Louis, Missouri; Edinburg, Texas; Flint, Michigan; Cleveland, Ohio; Buffalo, New York; Milwaukee, Wisconsin; New Orleans, Louisiana; El Paso, Texas; Baltimore, Maryland; Toledo, Ohio; Stockton, California; Lowell, Massachusetts; Tulsa, Oklahoma; Detroit, Michigan; Memphis, Tennessee; Newark, New Jersey; Barstow, California; Youngstown, Ohio; and Brownsville, Texas.

For about two months, a lot of people were on the verge of saying racism was over. Then Oscar Grant got shot in the back in the BART station in San Francisco, California, during the early morning hours of January 1, 2009.[18] It would be easier to deal with conflict if everyone cared about the same things, but the injuries we suffered from most were felt personally, not philosophically.

While considering hard facts about the life of Richard Wright, James Baldwin wrote this about racism: "One is always in the position of having to decide between amputation and gangrene."[19] A kind of death is implied, localized at first—how the body learns to absorb the fear of others.

In 1845 Frederick Douglass wrote this about the pursuit of freedom: "In coming to the fixed determination to run away, we did more than Patrick Henry when he resolved upon liberty or death.[20] With us it was a doubtful liberty at most, and almost certain death if we failed."[21] When it was our moment to act, many of us still wanted to run, but to where we did not know.

One morning two musicians on the subway complained about how no one looks a stranger in the eye anymore. They claimed everyone is afraid of each other. We wanted to shout—*people aren't interested in anyone other than themselves*—but didn't think anyone cared enough to listen.

Amongst the civil rights generation, the name of the virus was still being whispered in the same way our parents talked about cancer before each of them was diagnosed with it. By the time African Americans composed 49 per-

cent of those newly infected with HIV, the Centers for Disease Control and Prevention (CDC) recommended that testing be mandatory for all African Americans living in certain cities. This approach reflected the mistaken impression that high rates of transmission in black communities validated stereotypes about desire, deviance, and sexuality, rather than evidencing a widespread lack of economic opportunity and self-esteem.[22]

One of the biggest challenges in mapmaking has to be accurately representing those places with the least growth. The mapmaker faces the problem of determining what to show. Potential use or lack thereof? What good is a road no one travels on? Is a neighborhood no one lives in still a community?

These were some of the blackest cities in the United States: Washington, DC; East St. Louis, Missouri; Detroit, Michigan; Baltimore, Maryland; Jackson, Mississippi; Birmingham, Alabama; Richmond, Virginia; Memphis, Tennessee; Gary, Indiana; Atlanta, Georgia; Oakland, California; Louisville, Kentucky; Baton Rouge, Louisiana; Jersey City, New Jersey; Mobile, Alabama; Chicago, Illinois; Norfolk, Virginia; Philadelphia, Pennsylvania; Cincinnati, Ohio; Charlotte, North Carolina; and Rochester, New York.[23]

The value of the echo is that it teaches listening, though we all know that at times throwing your voice out there is the only way to deal with obstructing surfaces. One clear echo was the blackest and the poorest at the same time.

It didn't matter that critics still debated the relevance of hip-hop in the broader culture; clearly, it had already transformed the way people mix it up around the world. But if anybody could be president, this was the beginning of the end of the culture of distraction or what we used to call "celebrity."[24]

The weekend of President Obama's inauguration, we rode down to DC on the train. People waved welcome signs along the tracks in South Philadelphia, Pennsylvania. Days earlier in New York, a plane had crashed in the Hudson River. No one knows why everyone survived other than the fact that some luck is unfathomable.[25]

A young boy sitting with his white mother on the train considered the map in his hands easy reading. Most people didn't stare at him, except the few who wondered how he came to be so good with direction. The boy, too confident to notice their attention, pointed out the attractions in each city along the route. Through his comprehension of geography, the boy told all studying him—*you have no idea who I am.*

In his inaugural address, President Obama referenced what George Washington said during one of the most difficult times in the American Revolution. "Let it be told to the future world that in the depth of winter, when nothing but hope and virtue could survive, that the city and the country, alarmed at one common danger, came forth to meet it."[26] We came forth as well, everyone out in the cold, awaiting direction on our next move.

One of the hardest concepts about America to reckon with had been that it would always be a land of fractured allegiances.[27] Demands for equality and justice were unending, and the means by which we sought them defined how close we were to winning or losing our ideals. It seemed there would always be a struggle for America to become itself. No wonder that there were times when we all got tired of talking about it.

Those who marched from Selma to Montgomery, Alabama, in 1965 experienced rancor in the weapons, hoses, and dogs turned on them.[28] For years after that, there were those who should have died from disappointment but chose to spread their anger around like a virus.[29] And there were those who let go of their anger because they wanted to live, but every step they took after that was just an inch or two below ground level.

Even though a tension between the city and country in the United States had always played out in political debate, we were thankful that our dream for America still included both a community one could feel and a community one could see.[30] Making a justification for the further development of suburbs after the influence of a black middle class had been grossly overstated, however, was much more difficult.

Before there was any evidence that they would survive the act of treason, the men who signed the Declaration of Independence wrote this about the new democracy: "We mutually pledge to each other our lives, our fortunes and our sacred honor." And while some of us knew that a willingness to commit treason is sometimes the truest test of a patriot, the faith it took to believe in America this time around required no less of a conviction. This was when we started to show up in person, all of us coming out in the cold looking for one face to remind us of where we could have been going, in what direction.

Notes

1. At the time of our conversation, approximately 25 percent of the residents of Côte d'Ivoire lived below the international poverty line. In Detroit, Michigan, unemployment rates were rising and would reach nearly 16.1 percent within six months. See "Metropolitan Area Employment and Unemployment Summary."

2. Occasional touching of coworkers was considered to be awkward except when the intimacy of the conversation already extended beyond what might be considered casual.

3. For additional insight, see Rudder.

4. Road also implies a cut path, a lack of originality, a charted destiny, and the attempt to follow.

5. H. C. Carey, noted mapmaker, was the author of *Carey's School Atlas*, published in 1825, priced at $1.00 plain and $1.25 colored. Maps of England, Scotland, Ireland, France, Spain, Italy, Germany, Asia, North America, the United States, and South America were contained therein.

6. See Carey.

7. Michael Jackson (1958–2009) was an American entertainer who was, at one time, the best-selling singer and composer of popular music worldwide. At the time he died, many claimed he had been the most popular celebrity of all time.

8. The "middle class" was said to be the social class between the lower and upper classes, though its precise boundaries were always difficult to define, especially in times of economic tumult. Eventually it became known as a temporary state through which one passed en route to the upper or lower classes rather than a position in which to maintain a lifestyle. The "black middle class" was a post–World War II invention created to relieve concern about the long-term effectiveness of coercive segregation.

9. Fanon, *Black Skin, White Masks*, 109. Frantz Fanon (1925–61) was a psychiatrist, philosopher, revolutionary, and author from Martinique, who was considered an expert on the psychological effects of racism and colonialism.

10. It is possible to form the word "no" twenty-six times from these names as they are listed in order.

11. See Eckholm. *Victims . . . of murder . . . went up . . .* this route to ascension seemed unnecessarily steep.

12. "At least six people have been shot to death and more than two dozen others wounded in shootings since Friday afternoon in Chicago. At one point, 18 shootings had occurred in 17 hours." See Bradley.

13. In 2009, *RedEye* tracked all murders that occurred in Chicago. "In every Thursday's paper, *RedEye* will publish a map of the homicides from the previous week. This interactive map also will be updated weekly." See Swartz.

14. See Bernstein.

15. "To bleed" could imply falling in love, which might or might not play out as tragedy.

16. Proposition 8 was a ballot proposition against gay marriage that passed in the general election on November 4, 2008, and went into effect the next day.

17. Oprah Winfrey (b. 1954) is a popular American media personality and entrepreneur whose brand includes a television talk show, a production company, several magazines, a cable network, and many other successful projects. While her initial target audience was women in the United States, her advice on personal challenges and ability to make anyone who appeared on her show famous appeal to almost everyone.

18. Oscar Grant, a twenty-two-year-old unarmed man, was shot by a BART officer in the Fruitvale BART station in Oakland, California. When killed, he was in a submissive position. See "BART Police Shoot and Kill Man."

19. This metaphor is excerpted from "Notes of a Native Son" (Baldwin, 603).

Richard Wright (1908–60) was a writer born into a Mississippi family of sharecroppers. In 1927 he moved to Chicago, a city that would inform his most famous and controversial book, *Native Son*. James Baldwin (1924–87) was a writer born in Harlem, whose work in essays, plays, and fiction documented the complexity of changes that came as a result of the civil rights movement. His work also explored the complications of expressing sexuality within an African American community struggling for acknowledgment and validation in the larger society.

20. Patrick Henry (1736–99) was a prominent, radical figure of the American Revolutionary War. In a speech given about patriotism in 1773, he shouted the phrase "Give me liberty, or give me death," which became a battle cry for like-minded individuals seeking to end British influence over the American colonies. After the ratification of the Constitution, Henry served as the governor of the Commonwealth of Virginia for several terms.

21. Douglass, 57.

22. From the Centers for Disease Control website, "According to the 2000 census, blacks make up approximately 13% of the US population. However, in 2005, blacks accounted for 18,121 (49%) of the estimated 37,331 new HIV/AIDS diagnoses in the United States in the 33 states with long-term, confidential name-based HIV reporting." See "HIV among African Americans."

23. Location, location, location.

24. Celebrity was a global cultural phenomenon that reached its peak during the first decade of the twenty-first century. Film and musical performers along with the help of hired agents and publicists worked to hold a position in the center of the public

eye. The attention they received, often inversely proportional to their talent (with a few notable exceptions), served as a distraction from the global consolidation of capital systems among a few key corporations whose influence, though not recognizably coercive, was similar or broader in scope than those ideological, transnational armies professing a desire to destroy or create influential nations.

Celebrities who attended the inaugural balls went with the expectation that they would be recognized for bringing something distinctive to the party. But now that it appeared that anyone could be president, it mattered less that some of us could be pop icons.

25. This notable landing, called the "Miracle on the Hudson," was executed by a seasoned pilot, Captain Chesley "Sully" Sullenberger. After the crash, Sully testified before the National Transportation Safety Board about the danger of having so many inexperienced pilots in the air. See Levin. Since the terrorist attacks of September 11, 2001, airlines had been faced with drastic cost-cutting measures in order to stay in business and as a result employed more overworked, underpaid, and novice pilots than ever before. See Marlantes.

26. See "Transcript."

27. So it was going to be until we quieted our call for the tired, poor, huddled masses yearning to breathe free, the wretched refuse of distant teeming shores, the homeless and tempest-tossed to come home to our lamp-lit golden door.

28. "On 'Bloody Sunday,' March 7, 1965, some 600 civil rights marchers headed east out of Selma on U.S. Route 80. They got only as far as the Edmund Pettus Bridge six blocks away, where state and local lawmen attacked them with billy clubs and tear gas and drove them back into Selma. Two days later on March 9, Martin Luther King, Jr., led a 'symbolic' march to the bridge. Then civil rights leaders sought court protection for a third, full-scale march from Selma to the state capitol in Montgomery." See "Selma-to-Montgomery March."

29. Cancer is not a virus and cannot be spread from person to person. Still, no one in the scientific or academic communities could account for the frequency and virulence of it among the civil rights generation without speculating that at its root was either a long period of dormancy or transmission through political participation.

30. Many assumed "home" was where these imagined spaces converged.

CITYSCAPED

Ethnospheres

Discursions, Excursions

We begin with neologism, with fantasy logos, tongue dancing, mind tripping. Writing is graphing, lining up phonemes with ideas, emotions, and intentions, hoping to shake out the semblance of a message. Writing is long-form neologism for the memory. We force each other to suss out meaning in the order of our "original" strings of words. Really we are excavating, exacerbating the distance between the reader's own sense of morphology and the sensations that arise as they read our danced-out tongues, now extended into fingers, graphing a line of verisimilitude. Right there, our body is inserted into the paragraph, stretching from idea to period, demanding scansion to mark heartbeat and pulse. When we write, our mind dances as we calm our racing thoughts. In this chapter, I seek to reveal choreo-graphy, dance writing, in the process of describing a body in habitual motion.

1. Walking

around
through
in
toward
away
against
down
up
under
(with)

The heel strikes the floor. Unaware of the ramifications of its thud, yet fully aware, it calculates, sending data up the muscles of the leg, triggering cascades of neural communication strings along the spinal overpass that radiate into muscular realignments, confirmations. Pulsing distance, rate, height, sonic quality, even the density of the flooring, the brain starts to search for materials that match the sensational experience the heel now finds itself having. Foam? Cement? Wood: hard wood, soft wood, sprung wood? Metal: steel, iron, aluminum? Tile? Marble? Brick? Pavement? Pavement, cement with quadrangular variation at precise moments aka distances immediately preceded by a large echo of click-clack strikes against tile.

Meanwhile, above the sensorial fracas, the body moves through a series of linguistic spaces, meant to explicate, simplify, and convey the meaning of the motion. Around, through, in toward, away, against, down, up, under, with . . . what is that body doing? The prepositions stack up, almost as commandments, literalizing this very simple, yet intricate execution: walking in a building, through the foyer to the door and exiting onto the pavement out front. In this moment of stepping, we begin our journey into logos. And you thought you were just headed home.

2. The Social Life of Steps

Walk this way! Talk this way! Our syntax is showing. We adjust the space to our body metrics. The length of our legs, arms, torso, neck. Do we drop the corner when we turn, rounding it off for the nearest arc, or do we accept the so-called inevitability of the straight line? Places, noun-like in their presence, morph through our corpo-morphology; a sidewalk becomes a plaza; a stairwell, meant to facilitate movement from one altitude to the next, looks like a comfortable bench. That heel on the floor has created a tidal wave of experience. Simultaneously in the present moment, it also is reaching back, back to when we first learned how to put the heel on the floor, or realized that perhaps we would never be able to do that. The wave rushes up the legs into the spinal column. Our extremities must reorganize around this momentum. How do we accomplish this? The syntax of the everyday, of our first days, flood back into our system, making it so simple to move, but it also marks us in a specific class, identity, religion. We are moving annotations.

3. Psychology of Footprints

Did the walker stride or mince? Were they strolling or determined? Were they coming toward me? Are they moving into my energetic-spatial field aka my personal space? Is my personal space threatened, am I threatened? Am I being invited, is the position of the foot somehow making the hips

FIGURE 10.1. "Dancing Darkey Boy" (video capture). From *Vaudeville: An American Masters Special* (New York: Thirteen/WNET, KCIT, Palmer/Fenster, 1997).

and heart more vulnerable on the walker? Is there space to join? Wait! Are they not from here? No one walks like that here. I don't recognize that ordering of flesh, rhythm, bone, and intention. A different place. They are not from my block, my neck of the woods, my beachfront, my campus. Who are they? What are they? Do I belong to them? Are they lost? Am I lost? Is my corpo-real unreal if that corpo-real can move like that and continue to exist?

4. Retracing↔Mapping

So every step is a new one, and ancient as the geological record. You walk just like your mother. How demeaning is that? But can it be helped without conscious repatterning of your movement repertoire? Where else and how else do you become aware of how to move as a biped? Here is where conditioning resides in our exchanges one with the other, but it is also where a sense of "history" could be located—marking the high points, or important points—the experiences that marked your biological processes: etched themselves into your flesh memory. Habitual movement and conditioning does not necessarily have to become a linear procession of time, however. Since repetition is so much a part of the walking experience, it would seem then that our sense of past, present, and future in lexical terms is just a way to avoid the spatiality of cognition.

5. Geography of Meandering

Your body never gets straight to the point. To get things done, a series of inter-fluid pathways must be fired back and forth along your cerebral fluid—which appears in differing quantities throughout your organism. You look at the sidewalk; it appears to go straight to where you are headed, but for a moment, you hesitate about the destination. *aPersonaFloweraTree* catches your eye. *aNiceWindowDisplayaHotDogVendoraPanhandler* all pull your attention. The sidewalk appears to move, but it is static and your memory of this moment, already forming, will not be.

6. Choreography of Un-alikes

The sidewalk facilitates order, external patterning of footprints. This choreography of power appears natural and easy, like your heel striking the pavement. One foot in front of the other. This thoroughfare, shared with a vendor, someone reading while walking. A couple stopped to kiss; a gaggle of young thirtysomethings posing for a camera that is not there; the panhandler and the garish window display could easily dissolve into chaos were it not for the decorum demanded of public space. But so many bodies experience the public as punishment, as a disciplining force. In a neighborhood, transitioning from one social class to the next—gentrifying—the dust from generations of soles attached to bodies that look like me, a geography of meandering, holds no sway against the "real use value" of the sidewalk. Step aside, or buy your own right of way.

7. Social Construction of Space

Really, as de Certeau described in *The Practice of Everyday Life*, street names radiate like so many constellations, distant stars with no tangible referent to their perceived location. My turf, my hood, my route to work, my newspaper vendor, my shortcut—we socialize space, not in it. The repetition of passing by, our desire to keep it real, through the same ole same, not stuck in a rut, but in a groove . . . Spaced out in this manner, the body in motion emerges tagged and ready for identification, inclusion or exclusion. Four walls, a floor, a roof do not always equal home.

8. Configuration of Spatial Consciousness

Here fluidity as a metaphor becomes problematic. Striated with overuse. With tendencies toward identifying with one corpo-reality over another, the fluid in the body system begins to congeal. We call it euphemistically "conditioning," a good thing when you are at the gym, a bad thing when you are in jail, a deterrent to your success when someone decides to grant you limitations equivalent to your epidermal reality, as if you start and stop at your skin. These bodies, our bodies are not so much people aware of people as corpo-reals aware of muscle memory, strolling socializations bounded by unrecognizable locations.

9. religious/racialized/gendered/classed

corpo-benedictus, corpo-fanatica, corpo-epidermus, corpo-phallus, corpo-vaginus, corpo-hermaphroda, corpo-consumus, corpo-supportus, corpo-polis—how many bodies do you push your fluid through during the day? Are you aware, or performing to meet the expectations of a corpo-generus?

10. Socialization of Strolling

Through the way in which we "carry" our bodies in space, mincing steps, strolling, staggering, swaggering, waddling, gliding, switching, and so forth, we communicate our emotions, our sense of belonging, cultural history, ethnic identity, and gender identity. How we walk through open space can also reveal our subtle fears of unknown people, of Strangers. Other times, the way we appropriate a space designated for one use for another reveals our out-of-placeness, perhaps rootlessness and our ability to re-create a familiar zone of use around us and others like us. Walking sets us apart and brings us together, even though we are always already each other, fluid system to fluid system.

archiving, jiving, repeating

We want to remember all of this, right?

Boogaloo, Chili, Swing Out, Two Step, Slide, Bus Stop, Prep, Running Man . . . can we trust all of this to some fool's tendons or a scratchy old video-tape? Methods change, but the fact remains: landscapes don't mean the same thing to every body. Dance moves, are they really any different? Aren't they just moving landscapes from a bacterium-eye's view?

A soul is wrapped up in the phrasing of those moves. How dare we mishandle it, disregard its gift by trying to remember it! This ain't no oral culture! If we don't put the definition in the dictionary, the ad reps will, and then what will our shit mean? Really, do we want to have the body of a Julia Stiles, Britney Spears, or Wade Robson, the voice of a Christina Aguilera or Teena Marie DEFINING our shit? We ain't talkin' about money yet, either!

Write it down, commit it to memory? Is your dark ass submissable as evidence in a copyright dispute? Write it down, apply for the l'il ass™ and HOLD ON TO IT. Don't worry about getting paid. That ain't the point, at least not yet anyway. Stake your claim now; collect on the infringements later.

The pain point with nonessentialism is the recognition of jurisprudence: "white man's law." Here the performatives fly, creating value for the unmarked bodies in "our" kinematic clothing. "You dance really well (for a white girl)! I could not believe how you were able to rise to the challenge of hip-hop choreography." From any episode of *So You Think You Can Dance*.

But the marked body, the targeted body, in a de-essentialized practice, does it not still bear a burden of proof as exceptional? 1 2 3 and 4. Structure and stricture. Those allow space for adjudication. Improvisation? That's just darky bullshit.

Mindless repetition is the goal, the target. Wherein is freedom enacted? My sinews search through their archives for moves to turn a dance floor into a home site. What surfaces are not always "true" to the mark of my skin, my so-called heritage?

Repeat this! "Kenny G put a copyright on the technique of circular breathing!" Did he invent it? Of course not, but some ill-informed wonk in the U.S. Patent Office approved the application because WE did not write it down.

C A N N O N B A L L A D D E R L E Y.

We didn't write that down. We have to stake a claim beyond our bodies and write this shit down. Keep depending on the good graces of the melanin-deprived and see where that gets you. Chitlin Circuit. OK. Yeah, that still pays, but when do we get to make Art with the capital A always evident? Why we got to be popular? Always jive-timing it . . . colorstrucked time bomb

If the city is planed, ordinated, its memories adhere to skin, intrude into muscle, force weight shifts and sighs, toying with biochemical realities. Entrained, a body instigates experiences of a city on the butterfly wings of communal memory. Redlining gives way to bloodmemory birthing maps in response to here that is not now, but always and forever a relic . . . a reaction . . . a maneuver.

The little darky on the dock taps and taps, sending out code, hoping that someone will answer back, let him know he is safe. Smiling white faces are just as frightening as scowling, screaming ones. He cannot tell the difference. He has been trained that the absence of lips makes it difficult to read their faces, and their determination to not love what the body can do makes it a dangerous thing to act on their gestures. So he keeps dancing. And dancing. He smiles out of fear and anxiety. No, he smiles as a reflex. The code

FIGURE 10.2. "Dancing Darkey Boy" (video capture). From *Vaudeville: An American Masters Special* (New York: Thirteen/WNET, KCIT, Palmer/Fenster, 1997).

he stomps out is pure joy in other realms. A communication device and an esoteric text; his clicking and clacking reverberate across dimensions. He is safe. He knows that in his heart, but can he believe his eyes?

They are throwing things at him. He can't stop and see what it is, just in case they are actually angry. He needs the joysong to continue to hum around him, protect him with its ancient lightness. He keeps going. Does he slip on the coins? They throw things at him. Is he now extracted from his labor? Is he surplus, or his feet? Is it in his smile, the extraction point? Maneuvering, manipulating, he seems trapped. He keeps dancing.

The coins ring as they hit the boxes around the one he is on. When he started he was just standing on the dock. One set of meaty hands lifted him up and put him on a stack of crates, so that more people could see. They belonged to someone who was worried for his safety. A brawl had already broken out because someone who thought themselves too important to be in the back could not see and swiped at someone else who thought themselves righteous because they were there first.

"Look at l'il darky go!" This is what made the docks so exciting. Darkies and their smiles. Their sounds. Their joy?

"They *love* working like this."

"It's not even work to them."

"What makes that l'il fellar move so like that?"

Wonderment at the deployment of his texts, the laughing and smiling faces, faces that appear around lynched darky bodies as well, are drowning in the joysong. Unable to venerate the body, they pay for the right to see the labor. The boy dances like a hawk running to take flight. The boy dances like lightning striking an old tree. The boy dances like two old hands clapping to start the Feast. The boy dances like bones hitting the mat, telling the truth. The boy dances like Anansi weaving a web of imbrication, coating the story in protective plates of intrigue, science, and love. The boy dances, dances, dances.

The footage of his feat is the actual artifact. His tapping evidence not of his passing, but of the development of camera technique. He is dead, but his tapping has not stopped.

Roll the reel again.

PART IV / Hi-Fidelity Black

"RIP IT UP"

Excess and Ecstasy in Little Richard's Sound

My mother had all these kids, and I was the only one born deformed. My right leg is shorter than the left. I didn't realize that my leg was small. I never knew about it. Yet looking back, I can see why my mother and them was always so careful about me . . . cos they knew something I didn't. My mother used to let me get away with so much. I lived through a lot, and a lot of it was the way I walked. The kids didn't realize I was crippled. They thought I was trying to twist and walk feminine. But I had to take short steps cos I had a little leg. I used to walk with odd strides, like long-short, long-short. The kids would call me faggot, sissy, freak, punk. They called me everything.

—Little Richard, in Charles White, *The Life and Times of Little Richard*

I

In the passage of autobiographical reflection offered as an epigraph to this chapter, an adult runs his fingers against the grain of memory, touching and feeling his way back to a proto-queer childhood. In his recollection, disability and effeminacy merge as that which the body experiences, but which is not yet available to conscious recognition. This body that is not yet known is then recollected in memory, but not in order to achieve a mastery over it or to impose a retrospective coherence. In this case, the child is not the father to the man. Rather than a developmental narrative, what we hear from Little Richard is the long-short, long-short of the body's movement, its odd and individual gait. If we suspend the knowingness that would define this long-short, long-short movement as a crippling or deformity, we may begin to see that what this passage highlights is the way such concepts—"crippling," "deformity"—

help instate the injury they purport to describe.[1] So we should not say the adult has put away childish things; we say rather that his recollection is what puts his childhood into stride.

So we both encounter and hear a body out of joint. Such out-of-jointedness, the passage reminds us, has repercussions on the playgrounds of everyday life. An "odd stride" selects a body for injurious interpolation. The long-short, long-short of not-knowing brings down a rhythmic pattern of abuse. In Little Richard's retelling, we quickly recognize the ever-suspect figure of the mama's boy, a product of excesses of care and protection. It is important to realize that the proto-queerness of the mama's boy is not reducible to sexual orientation, preference, or identity. Rather than sexual essence, there is sexual existence, or, following Heidegger, what we might call ek-sistence. "The ecstatic essence of man consists in ek-sistence," Heidegger notes in the "Letter on Humanism." "In terms of content ek-sistence means standing out into the truth of Being" (Heidegger, *Basic Writings*, 229, 30). To be, in Heidegger's existential phenomenology, is to be thrown out into a clearing, to occupy an ordinariness irreducible to any average or norm, a singular long-short, long-short stride. But because we are talking about a man who would become a great figure of musical crossover, the self-styled "architect" of rock and roll, it would be sensible to consult Marx as well in ascertaining this movement of constitutive out-of-jointedness in relation to a sociological given: "To say that man is a *corporeal*, living, real, sensuous, objective being with natural powers means that he has *real, sensuous objects* as the object of his being and of his vital expression, or that he can only *express* his life in real, sensuous objects. . . . A being which does not have its nature outside itself is not a natural being and plays no part in the system of nature" (Marx, 390). The early Marx anticipates Heidegger in his insistence that "being" be thought of as "besidedness," in his claim that species being is also a constitutive outside. It is this besidedness, this out-of-joint bodying, which produces the real, sensuous object and its relation to self-expression.[2] The historical critique of American popular music is shaped by powerfully emotive concepts of cultural theft and appropriation. But to think of being as besidedness should introduce a hesitation in our analysis of property and the proper. Capitalism, for Marx, does not simply alienate what is essentially ours; it interposes a system of abstract equivalences, the commodity form, which alienates us from estrangement. It is a naturalized ideology of norms and of the proper that a black existence in rock might subvert. Among its most potent effects is the fantasy of identity and belonging. But queerness emerges not as the truth of this identity or belonging, but as its ecstatic outside. Things are queer (Weinberg). In Richard's memoir, things give their outness to a memory as it narrates the modulation between caring, permissive "mother and them" on the one hand, and abusive, fearful kids on the other. And because Althusser's allegory of interpellation shadows any text concerned with the hailing language of injurious speech—"The kids would call me faggot, sissy, freak, punk"—it is surely worth lingering a bit longer in this modulation of what Marx redundantly calls "*corporeal*, living, real, sensuous, objective being."

In Althusser's allegory, the command of the police brings us out of ourselves, and into a lockstep (Althusser). "Hey you!" The policeman shouts. But it is important that the echo of the policeman's call not drown out the scattering of other voices at play in the passage I opened with. Even in their viciousness, they do not cohere into any single stable interpellation. Little Richard reminds us that, to the contrary, "They called me everything." In assaulting him with every name in the book, interpellation disrupts its own project of cohering the queer and disabled body into a stable abjection. Instead, it unlocks a series of affinities, a series that points into a line of flight, on beyond "faggot, sissy, freak," and "punk," toward "everything." This is the first historical excess we must register. Because no one word can halt him, command exhausts itself in inventing names, all of which fail to bring his long-short, long-short to a halt. He crosses over.

This is all to say that it is not simply insult, not insult alone, which inaugurates the black queer subject. Properly speaking, it is not even subjectivity we are discussing, but a brushing up against the memory of a body's outness, its prodigal wandering from the care and permission of mother and them, and into the range of the kids' verbal fire, and beyond. "My mother had all these kids, and I was the only one born deformed." Pace Erving Goffman, this deformity is not first registered in the bodily schema, still less in a stigma negotiated against a cruel, normalizing world (Goffman). Rather, it is established first in the arena of the "not known." "I never knew about it," he insists. This not-knowing is not an absence but a presence and a movement registered in the figure he cut. At fourteen, this proto-queer child walked out of a home reverberating with his father's voice saying, "My father had seven sons and I wanted seven sons. You've spoiled it, you're only half a son."

Already, his walk had broken out into a run—"Daddy was always criticizing me for the way I walked and talked and for the people I was *running* with" (White, *Life and Times*, 21). When B. Brown and His Orchestra came through town, this child got one whiff of the life of the traveling show and started to travel. Eight years and many costume changes later, he sat down

FIGURE 11.1. Awapbopaloobopawopbamboom: Little Richard performing, 1957.
Photograph: Michael Ochs Archives. Copyright, Getty Images.

in a recording studio in New Orleans to record the single that he pegs as the
greatest achievement of his life. "It took me out of the kitchen," he told an
interviewer in 1999 (referring to a day job in a restaurant). "I thank God for
'Tutti Frutti'" (Crazy Horse, 4).

II

If I have belabored a reading of a short autobiographical passage, it is in order to open out an alternative approach to the work and influence of Ricardo
Wayne Penniman, better known as Little Richard. Born in 1932 to Leva Mae
and Bud Penniman of Macon, Georgia, Little Richard is today enjoying

something of a critical renaissance, and, as of this writing, still performing rock and roll and preaching the gospel word. From the revisionist blues
historiography of Marybeth Hamilton and W. T. Lhamon's cultural history
of the 1950s to Kandia Crazy Horse's audacious project of black rock reclamation, Little Richard increasingly figures as the missing link for a number
of theoretical and musical projects interested in breaking out of masculinist and heteronormative accounts of American popular culture (Hamilton;
Lhamon; Crazy Horse). From Frank Tashlin's rocksploitation comedy, *The
Girl Can't Help It* (1956) (Little Richard sang the title song), to his turn as
Orvis Goodnight in *Down and Out in Beverly Hills* (1986), Richard has been
an outrageous and iconic presence in visual culture. His flamboyance and
self-regard is as easily and frequently parodied as that of Rick James, but that
individuality, like James's, shines through even the fiercest caricature. Like
an itch that popular memory must continuously scratch, Little Richard has
been recycled as both buffoon and genius, spectacle and virtuoso. His is an
ambidextrous legacy that distills the dilemmas of black musical crossover.

"Awapbopaloobopawopbamboom" indexes a cultural moment redolent
of the absurd, the freeing, the innocent, and the carnal. This is so even when,
as in *The Girl Can't Help It*, the camera of cultural memory persists in visually segregating black performance into its own separate history. Arthur
Knight has shown how in the classic Hollywood musical, the film cut silently
separates the races even as the diegetic sound crosses over, rendering the
technical fantasy of racial consumption without contamination (Knight).
If black performance in Hollywood in 1956 was permissible only within an
internal proscenium such as a nightclub stage or a television set, then black
bodies served primarily as a visual metonymy for their presence on the
soundtrack. So Little Richard's exuberant performance in that film, along
with that of Fats Domino and many others, brings to the foreground the
aesthetic and political dilemmas of the commodification of black sound.

In a key scene, Little Richard performs "She's Got It" at the piano as Jayne
Mansfield sashays through the segregated nightclub where he is performing. The film stages and represses a miscegenation fantasy. Acceding to the
paranoid restrictions upon black male sexuality, critics sometimes interpret
Richard as parading his own vanity and outrageousness to dampen racial
anxieties. But his ecstatic performance also records, in its queer narcissism,
the unmistakable suggestion that Mansfield is not the only "she" who's got
"it."[3] Such an exchange of position between lyrical subject and object is not
unusual in Little Richard's recording career, as one of the first tracks he laid
down for Specialty Records in 1955, a song named "Baby," indicates. In it he
ad libs, "Baby, don't you wish your man had long hair like mine? / Baby, I'm

the sweetest man in town" (Little Richard). Notionally heterosexual, the line issues an odd invitation to a woman to imagine her man as both "sweet" (southern black slang for gay) and as pretty as Little Richard. Beautiful long hair signifies, and signifies on, femininity, whiteness, and artifice, in a joke straight out of a drag queen's repartee with the straight couple slumming at her show. The lyric puts both Baby's and Little Richard's business out in the open for all to see. Richard's male dandyism would subsequently influence the look of Jimi Hendrix and Prince. In 1956 such sweetness on the part of black men could be misread as "safe," but before we name this strategy emasculation, we should consider what alternative history of black male sexuality might be there for a telling that never fully conformed to the policing white gaze.

The flamboyant queerness of Little Richard—hardly a figure on the margins—has been, one might say, hiding in plain sight. It was hardly predictable that the mid-twentieth-century demand in segregated America for black musical acts to feed white musical appetites would produce this vision of what, in the black vernacular, could only be called a freakish man. Little Richard managed to convert his first hit into a meteoric, three-year career in rock that left a legendary persona name-checked by every figure in the rock pantheon. Elvis called him "the greatest," and the Greatest, Muhammad Ali, called him "my favorite singer." Jimi Hendrix said, "I want to do with my guitar what Little Richard does with his voice," and in perhaps the most arresting "tribute" collected by Richard's biographer, from whom I have gathered these testimonials, is an anecdote told by John Lennon:

> Elvis was bigger than religion in my life. Then this boy at school said he'd got this record by somebody called Little Richard who was better than Elvis. . . . The new record was Little Richard's "Long Tall Sally." When I heard it, it was so great I couldn't speak. You know how you are torn. I didn't want to leave Elvis, but this was so much better. We all looked at each other, but I didn't want to say anything against Elvis, even in my mind. How could they *both* be happening in my life? And then someone said, "It's a nigger singing." I didn't know Negroes sang. So Elvis was white and Little Richard was black. This was a great relief. "Thank you, God," I said. "There is a difference between them." (White, *Life and Times*, 225–26)

The relief felt by Lennon at the racial abjection of Little Richard—an abjection that somehow combines a privileged unknowingness about the origins of rock, even the tradition of black vocal performance, with a ready-at-hand insult—supplies an opening to his own possessive investment in whiteness (I don't have to be as good as this black voice; I need only be as good as Elvis) but cannot fully repair the fracture left by the dispossessive force of Little Richard's sound, which throws Lennon out of himself, leaving him speechless, wordless, experiencing his life as the impossibility of a simultaneous, mutually exclusive happening. The "relief" felt by the reordering of sound into color-coded genres, supplying the possibility of a musical "crossover," thus represses a prior and more fundamental sonic encounter with ek-stasis.

The color coding of black performance into segregating genres enabled the exploitation of singers like Big Mama Thornton and Little Richard, leading Norman Kelley to acidly characterize the commercial music industry as a structure of stealing (Kelley). "It didn't matter how many records you sold if you were black," Richard recalled. "The publishing rights were sold to the record label before the record was released. 'Tutti Frutti' was sold to Specialty for fifty dollars." Under such an arrangement, mechanical performances of his songs such as airplay accrued Richard half a cent. Sarcastically reifying this accounting principle in a manner that recalls his own recollection of being called "half a son," Richard exasperatedly asked, "Whoever heard of cutting a penny in half!" (White, *Life and Times*, 57–58). It would hardly be consolation for him to learn that such exploitation was standard within the culture industries, that race in this case was a metonymy of the general dominance of capital over labor. For black musical labor before the civil rights era was asymmetrically produced along racial as well as class lines. Fair accounting practices in an industry that immediately rerecorded many of Richard's hits for release by white artists like Pat Boone, on the understanding that airplay would prefer a "white" voice, would hardly have placed more than a fig leaf over structural racism.

The affective labor of performance, existing under conditions of unfreedom, and in fact called into existence by those conditions, nevertheless is not fully subsumed by those conditions. One challenge is how not to fall back upon a compensatory structure of musical feeling as a consolation for the market's rigors. Another is not to mistake the uses of the sacred as a haven in a heartless world. The question I pursue here is the question of what is in the commodity, but not of it, which might be thought of as something other than a property, whether individual or collective, and which thereby might refigure our histories of capitalism so as to allow a greater sensitivity to what Moten has called the resistances of the object.

In an article on the political economy of the race record, David Suisman contrasts the "radical experiment" of the petit bourgeois Black Swan records with the "credulous" attempt to found social change in the actual "composition or performance" of music itself (Suisman, 1297, 1324, 1323). Such a definition of the political economy of music is one I break with here,

radically reducing as it does the phenomenology of performance to a deriva-
tion of macroeconomic processes. Such an approach, notionally in the spirit
of Adorno and Horkheimer's critique of the culture industries, is, I would
argue, diametrically opposed to the authors of the following observation: "A
technological rationale is the rationale of domination itself" (Horkheimer
and Adorno, 121). The radical experiment of autonomous or black-owned
business enterprise may or may not be ultimately congruent with capitalism, depending on the angle of one's ideological vision. But to separate it
from questions of music-making and performance is to reify the system of
abstract equivalences in capitalism, and is thus to perform political economy
rather than, as Marx attempted, to *critique* it.

It is such a critique of the political economy of music—in which performance and composition are critical—that occupies my present concern.
What is the temporal register necessary for "Tutti Frutti" to be heard once
again? If crossover gets caught in an upward redistribution of cash flow and
enjoyment, is there nevertheless not an excess within the commodity form
and within the labor discipline entailed in its production? If crossover only
gets half a man for half a cent, what about the other half, dragging behind,
inside, outside? This is another way of asking the question, what does the
scene of production produce other than the product?

Part of my answer lies in the scenes of performance that exceed the recording session that is their occasion. Indeed, I want to argue that what labor
discipline encounters, rather than a live performance and its recording, is a
sound filling a space, an auditorium, that is singular, a full plenum, and that
evades the repetitious, duplicative process of commercial recording. This argument is a little bit different than the now-familiar claim that performance
is only in its now, in a burdened live (pace Phelan). The auditorium is neither
the real space in which sound is heard or recorded nor the future spaces in
which it might be replayed, but the virtual space that transects both, the void
into which the voice is thrown, the "there" in which its ek-sistence subsides.
Sound escapes as it reverberates and echoes, as it catches and burrows in the
ear, as it drives the body into frenzy, a singular voice that is out of body and
out of time, that is present even when it is not audible.

In the most apt expression of such an auditorium, we might consider
how Richard describes his own impulse toward one-upmanship: "I couldn't
allow anybody to take an audience from me. . . . And I truly did feel in my
heart that nobody could take a show from me. I didn't care how great they
were. I didn't care how many records they had. I would say 'This is my
house'" (White, *Life and Times*, 85). Liveness here operates in tandem with
recording, each pushing the other toward excess. Claiming the house, the

auditorium, as his own, taking it from any other act on the bill, no matter how famous, Richard also takes it from himself, from the prior recordings that had brought his audience to that room to begin with. He is describing an indefinitely extensible space, one forever reaching for the next level or plateau (Deleuze and Guattari, 21). The ecstatic exclamation "This is my house!" extends the zones of intensity created by Little Richard's sound, and this conflation of crossing over and bringing down the house radically challenges the planned obsolescence of the culture industries.

III

The convenient definition of rock as black music played by white people manages to explain away someone like Little Richard, like a historical scaffolding that has been wheeled away from the edifice of rock. This ignores the ways and degrees to which black sounds continue to animate the "whitest" of rock, from Lenny Kravitz channeling Jimi Hendrix or Slash fronting Guns N' Roses to Fishbone's saga of being perpetually on the brink. As Kandia Crazy Horse notes, the struggle to be recognized within rock is an enduring dilemma for black musicians, one compounded, ironically, by the dependence of rock on its myths of an authentic folk music somehow converted or transformed by true rock musicians. Marybeth Hamilton foregrounds the gendered dynamics of this operation in "Sexual Politics and African-American Music; or, Placing Little Richard in History." Insofar as rock recognizes its black roots, it is in the blues. And yet the blues is always already figured as a rural, earthy, masculine tradition that would exclude an urban, glamorous, effeminate performer like Little Richard. In her article, Hamilton notices the marginalization of black rockers in most histories of black music and argues that rock "is perceived as a factory product that diluted, even perverted, black performance traditions for sale to undiscerning consumers who, if anything, preferred the fake stuff to the real" (Hamilton, 163). In this critique, the scene of production produces only the product, never the worker as well, or if so, only as another commodity, an objectified black soul reified into acetate.

This ostensibly Marxist critique of the "factory product" is actually quite conservative, insofar as it ignores Marx's insistence that all social existence, and therefore even the utopia of unalienated social existence, is produced out of a relation to real, sensuous objects. Instead, and perversely, the mechanized factory production of music is feminized, a form of "housework" in contrast to the masculine "fieldwork" of the authentic blues. Reading the work of both black and white scholars, Hamilton detects an unspoken syllogism at work: authentic is to sellout as masculinity is to effeminate. Black music—whether secular or religious—comes out of a southern, rural, folk scenario for which sexuality and effeminacy stand as divisive, differentiating principles that confound and disrupt in the way that the market is imagined to confound and disrupt our natural wants and desires. In particular, the use of objects to produce an alluring surface—cosmetics, hair pomade, clothing—is conflated with their status as commodities under capitalism, ignoring their function as equipment of self-fashioning.

This self-fashioning crosses over the visual/audible divide. Can authenticity sound like "The Girl Can't Help It"? Or "Good Golly, Miss Molly"? In such songs, we hear the aural traces of Little Richard's prior incarnation as the teenage Princess Lavonne, a "minstrel-show drag queen" plying the southern black audience Chitlin Circuit (Hamilton, 162). But despite the appearance of the telling word "Molly," it is important not to rush too quickly to decode these songs as "secretly" about drag queens. First of all, this was hardly a secret. But secondly, the southern, pre–civil rights, African American gender system these songs index cannot be reduced to the image of the transgressive transvestite any more than Little Richard's reference to "mother and them" boils down to an Oedipal narrative. The performance knows more than the words tell, and the possibility of a black spectacle is exploded by the interanimation of an eroticism that is temporarily without boundary. What is going on is an ecstatic outness that in Baltimore in 1956 had white girls in fits, throwing their panties at the stage as songs about the gendered strife of everyday black life in the South were recognized, impossibly, as songs about them.

How are we to approach this dialogic play between black and white, sex and fun, sense and nonsense? Is there a risk here in that making rock about everyone, we lose the specificity of the black drag presence in Little Richard? What about the closet, and the compulsory encoding of queer life? Sure, the original lyrics to "Tutti Frutti" reveal what the seeming nonsense of the recorded version encodes: "Tutti Frutti, good booty / If it don't fit, don't force it / You can grease it, make it easy" (quoted in White, *Life and Times*, 55). Clearly, some encoding is at work in the version that made it to vinyl. A song about the pleasures and risks of anal sex was not going to make it onto the airwaves of America in the 1950s. But I want to insist that, at the level of phonic materiality, one song like this nevertheless did; that Little Richard got one over on the American public, and that what is translated between the barrelhouse bawdy and the nostalgic innocence of rocking around the clock was precisely that not-knowing, the freedom that came from it, and the irruption of youthfulness that was a newness entering the word along that slide. "If it don't fit, don't force it. You can grease it, make it easy." Sexuality is not so much unveiled as invented. The affective bonds forged by this advice were promiscuous in the best sense of the word, and provide an interpretive key to what W. T. Lhamon calls Little Richard's musical "cubism," his modernist triangulations of folk relationships, his complex, fragmented portraits of a folk divided among themselves (Lhamon). This aesthetic strategy is brought forward in a series of sexual personae and struggles set forth by the long-short, long-short rhythm of a locomotive that opens the track "Lucille."

Lucille won't do her sister's will, the singer sings, but he loves her still. What is this love, this homosocial triangle in which the narrator finds himself between two sisters, one willing and one willful, and discovers in their difference the route to his own ecstatic outness, sonically registered with such abandon on the record? Such a tangle of antagonisms and identifications is no more clearly present than in the story his producer Robert Blackwell tells of the origins of the song "Long Tall Sally":

> I got a call from a big disk jockey called Honey Chile. She *had* to see me. . . . So Honey Chile said to me, "Bumps, you got to do something about this girl. She's walked all the way from Appaloosa, Mississippi, to sell this song to Richard, cos her auntie's sick and she needs money to put her in the hospital." I said okay, let's hear the song, and this little clean-cut kid, all bows and things, says "Well, I don't have a melody yet. I thought maybe you or Richard could do that." So I said okay, what *have* you got, and she pulls out this piece of paper. It looked like toilet paper with a few words written on it:
>
> *Saw Uncle John with Long Tall Sally*
> *They saw Aunt Mary comin'*
> *So they ducked back in the alley.*
>
> And she said, "Aunt Mary is sick. And I'm going to tell her about Uncle John. Cos he was out there with Long Tall Sally, and I saw 'em. They saw Aunt Mary comin' and they ducked back in the alley."
>
> I said, "They did, huh? And this is a song? You walked all the way from Appaloosa, Mississippi, with this piece of paper?" (White, *Life and Times*, 61)

Enortis Johnson's picaresque narrative, the family illness that set her in motion, is full of endearments and a child's petulant determination to tell. It marks a line of flight directed toward the culture industries, a deliberate pursuit of commodification that, in its not-knowing, produces a dwelling that the commodity can hold but not capture. It was only by not knowing how to write a song, more precisely, by not knowing that she was not supposed to be able to write a song, that Enortis Johnson ended up writing a song. Here we glimpse the secret prehistory of the "do-it-yourself" radical aesthetic some have traced to the European avant-garde but that I want to see prefaced here, a punk attitude that rose up in Enortis from Appaloosa, and set her flowing.

What is black rock? What is the sound of crossing over? Maureen Mahon pursues the question rigorously in chapter 5 of her recent monograph, *Right to Rock*, varying between the view of New York–based guitarist Kelvyn Bell that "black rock to me is funk. . . . Funk really means an emphasis on the rhythms that are African-based, heavily African-based" and Beverly Milner's insistence that blacks also play "'pure' rock, you know, 'white boy rock.' We like to bang our heads" (quoted in Mahon, 138–39). We might split the difference and argue that black rock *cuts* rock, invaginating the culture industries with what Moten calls a "radically exterior aurality that disrupts and resists certain formations of identity and interpretation by challenging the reducibility of phonic matter to verbal meaning or conventional musical form" (Moten, *In the Break*, 6). This cut, Moten insists with Nathaniel Mackey, must be thought of as a "sexual cut": "Indeed, one of the things that is most important and worthy of attention in the moment I'm trying to touch on here, the period between 1955 and 1965 when the avant-garde in black performance . . . irrupts into and restructures the downtown New York scene, is precisely this sexual differentiation of sexual difference that occurs at the convergence of fetishized, commodified, racialized consumption and aesthetic rapture, that occurs as militant political and aesthetic objection" (Moten, *In the Break*, 152). Could we think of Little Richard's rock in the orbit and ambience of this avant-garde? As containing a militancy even within the fraught terrain of the popular, the factory-produced, and the sexual that reveals a folk divided against itself along the lines of a "sexual differentiation of sexual difference"? The decade Moten specifies (1955–65) is, after all, precisely the decade Little Richard began on September 13, 1955, not in downtown New York, but in the legendary J and M Recording Studio in New Orleans, just north of the French Quarter and across the street from Louis Armstrong Park, formerly Congo Square, where slaves were permitted to gather weekly for several hours of singing, drumming, and dancing. Benjamin Latrobe in 1819, like Frank Sinatra in 1957, heard something martial in the pounding, rhythmic music of the slaves, like "horses tramping on a wooden floor." If there was a war going on, it was between Little Richard's crossover sound and its co-optation by Pat Boone's covers, which Little Richard responded to with a deliberate speeding up "faster and faster until it burned. . . . Let's see Pat Boone get his mouth together to do *this* song" (White, *Life and Times*, 62).

Moten's deconstruction of an ostensibly white, downtown New York–based avant-garde, his infiltration of that narrative with the suppressed stories of "militant political and aesthetic objection," clears some of the space we need for other histories of the 1950s, cultural histories that refuse orthodox distinctions between high and low art, between popular culture and the avant-garde, distinctions that still seem to confound. To hear Little Richard's speeded-up scream alongside Abbey Lincoln's howl is a way for its auditory performance to outlast the moment of commercial ephemerality. If a gold record is a flash in the pan, "Long Tall Sally" is a historical slow burn, a sound image awaiting our re-audition to restore the disjunctive temporality of "afro-sonic modernity" encoded in its grooves (Weheliye). It is not paradoxical to assert that Little Richard's speed also stops time, halts the commercial, homogeneous time along which profits are charted and surplus values are extracted. Each re-audition restores an antiprogressive, anticapitalist promise:

> Saturday night and I just got paid
> I'm a fool about my money, don't try to save.
> . . .
> I'm gonna rock it up,
> Rip it up, and ball tonight.

The exuberant abandon announced by the opening lines of Little Richard's hit single "Rip It Up" (1956) finds a counterpoint in the unexpected restraint of the song's chorus, where Little Richard's growl softens into a falsetto, and the release promised by the propulsive energy of the first bars finds it is unexpectedly contained by a musical sublimation. The barbaric yawp that punctuated this and other Little Richard songs from the miraculous three years of 1955 to 1957 is enfolded in a dialectic of containment and release, as musical form abbreviates and gives shape to the anarchic, youthful energies that want to rip it up and ball tonight. Rip money into a ball and have a ball (have a party, have sex), this is the secret preserved somehow even in the negations of contemporary "bling" culture, which in its near manic identification with the acquisition of wealth can never fully evade its own pleasure in seeking money destroyed, theatricalized, burnt up, and spilled out. Little Richard's song encapsulates rock's rebellious premonition of what Georges Bataille called a "general economy," one characterized not by the thrift, scarcity, and alienation of capitalism, but by an abundance and superfluity that cannot be used but must somehow be wasted, spilled, and depleted (Bataille). The core of rock and roll's politics, "Rip It Up" suggests, lay not in the countercultural negation of the 1960s-era protest anthem, but in the impossible innocence of rock's dawn in the 1950s, when it dared speak the pleasures of the flesh across the threshold of race.

Mainstream and margins then are assemblages of one complex, unrepresentable whole. The forms of antagonism at play in the freest of the free spirits of performance art are also figured in those most rigorously self-disciplined by the terms of commodity fetishism and musical wage slavery. We can begin to see an approach that might harmonize the cultural agendas of an Enortis Johnson, homely representative of the folk, and Little Richard Penniman, representative of some sort of black sexual underground, such that rather than seeing his nonsense as the coding of a secret, sexual sense, we might release both into a semiotic play that is only cut by the ideological closure of race. The glossolalia of the carnivalesque upwells from the lower orders and regions of the body, ripping it up, balling it up, having a ball. Words establish unusual relationships among themselves. Enortis Johnson's agenda merges into Little Richard's pop cubism, sexually differentiating the folk, the vernacular, in a way that will always be a surprise, will always be a scandal, for ideology.

This rock-musical dialogism, of which Greil Marcus's *Lipstick Traces* stands as an almost solitary monument, places us within a different kind of temporality, one we can align with the inspiration heard from this off-again, on-again preacher of the gospel:

> Once there was a man called the prodigal son. He came to his father and said, "Father, give me all of my belongings. Give me *all* the goods that belong to me. I want to go *out*! I want to *taste* the world! I want to see what the world is like." His father didn't *want* to give him those goods, but his father had so great a love for his son. And *he gave* his son his goods and his son went away into a *foreign* country. Living a rowdy life, doing things that God would not like to see his children to participate in. One day the boy got *hungry*! One day the boy got *raggedy*! He didn't have *any clothes* to put on. He didn't have *nothing*, He was *raggedy*! Eating down with the swine. He said my father have many servants, that have enough food to give me. I will arise.

So begins the spoken/preached prelude to Little Richard's rendition of the gospel song "Coming Home," recorded in 1959 in New York City, shortly after his climactic abandonment of rock and roll in 1957 and the prodigal's return. Clearly, one hears in his rendition of the allegory the contours of his own life, recounted in a public recantation. But the terms upon which the prodigal returns are never simply the negation of his secular, wandering, irresponsible ways.

The home he returns to is not the one he left. The means carried over from commodity production into the adjacent halls of spiritual productions return our attention to the outness of the prodigal's return, the strange, estranging *ease* of his return, his unrepresentably, irreducibly queer space within the community. "Ease is the proper name of this unrepresentable space," Giorgio Agamben reminds us. It "designates, according to its etymology, the space adjacent (*ad-jacens, adjacentia*), the empty place where each can move freely . . . the very place of love" (Agamben). The ecstasy that invaginates the secular commodity grain of Richard's voice with a transgressive, prodigal spirit should not, however, license a return to religion or metaphysics. Take it from Agamben, or if not, take it from Little Richard. For in the grain of Richard's preacherly cadence, in its auspicious theatricality and ecstatic outness, you can still hear the drag and lisp of his long-short, long-short stride.

Notes

1. The injury of abuse is metaphorically condensed onto the "disability" of the body, which is disabled in relation to a norm. Knowing one's disability is therefore a declension from the "not-knowing," effecting the metonymic displacement of injury into a rhythmic, off-kilter movement. I borrow the concept of "instatement" to name this process from Sappol (12). See also McRuer.

2. Fred Moten calls this phenomena "objection" when he asks, "What's the revolutionary force of the sensuality that emerges from the sonic event Marx subjunctively produces without sensually discovering? To ask this is to think what's at stake in the music . . . the ontological and historical priority of . . . objection to subjection" (Moten, *In the Break*, 12).

3. In his biography Little Richard confirms this image of gay male narcissism, remembering, "My whole gay activities were really into masturbation. I used to do it six or seven times a day. In fact, everybody used to tell me that I should get a trophy for it, I did it so much. . . . Most gay people fall in love with themselves" (White, *Life and Times*, 72).

DON'T STOP 'TIL YOU GET ENOUGH

Presence, Spectacle, and Good Feeling
in *Michael Jackson's This Is It*

There's a fantastic moment I can't shake in Columbia Pictures'
Michael Jackson's This Is It (2009), the film posthumously cobbled
together from raw video footage of Michael Jackson during his final rehearsals. While restaging synth-funk jam "Smooth Criminal"
(1988) at Los Angeles's Staples Center, codirector Kenny Ortega asks
the wiry pop superstar, who is facing stage front, how he will see
an important visual cue on the gargantuan one-hundred-by-thirty-
foot HD 3D screen behind him. With scarcely a moment's hesitation,
Jackson replies: "I gotta feel that . . . I'll feel that, the screen behind me."

"I'll feel that": an essential cue in a multimillion-dollar live theatrical extravaganza hinges on Jackson's ability to intuitively feel
that which he cannot physically see. Ortega seems secure enough
to surrender the moment to Jackson's tremendous self-confidence
in his own peerless rhythm and timing. No visual proof is required.
In the moment in which he must be in the moment, Michael has
faith that he'll ride the energy of that moment.

But Jackson's timing is beyond extraordinary. It's extrasensory.
As default custodians of improvisational musical traditions, black
performers have always been clairsentient futurists, architects
of a sentimental avant-garde tradition. The ability to improvise,
to think on your feet, is rooted in intuition: gut feeling, muscle
memory, the hunch. To feel something is to know it. Black music is
paraperformative—"feeling beyond" emerges as the way to higher
knowledge. Like a precog, Michael Jackson can sense and therefore *know* a future cue he could not physically see on the screen
behind him. He bends and manipulates temporality and sculpts

the total environment into his vision. Vibrational connectedness to your surroundings—to feel and honor the auratic energy in a space, to be highly present in the moment—is the prerequisite to feeling the future.

Critics have long derided Jackson's heart-on-your-sleeve sentimentality and his schmaltzy pleas for charity on songs like "Heal the World" (1991). But they ignore the implicit relationship between Michael's penchant for feelingful connection and communion with others—his utopian belief in the social whole, multi-oneness, that everything is present in everything, which is how you'd have to reread his charity anthem "We Are the World" (1986)—and his clairsentient ability to feel into the future. Jackson's other-worldly perceptual skills, which always already inform and are informed by his immense gifts as a singer, dancer, producer, actor, and stage and studio auteur, explain why director Kenny Ortega confesses in a scene from the extras to the DVD release in 2010 of *This Is It* that despite the outsize techno-logical grandeur of the production, at the end of the day "technology didn't run the show . . . Michael ran the show."

Before it became a film, *This Is It* was a planned series of fifty sold-out concerts at London's mammoth O2 Arena, produced by promoter-behemoth AEG Live and codirected by Ortega, whose adventurous résumé includes choreographing spectacles like the Olympics and the Academy Awards and directing the Disney mega-smash *High School Musical* series. Jackson had hoped to make a career comeback with the concerts. He'd neither recorded new material nor toured in years and had most recently been living in a kind of self-imposed exile in the Middle East with his three young children after having been acquitted in 2005 in a controversial trial centered around child-molestation charges. He'd slogged through decades of disastrous press surrounding his bizarre personal life, various financial setbacks, and on-again/off-again prescription drug abuse. For some, Jackson's so-called wackiness had begun to overshadow, if not erode, his sizable musical legacy. The London concerts, set to launch on July 13, 2009, were to consist of newly staged excerpts from Jackson's greatest-hits catalogue. Fans would vote for the set list in advance. On the morning of June 25, the fifty-year-old singer, in the midst of final dress rehearsals at the Staples Center, unexpectedly passed away from cardiac arrest at his Holmby Hills mansion. Dr. Conrad Murray, hired by AEG Live as Jackson's personal physician, allegedly administered an illegal and lethal overdose of the anesthetic Propofol to the superstar, who reportedly suffered from chronic insomnia. Months later, Murray would be officially charged with homicide.

The shock of Jackson's death prompted an unprecedented global outpour-ing and a veritable tidal wave of media frenzy. In early August 2009, AEG

FIGURE 12.1. "I'll Feel That." Promotional materials for *This Is It* (2009) map Jackson's intuitive memory onto his silhouette, effectively materializing his embedded awareness of his vast influence and storehouse of memory.

Live cemented a deal with Jackson's estate and Columbia Pictures to help minimize the financial fallout from the canceled concerts. Luckily for all parties involved, AEG had hired commercial director Tim Patterson and collaborator Sandrine Orabona months prior to document behind-the-scenes rehearsal moments and conduct original interviews with the cast and crew. According to the opening credits, the footage was supposedly intended to be used for "Michael's personal library and as original film content for the show." Patterson and Orabona had shot close to 140 hours of raw footage at the time of Jackson's death (Jackson, "'Michael Jackson's This Is It'"). Columbia Pictures (a division of Sony) agreed to buy the content for $60 million in order to use it as source material for the proposed theatrical film. By mid-September, concert helmer Kenny Ortega, who had also signed on as film director, had whittled down the raw footage into a manageable 112-minute cinematic experience, working closely with Patterson, commercial director Brandon Key, and frequent Ortega collaborator editor Don Brochu (Fritz). The patchwork audio, culled from multiple sources, had to be carefully restored by a skilled team that included tour audio supervisor Michael Prince and veteran front-of-house mixer Bill Sheppell (Jackson, "'Michael Jackson's This Is It'").

Michael Jackson's This Is It was released on October 28 to mixed-to-positive critical reviews and robust box office. Domestic sales underperformed Columbia's expectations. Early hype estimated an unlikely $250 million gross in the first five days. According to website BoxOfficeMojo.com, it ended 2009 as the forty-sixth top grosser, with a domestic take of approximately $72 million. The film raked in $260.8 million worldwide (http://boxofficemojo.com). At the time of this writing, *This Is It* holds the record as the highest-grossing documentary or concert movie of all time (assuming it can be rightfully classified as a concert movie), beating out previous concert film record holder *Hannah Montana / Miley Cyrus: Best of Both Worlds Concert Tour* (2008) (Bowles). The *This Is It* DVD release in February 2010, accompanied by newly shot interviews and unreleased footage, also brought commercial success. After his modest film debut in *The Wiz* (1978), Jackson had several nonstarter attempts to establish himself as a box office presence. Ironically perhaps, the pop superstar became something of the film star in death he'd always aspired to be in life.

Because of Jackson's instantiation in sentimental pop spectacle and tabloid gossip, critics and audiences alike often misread him as a frivolous entertainer rather than a serious auteur. In fact, he spent his adult professional career as both the showman *and* the auteur; or, more to the point, he rendered the dichotomy between the two irrelevant and false.[1] Prior to its release, some feared that *This Is It* would be a hastily assembled hatchet job in which Michael, due to the shady circumstances of his passing, would be portrayed as a drug-addicted, aged pop star too feeble and disoriented to move or sing meaningfully.[2] To the surprise of many (perhaps everyone except his die-hard fans), Jackson emerges in the "finished" edit as a remarkably limber and *coherent* showman with clear and forthright artistic and directorial vision.

That's partly because the film completely decontextualizes the "found" rehearsal footage on which it relies—there's no superimposed voiceover, no times or dates given, no interviews with Jackson even. Instead, the film puts forward a normalizing and revisionist rendering of Jackson: the superstar free from, and absolved of, his infamously controversial baggage. That revisionist rendering is in some ways a refreshing revelation. By returning all the focus to Jackson's inestimable performance skills, *This Is It* indirectly confronts the misconceptions about Jackson's artistry.

But that limited focus also means transgressive aspects of Jackson's star discourse—including his radical androgyny, "queer" paternity, and long history of racial transmogrifications—are suppressed in the world of the film. Decontextualizing the footage reconsolidates the Jackson mythos by reauthenticating the superstar as "normal." The filmmakers in turn market the movie as a must-see revelation of the "authentic" Michael Jackson: a "cleaned-up" Jackson might more effectively ascend into franchise nirvana as a merchandising cash cow. As one critic notes: "One can't help but worry that, rather than a bittersweet farewell, the film will merely serve as the opening salvo to a flood of posthumous releases and merchandising that will make Tupac Shakur's estate seem a paragon of restraint" (Barker).

That said, *This Is It* surprises with effervescent moments of good feeling that exceed the film's conservative attempts to rescript and rebrand Jackson as "authentic" and therefore normal. Few film critics were willing to deal with the staggering phenomenological implications of the project in their reviews. Watching *This Is It*, you're constantly aware that Jackson is far more unreal than real. In fact, he's sort of *out of this world*. During feverish renditions of tunes like "I Just Can't Stop Loving You" and "Billie Jean," Jackson looks like a fierce ghost, a benevolent badass who knows how to expertly craft a spectacular concert even as he can't help getting caught up in the spirit of his own innervating songs. The film's most unforgettable scenes find Jackson shimmying and boogieing in exuberant joy, sharing and flaunting his formidable singing and dancing with his coworker cast and crew. Some will argue that soulfulness is a dying art at a time when postproduction technologies (like Auto-Tune) have regressed performance expectations. But *This Is It* affirms the recalcitrant power of spirit—of energetic good feeling between artists bent on getting together and sharing together even in the context of late capitalist techno-megaspectacle.

Spectacle and Non-spectacle

This Is It borrows its ambiguous title from the unrealized London concerts.[3] The title suggests an unguarded offering, an authentic revelation, laid out in front of you. "It" suggests *thereness* as a response to fans' anticipation, as if to say: "Here you go, this is what you've been waiting for." Kenny Ortega re-counts the title's existential origins: "[Michael would] call me up every once in a while or come to visit me on set and he'd say: 'There's nothing out there that has enough purpose behind it for me to want to do it.' Meaning in the live arena. Then, suddenly, I get this phone call and he said: 'This is it.' And during the conversation he said that, like, five times. And I kept laughing and saying: 'You should call the tour *This Is It* because you keep saying it.'"

Jackson long despised the grueling rigors of touring. Since the late 1980s, he publicized each of his solo tours as his last. These pronouncements were always, if nothing else, cunning marketing strategies to entice audiences to buy tickets in record numbers. The title *This Is It* sounded an alarm to fans that there would be no more concerts to follow, as if to say: "You're not get-ting any more." It also suggests finality, and, by extension, freedom. At the press conference on March 5, 2009, at the O2 Arena, Michael referred to the concerts as "the final curtain call." Those portentous words ultimately rang true, albeit not for intended reasons.

Associate producer and choreographer Travis Payne gives an explanation for the title's ambiguity: "As we went through the process, 'This Is It' began to take on many different meanings. 'This Is It,' a call to action for our planet. 'This Is It,' the last time you'll see me in this scenario. 'This Is It,' the show to come see this summer. Also, 'This Is It' for all of us (dancers) was what we had worked our entire lives to get to. It was a culmination of all those things" (quoted in Lee, "For Michael"). Some critics found the declamatory title ironic, given the fact that the concerts never actually took place. With no "there" there, no culmination or climax, the film comes off as immate-rial, neither here nor there. In an acidic *Sight and Sound* review, Mark Fisher asks: "Has there ever been a less apt title for a film than *This Is It*? 'This' is very much not 'it'—this film is the making-of feature for a spectacle that never happened." From this perspective the film is nothing more than an unspectacular rendition of a non-spectacle.

The song's convoluted birthing process parallels the haphazard genesis of the film itself. Both the song and the film force us to contemplate the com-plex relationships between the spectacular and the mundane, the finished and the unfinished. I recall first hearing the song "This Is It," released over the Internet in early October 2009. The elementary lite-inspirational chord progressions and uneventful romantic lyric of "This Is It" ("I never heard a single word about you / Falling in love wasn't my plan / I never thought that I would be your lover / Come on please, dear, understand") felt to me brazenly anticlimactic and *un*spectacular, especially given the song's status as the first posthumously released single from the Jackson catalogue.[4] "This

Is It" was just ho-hum, neither here nor there. In the *Los Angeles Times Pop & Hiss* music blog, Todd Martens goes a step further, calling it "a trifle, and while it's one that certainly won't embarrass Jackson's legacy or break the hearts of fans eager to hear Jackson's voice again, it does bring the fallen pop icon a little back down to earth" (quoted in Jones, "Michael Jackson's 'This Is It'"). The *New York Times*' Jon Caramanica had little positive to say about the tune, noting: "It never fully resolves, working at one melodic and emotional pitch and then fading out." He continues: "But as a musical artifact, it's better as suggestion than song: what I hear here is how Mr. Jackson might have sung these words in a proper studio setting, perhaps in a roomier arrangement with more motion in the rhythm" (Pareles; Caramanica).

It's worth noting that the song does perfectly complement the film for which it was produced. To be sure, the song is mundane and has no real musical resolution, but then neither does the film. (Neither song nor film *could* have a satisfying conclusion. Due to Jackson's death, finality was always already impossible, never an option.) "This Is It" may be little more than a dressed-up recorded demo, a suggestion of what might have been had Jackson lived to see its completion. Truth be told, the film itself is not much more than a slickly edited compilation of rehearsal scenes that only suggest what the O2 performances might have been had the circumstances been different. The song "This Is It" was born from an unreleased demo, a sketch, a trace, an unfinished work in progress. It was always already ephemera, never likely intended to be the main event, the finished centerpiece. Its history therefore parallels the history of the film itself. The unfinished rehearsal footage that constitutes the movie was itself ephemera, surplus documentary content, a side dish never intended to be served as the main course. In his *Hollywood Reporter* review, Kirk Honeycutt calls *This Is It* "the first concert rehearsal movie ever." While films like the Beatles' *Let It Be* (1970) have flirted with the rehearsal film format, *Michael Jackson's This Is It* can certainly claim the crown as the first mainstream motion picture in which the exclusive attraction is a rehearsal rather than a full-on concert. In the absence of any sort of culminating performance, the rehearsal process becomes reconstituted as the show itself, the finished product. The part stands in for the whole, as in synecdoche.

As a result, *This Is It* manages to invent a completely improvised film genre, perhaps one never to be repeated again. It's halfway between a flamboyantly spectacular blockbuster (in that it presents scenes from the groundbreaking live theatrical spectacular) and a gritty indie "found footage" reality documentary. In designing his concerts, Michael and the creative team were striving to create the greatest show that had ever been seen. Jackson had long described himself as a "fantasy fantatic," a devotee of the Cecil B. DeMille school of bigger is always better. He spent much of his post–*Off the Wall* career in monomaniacal pursuit of crossover music as blockbuster entertainment, and he was intent on forever smashing sales records—even his own. *This Is It* proved to be no different. During the film, Jackson talks about his desire to bring his audience "something they've never seen before." The concerts were to break ground on several levels. For one, they were to introduce the world's largest 3D HD screen, supposedly capable of providing an unprecedented immersive live experience. For the staging of "Smooth Criminal," Ortega would use green-screen technology to splice Jackson into existing footage from classic Hollywood films. At the end of the screened footage, Jackson was to be filmed jumping through a window; shards of glass would appear to fly into the audience. (Jackson apparently referred to the live 3D experience in upgraded terms as 4D as he intended to break the fourth wall by having the cast move from screen onto stage into the audience.) Throughout the show, expensive sci-fi-style costumes were decked out in unprecedented numbers of Swarovski crystals. Costume codesigner Valdy deployed never-seen-before Philips Lumalive LED textile technology to illuminate Jackson's fashionable garments on stage. And in another exciting green-screen dance sequence, eleven of Jackson's backup dancers would be filmed performing choreography; they'd be replicated through technology to turn into a virtual army behind him on the screen. Aerialists and massive pyrotechnics that circled the stage perimeter in record time were also part of the plans. And during pro-environment "Earth Song" a menacing on-screen tractor bulldozes a jungle before emerging "out of" the screen to physically appear on the stage. In the DVD extras released in 2010, AEG Live CEO Randy Phillips confirms that Jackson only agreed to perform fifty shows (only about twenty were originally scheduled) if the *Guinness Book of World Records* would be on hand to memorialize his achievements, as they had done more than twenty-five years earlier in the immediate aftermath of *Thriller*'s boundary-breaking success.

There is no term that accurately summarizes the Michael Jackson aesthetic, but I'll venture one: *techno-megaspectacle stadium pop soul*. If that descriptor sounds positively "off the wall," you bet it is. At the time of his death, Jackson was the sole creator and exclusive custodian of that outsize vision of campy excess: no other artist in recorded music had the clout and the cash—or the cojones, frankly—to deliver a smorgasbord of naked sentimentality, stripped-down soul, James Brown–influenced funk, Broadway musical theater, inspirational gospel, easy-listening schmaltz, B-movie horror, disco cheese, West Coast pop-locking, Jim Henson–inspired puppetry, and whatever else he deemed fit to throw in the pot, all somehow wrapped in the package of sci-fi techno-megaspectacle. Critics have always made an easy target of Jackson's affinity for colossal spectacle. Sean Burns of *Philadelphia Weekly* lambasted the film, calling it "a mechanical, over-choreographed spectacle, drowning out the music with precision timed pyrotechnics, on-stage bulldozers, 3-D movies, and even a computer-assisted, black and white machine gun battle against Humphrey Bogart." *Hollywood Reporter*'s Kirk Honeycutt anticipated the by-the-books critical ire: "Make no mistake this was a show intended for a stadium with a dazzling, mixed-media staging. One can even imagine a music critic in London fuming about overproduced numbers that don't trust Jackson's great song catalog to deliver the goods."

In spite of its radical innovations in technology, the O2 shows by and large consisted of a recycled set list, and many of the live stage renditions were relatively low-risk variations on visuals from Jackson's classic music videos. *Sight and Sound*'s Mark Fisher argues:

> If Michael Jackson had lived and managed to perform the 50 (50!) shows planned for the O2 arena in London, they would have been part of the dreary gloss of late capitalism, part of the sense of heavy inevitability and predictability that now dominates the entertainment industry: another super-slick spectacular centered on an ailing pop star long past his best. Yet Jackson's death lends the never-actually performed shows a kind of epic grandeur, now that all the kitschy contrivances, familiar gimmicks and well-rehearsed routines have become the stage set on which the King of Pop's final tragedy was to be played out.

Notably, *This Is It* arrived in theaters two months before the release of James Cameron's acclaimed sci-fic epic *Avatar*, a film that quickly broke box-office records to become the top-grossing movie of all time, grossing over $2 billion. Though they're wildly different types of movies, *This Is It* in some ways prefigured *Avatar*'s curious mix of immense spectacle, immersive 3D technology, maudlin sentiment, and back-to-nature themes. I often think of Jackson's proposed concerts as a sort of live UK theatrical analogue to Cameron's sci-fi techno-megaspectacular entertainment. While cultural theorists from Malcolm Gladwell to *Wired* magazine editor Chris Anderson spent years predicting that the widespread availability and accessibility of niche products on the Internet would wipe out hit-driven economics and render the blockbuster irrelevant, *Avatar*'s runaway success seemed to have driven a final nail in those theories' respective coffins.[5]

Jackson's posthumous sales records in some ways did for the music industry what *Avatar* did for the film business. According to *Billboard*, Jackson moved a whopping 8.7 million albums in the year following his death, a remarkable figure considering that by 2009, the industry had long since found itself in a disastrous economic slump, with digital music sales failing to compensate for the concomitant loss in physical (compact disc) sales (Mitchell, "Music Biz Insiders"). The year 2009 became a more modest sales sequel to 1983, that celebrated year in which Jackson's groundbreaking success with *Thriller* almost single-handedly brought the music industry out of economic doldrums and reenergized sales momentum. In March 2010, Sony entered into a groundbreaking $200–$250 million recording contract—the biggest in history to date—with the Jackson estate to issue ten albums' worth of classic album reissues and/or unreleased material (Mitchell, "Music Biz Insiders"). Jackson's resurrection—his "comeback" in death—served as reminder of the role that "heritage artists" (the industry buzz term for veterans) continue to play in the shaping of the music industry's financial future. The *Independent*'s Pierre Perrone comments on Jackson's post-death economic impact: "The music industry, and especially the four major labels, have made a significant shift, and one emblematised by Sony's deal with the Michael Jackson estate: from a model predicated on signing new talent, with all the attendant pitfalls and shortfalls that entails, to one where the real money is made maximising revenue from tried and tested acts by selling their work to an older demographic that buys CDs at the supermarket."

Despite its claims to spectacle status, much of *This Is It* also looks and feels like an unspectacular independent documentary: the original budget for Tim Patterson and Sandrine Orabona's video footage was a whopping $80,000. *This Is It* also shares its aesthetic with the "found footage" genre. On one hand, found footage films can be experimental films that deliberately decontextualize "found" source material (from existing feature films, stock footage, educational films, military films, or anything else), all in the effort to convey a particular meaning that might deviate from the messages originally intended by the source material.[6] On the other hand, found footage filmmaking can also refer to nonfiction hyper-verité documentaries created from home movies or distressed footage, like Jonathan Caouette's disturbing *Tarnation* (2003) or Harmony Korine's polarizing *Trash Humpers* (2009). And what's more, films like *The Last Broadcast* (1998), *The Blair Witch Project* (1999), *Quarantine* (2008), and *Cloverfield* (2008) help compromise a newly emergent subgenre of found footage horror. These faux documentaries center around a patched-together edit of raw, amateur footage shot by deceased victims of some variety of supernatural attack. The film itself *is* the "recovered footage," supposedly found by government officials or other law-enforcement officials posthumously. These nimble horror films are often low budget and produced using DIY filmmaking techniques; or, in the case of J. J. Abrams's *Cloverfield*, they're studio films painstakingly designed to look low-budget. The films further distinguish themselves by deploying innovative word-of-mouth and viral marketing campaigns; several films in the genre have emerged as true sleeper hits. *Cloverfield*, for its part, reimagines a Manhattan monster invasion as if the only footage left to document the disaster was culled from an amateur handheld video discovered in the aftermath of the tragedy. The entire film is deliberately shot in single point-of-view, herky-jerky digital video. To ramp up the thrills and chills, films like *The Blair Witch Project* and *Cloverfield* project the illusion that the bleak unfolding action—raw, grainy, and amateurish—is hyper-authentic. In so doing, found footage films serve to showcase what film critic Karina Longworth has called "the bizarre beauty of degraded low-grade video."

In his *Cloverfield* review, Bruce Newman claims: "The film often sacrifices niceties such as sound quality for authenticity. This may be the first big-budget Hollywood picture in history to go to so much trouble trying to look like crap." He describes the film as an exemplar of voyeuristic web 2.0 aesthetics: "If this isn't exactly the first YouTube movie, it may be the first to fully discard what snooty scholars refer to as 'film grammar' in favor of a new video-based visual language employed by that Web site, as well as Facebook and MySpace." Though most would not call it a horror film (we'll deal with that in the next section), *This Is It* is like a twisted real-life analogue of the narrative conceit that powers films like *Cloverfield*: it's an edit constructed from valuable "found" handheld video footage (though it was never "lost" per se), more or less rescued in the aftermath of a singular tragedy, in this case the death of Michael Jackson.[7] Many of the same authenticity issues engendered by found footage films also engulf *This Is It*. The fact that some of *This Is It*'s low-resolution digital rehearsal footage was clearly not necessarily intended for main-event public dissemination certainly enhances the film's claims to realness. In a thoughtful assessment of the found footage genre, writer Landon Palmer notes that "the requirement of compelling content is probably why this [found footage] approach has been so popular recently in the horror genre—there's something exciting about *the extraordinary posing as the mundane*" (Palmer, "Culture Warrior," my italics).

Many film critics similarly admired the behind-the-scenes mundanity of the rehearsal footage that constitutes *This Is It*, for the voyeuristic "video-based visual language" of the project offered a new lens through which to view Jackson's creative output. Writer Alan Light argues: "The release of a work in progress may have been the only possible way out of the 'bigger is better' addiction that derailed so much of his art" (Light). But more to the point,

This Is It is an unspectacular DIY "found footage" documentary of an unrealized techno-megaspectacle, the London 02 concerts. In that sense, *This Is It* accomplishes the unique and improbable task of bringing Michael Jackson, whose bigger-is-better aesthetic and outsize recording advances made him something of a financial liability to record companies after the mid-1990s, into the twenty-first-century reality TV–YouTube–Twitter era. No small feat.

Freaky Ghosts and Inauthenticity

There's no goin' back. See to them, you're just a freak . . . like me!
—**The Joker, played by Heath Ledger, in *The Dark Knight* (2008)**

Who's the freak now? Freaky Boy, Freak circus freak!
—**The Maestro, played by Michael Jackson, in *Michael Jackson's Ghosts* (1997)**

The theatrical rerelease in 2000 of William Friedkin's horror classic *The Exorcist* (1973) was reedited to include "lost" footage, retitled, and resold to the public as *The Exorcist: The Version You've Never Seen*. Using that marketing ploy as a cue, we might say that *This Is It* attempted to sell the public "The Michael Jackson You've Never Seen." Particularly given Jackson's lifelong interest in magic, masks, and other forms of subterfuge, one can imagine that the mainstream release of rehearsal footage was not likely his intention in wanting to give fans something they'd never seen before. Jackson spent much of his professional life attempting to carefully manipulate and control his public image. The ethical question arises: would the superstar have wanted unfinished rehearsal footage in which he was not necessarily at "his best" to be publicly released? Jackson's family initially protested the release of *This Is It*. And a group of ardent fans launched a website, This Is Not It (www.this-is-not-it.com), to raise public awareness: they believed that AEG Live was using the film to conceal the company's exploitative mistreatment of an allegedly ailing Jackson.

Alan Light confronts these thorny questions of exploitation: "Though often raised in voices of hysteria, these are actually all fair questions, as they are with all outtakes, bootlegs, or posthumously released work by any artist" (Light). However, I'm much more interested in the way the producers of *This Is It* attempt to market the film as a singularly authentic revelation of the "true" Michael Jackson. "I think what we want out of this film," said producer Paul Gongaware in scenes from the film's DVD extras, "is for people to see the real Michael Jackson." Randy Phillips of AEG Live confirms Gongaware's authenticity claims, boasting that the film represents "unrestricted access to an unguarded genius" (quoted in Waddell). He continues: "There's nothing in it other than the credits that wasn't shot or recorded from March 5, when we did the press conference in London, to June 25, when he died. It's completely authentic. Nothing has been doctored" (quoted in Waddell). *This Is It* purports to be an unmediated voyeuristic experience. In other words, the intrinsic authenticity of the found footage—the idea that we feel that we're being allowed to see something we may not have been intended to see—allows the filmmakers to present its unique version of "Michael Jackson Stripped," the celebrity finally exposed for the true artistic genius that we always knew him to be.

The film would like us to have faith in its undoctored and unpretentious presentation of Michael Jackson—he's nothing other than what he is. But the finished product is of course highly mediated and, as such, it may be more valuably inauthentic than authentic. It's also been suggested that we might not have always been seeing the "real" Michael Jackson in the final edit. Whether the footage is real or false—and many if not most concert films augment original audio source material with outsourced sounds to produce the most effective final edit possible—we may never know fully. But the notion that the film could offer us an authentic and knowable and even singular Michael Jackson is a chimera. Michael Jackson's public image is an always already mediated construction. There is no authentically knowable Michael Jackson behind the mask, beyond the multiple discourses that constituted his star text. There are, and have always been, many Michaels. It all depends on how you look. *This Is It* has precious little interest in retelling the Michael Jackson story. The film offers no voice-over; no personal information about Michael Jackson; no mention of his legal or financial problems, his business dealings, or acumen; no mention of his children; and no interviews with Michael. What you see is all you get. For a celebrity who spent most of his professional career overdetermined by discourse, Jackson is completely *underdetermined* in Ortega's directorial vision. He exists in a vacuum.

"Underdetermining" Michael Jackson has its uses. As reviewer Josef Woodard notes: "What makes *This Is It* such a remarkable achievement, and a surprise to skeptics among us, is that it's an 'inside' job without that insider aftertaste—a raw, real document of this amazing performer at work. No apologia, the film contains none of the incessant nattering, irrelevant punditry, or tabloid spittle following (and preceding) his death" (Woodward). Because we weren't often invited to see Jackson in the process of making his spectacular music, the film emerges as a cinematic valentine to the artistic process. While the racist and primitivist imaginary assumes that performers of color are intrinsically more energetic and spontaneous than their white counterparts—which is another way of saying performers of color don't have to work hard to get good results—watching Jackson painstakingly shape his concert in collaboration with fellow musicians and a superbly talented band and crew is a telling reminder of the incredible labor that undergirds the best of black performance. We're confronted with the compelling results of Jackson's singular lifetime of skillful practice, from his grueling prepubescent pre-Motown work schedule in Indiana to his brilliant studio and soundstage work to his marathon world tours as an adult solo artist. The film implicitly confirms that Michael Jackson knows how to fiercely "work it" as a performer because he spent his life working hard at it. As a result, the strict focus on performances helps challenge the widespread benign critical indifference to Michael Jackson as musician and artist. *This Is It* serves, in some ways, as a critical intervention, reconfirming Jackson's artistry and giving us a valuable window into the ways that Jackson's profound sense of discipline manifests in his decisive, auteurist vision.

Sensual Presence

In *This Is It*, we are given a posthumous vision of Michael Jackson at the most "alive" and spirited we've seen him in years. Still, throughout the film, Jackson and the cast are mostly marking and blocking the concert, not necessarily performing "all out." Jackson apologetically pleads with his cast and crew that he is actively saving his voice, strength, and energy, sketching just enough of an outline of his performances so that his collaborators can develop the show appropriately but no more. Jackson drops and fudges entire lines, and sings off-pitch at others before self-correcting. He continually stops himself from getting too invigorated and caught up in the spirit of his own music, drawing a clear demarcation between the rehearsal and the full-out energy required for a successful arena show.

Toward the middle of the movie, Jackson closes a Jackson Five tribute medley with a lilting rendition of chestnut "I'll Be There" (1970). The band drops out as the song comes to a close. In the silent pause, Jackson talks through a spoken tribute that he'll give to his brothers and parents, and then he interjects the apology "trying to conserve my throat please so understand" before launching into a tender series of mellifluous vocal riffs on the phrase "I will be." Film critic Kirk Honeycutt notes in his review: "To be clear: No one should expect a concert film. Jackson clearly is conserving his energy, holding back on dance moves and vocal intensity. He is searching for his concert, the way a sculptor chisels away at marble to discover a statue" (Honeycutt). The tension between control and release in Jackson's artistic process seems to parallel the existential conflict that informed Jackson's personal life, as he often found himself caught between family obligation to ascetic Jehovah's Witness evangelism and the vision of hedonistic excess he created for himself at his infamous Neverland Ranch.

In another scene, at the close of the ballad "I Just Can't Stop Loving You," Jackson and duet partner Judith Hill riff on the oh-so-appropriate lyric "I just can't stop" to the delighted applause of the backup dancers congregated in the orchestra pit; they've basically become the default private audience during the rehearsal process. Ortega wisely intercuts the scenes of Jackson and Hill doing vocal improvisations with these scenes of the dancers watching from below, fawning in exultation and glee. As the riffing ceases and the song resolves, Jackson says to his adoring crowd: "Now don't make me sing out when I shouldn't sing." Playfully, the band launches into a gospel chord progression, encouraging and egging on the singer to lose himself in the moment. "You better sing!" and "You can allow yourself that one time," they tell the superstar. With a wink in his voice, Jackson politely retorts: "I'm warming up to the moment" and "I really shouldn't."

Jackson's ever-so-feigned attempt to contain the auratic energy that's bubbled over in the venue is instructive. Noticeably, Jackson and musical director Michael Bearden have arranged some of the songs in such a way that they've left deliberate pockets of space, often extending the ending of songs for maximum dramatic effect. In so doing, Jackson leaves room for an improvisational moment to occur, for the spirit to come down. Whenever a musician lands on a cue too early, we see Jackson firmly scold him to let the moment "simmer." "You're not letting it simmer," he chides. Jackson's use of a heat metaphor is hardly accidental. He amplifies the electricity of a dramatic moment by leaving pregnant silent pauses in the action—scheduled stops and starts—where the all-important energetic transfer between performer and audience can occur.

I've previously noted how *This Is It* concerts were seen by some as "low-risk" in terms of the heavy reliance on recycled choreography and technological spectacle to wow the audience. But the genuine risk of the shows is much more profound, tied to the suspense created by Jackson in these cultivated improvisational moments where silence and space is left for magic to happen—the proposition of danger without warning. These innervating moments humanize the techno-megaspectacle and reformat the canned nature of the film medium into a decidedly spirited, human affair. As director and designer Julie Taymor once noted: "Live performance will always surpass media like the Internet. Live theater, when things spontaneously happen, makes audiences feel like something special happened for them" (quoted in Rockwell, 105). *This Is It* rides on these moments of improvisational danger without warning, and in so doing, it surpasses many other "celebrated" concert films, including the Rolling Stones' corporate, sterile *Shine a Light* (2007), directed by Martin Scorsese.

Some film critics attacked Jackson's "imprecise" directorial language in the film. In one scene, Jackson instructs the musicians to let a moment "bathe in the moonlight," another metaphor he uses to milk a dramatic moment. Toward the end of the movie, Jackson leads the cast and crew onstage in a ritual hand-locked prayer. His speech, while positive and encouraging, quickly becomes rambling and cliché-ridden. And during a rendition of the Jackson Five's "I Want You Back," the loud volume levels in Jackson's in-ear monitor during the performance force him to stop the rehearsal temporarily. "I'm adjusting to the situation," he informs Ortega. Critics like *Philadelphia Weekly*'s Sean Burns managed to center on this scene, somehow, as proof of Jackson's prima donna insecurity as well as his inarticulateness: "The few times Jackson is actually heard speaking in the movie, he comes off like someone you'd hide from on the subway, unable to articulate a simple request to lower the volume on his headphones without shrieking 'There's a fist in my ear!' Regular communication with fellow human beings was clearly impossible for him by this point" (Burns).

Highly evolved collaborative listening and feedback—communion, if you will—runs throughout the film. Regular, heightened communication with other human beings is not only possible for Jackson—it emerges as the centerpiece of the entire film. The carefully cast, cosmopolitan backup dancers, whom Ortega calls "extensions of Michael Jackson," serve as the immediate audience in the film. They are both participants in the extravaganza and awestruck fans, stunned and honored to be working with one of their idols. (In fact, Payne notes that Michael Jackson cast the dancers based on energy. "Michael's very much about feeling," he says in the film extras. "Michael has to feel that energy, that confidence" (quoted in Lee, "For Michael"). Through slick editing, Oretga cuts away from the stage action to show us the grainy darkened footage of the exuberant dancers in the orchestra pit. The camera positions you to see what Jackson would see from the stage: the dancers throw their arms up in the air, applauding, sending out positive energy back to the stage. We see a visual representation of the electrical current passed between performer and audience, flesh and blood corroborating flesh and blood. "But once he starts dancing with hoofers young enough to be his children, Jackson, who died at age 50, radiates pure energy. It's always a pleasure to watch him move. Just as pleasurable is to see him beam that vitality to dancers and musicians, and see them beam it back" (Rickey).

In the past, I have criticized Jackson for staging class- and status-conscious music videos, like "Scream" (1995), that enforce a critical physical distance between the superstar as messiah figure and the masses (King). *This Is It* challenges those class and status implications through the presentation of black performance as labor rooted in shared collective good feeling. For the dancers, the work is labor that is not labor. They appear happy to share the stage with a peerless artist who served as the primary inspiration for the professional work that they do. Jackson's surplus performances—those scenes where he can't help but get carried away by his own grooves—are also about summoning an energy that is rooted in "giving back," even if only for a conservatively bounded moment, to his cast/fans. During the hard rock performance of "Black or White," Jackson directs Australian guitar phenom Orianthi Panagaris in a fervent guitar solo, instructing her to hold out a screaming guitar note much longer than she intuitively feels comfortable in the moment. Again, Jackson is milking the moment for dramatic impact. (He also would have likely taken a costume change during her extended guitar solo.) "It's time for you to shine," he announces, using his falsetto to demonstrate how he wants her to sculpt the temporality of her guitar solo. It's a telling moment that demonstrates Jackson's generosity of spirit: he self-effacingly wants her to have her moment.

These moments of shared surplus feeling between Jackson and his cast and crew inundate the entire film with radiant good feeling. As Roger Ebert notes in his film review: "These are working people who have seen it all. They love him. They're not pretending. They love him for his music and perhaps even more for his attitude. Big stars in rehearsal are not infrequently pains. Michael plunges in *with the spirit of a coworker*, prepared to do the job and go the distance" (Ebert, my italics). The film powerfully documents a cross-class artist-to-artist affinity that is rarely seen in the feature-film format, much less in everyday life. Through found rehearsal footage, we witness the love and the trust that musicians and dancers have for each other while collectively working toward a spectacular show that is a sum much better than its moving parts.

The top of the film presents a series of interviews of backup dancers testifying directly to the camera. The footage was clearly shot prior to Jackson's death, as the dancers use the camera as a sort of confessional, speaking directly to Michael, verbalizing their feelings about having been cast in the 02 shows. The last teary-eyed male dancer/interviewee, Misha Gabriel Hamilton, gives the most affecting speech: "I've been searching for something to shake me up a little bit and give me, uh, a kind of meaning to believe in something and this is it." And here we have the film's title, *This Is It*, redefined as faith itself, unshakable belief, the evidence of things not seen. This is indeed "it": the performance, the labor, the work, the camaraderie, the collectivity, the sharing, the collaboration, the energy, the electricity.

The Bluest Magic

What Black American culture—musical and otherwise—lacks for now isn't talent or ambition, but the unmistakable presence of some kind of spiritual genius: the sense that something other than or even more than human is speaking through whatever fragile mortal vessel is burdened with repping for the divine, the magical, the supernatural, the ancestral.

—Greg Tate, in "The Man in Our Mirror," *Village Voice* obit of Michael Jackson (2009)

If the film does have a climax, it's Jackson's otherworldly rendition of his synth-pop masterpiece "Billie Jean" (1983). Lighting designer Patrick Woodroffe bathes the stage in blue specials, creating a melancholic vibe. Had the concerts occurred, Jackson would have been dressed in magical remote-control-illuminated tuxedo pants, jacket, ankle socks, and glove. In the rehearsals, however, Jackson appears in a more modest blue-and-silver dinner jacket. The number itself is minimalist in its execution, a winnowing down of the show's proportions and scale. We're treated to Jackson, standing solitaire, on the naked stage. Ortega describes the bare-bones staging in the DVD extras as "a place for [Jackson] to invent." He notes that there is "stuff that should remain sacred," meaning he's left space in this number for Jackson to improvise and to call down spirit through his agile singing and dancing. The arrangement of the live rendition also leaves space for heightened drama and energetic communion. After a full pass of the song, all the instrumentalists gradually fall out and we're left with drummer Jonathan "Sugarfoot" Moffett powerfully beating out the song's shuffle rhythm in real time.

Grinding and isolating his hips, crotch, shoulders, torso, legs, and neck in impeccable rhythm, Jackson improvises to the muscular groove and gets carried away, set adrift on blissful funk. He flips the bottom of his jacket up in the air and kick pushes his leg. He twitches and glides, shuffling his feet, stopping time through rhythm and sculpting the energetics in the concert venue. His movement is a magical mix of pop-locking, mime, Broadway jazz, James Brown and Jackie Wilson funk, and much more. Jackson always claimed that he spent every Sunday, even into his adult career, locked in his bedroom, rehearsing his trademark dancing in worship of a higher spiritual energy. "Sundays were sacred for two other reasons as I was growing up," he once confessed. "They were both the day that I attended church and the day that I spent rehearsing my hardest. This may seem against the idea of 'rest on the Sabbath,' but it was the most sacred way I could spend my time: developing the talents that God gave me. The best way I can imagine to show my thanks is to make the very most of the gift that God gave me" ("My Childhood, My Sabbath"). In *This Is It*, "Billie Jean" emerges as a primal scene—Michael Jackson improvising movement to a single percussive groove, with no accoutrements—and it voyeuristically suggests what it must have been like to watch the singer practice those awesome dance moves in his room.

The compelling scene also documents the powerful energetic connection between Jackson and his drummer. Interviewed in DVD extras, Moffett describes the joyous intimacy that constituted his "duet" with Michael. It was "just him and me," he reminisces. "And I played my heart and my soul out to try to evoke an extreme [*sic*] great performance out of him and I would connect with him and I would watch him so closely. He was my dance partner and I will always treasure that. And, um, that's magic and life." Jackson's dancers provide another level of intimacy during the number: they watch from the orchestra pit, once again, in total adulation, enraptured in the moment. Ortega notes in the DVD extras: "You couldn't drag those kids away from being in front of the stage watching Michael. They were there every second they could be—glued."

For James Baldwin sensuality was inseparable from presence. "To be sensual I think, is to respect and rejoice in the force of life, of life itself, and to be *present* in all that one does, from the effort of loving to the breaking of bread" (*Fire Next Time*, 43). The quality of communion (or soulful getting-togetherness) that emerges most fully in sensual, everyday acts of intimacy, like breaking bread and loving, is also for Baldwin an augmented temporality, a being in and on and past linear time—being "in the moment" as a sensual engagement with the Other. This is yet another way in which Jackson is a brilliant communicator with fellow human beings—he's co-*here*-nt, he's highly in the moment with others. *This Is It* is ultimately a sensual film, one that rejoices and honors the vital life force even as it provides meta-commentary on the phenomenological "problems" of presence and finality. For all the modern talk of 3D and 4D technology as immersion and intimacy, Jackson cultivates intimacy with his body and soul. Sharing good feeling produces a proximity and depth and scale of immersion that no 3D glasses could ever provide.

As Jackson's breathless "Billie Jean" improvisation ends, to spontaneous applause from his private audience, Jackson humbly suggests: "At least we get a feel of it." "God bless you," he continues, responding to the augmenting enthusiasm for his performance. Musical director Michael Bearden, off-camera, mutters into his microphone: "I'm a fan." Ortega walks onstage to congratulate Jackson and announces "Church! . . . The church of rock 'n' roll!" It's a slightly odd observation, to be sure, but one that tacitly acknowledges the palpable spirit that has come in the room, summoned by the emotional power of popular music.

Ortega suggests that Michael should drink some water; he's expended a lot of energy. Jackson agrees, we assume, because he melodically sings the line "water." Someone, somewhere, should bring him some, it seems.

The image begins to fade, as all things do, and Jackson disappears, somewhere into the blue magical ether.

Notes

This chapter was originally published as "Don't Stop 'til You Get Enough: Presence, Spectacle, and Good Feeling in *Michael Jackson's This Is It*," in *Taking It to the Bridge: Music as Performance*, edited by Nicholas Cook and Richard Pettengill (Ann Arbor: University of Michigan Press, 2013). © University of Michigan Press, 2013. Reprinted with permission of the publisher.

1. Other critics long ago condemned Jackson outside of the courtroom. For those critics, Jackson's alleged improprieties with young boys (never legally proven) render any discussion of his artistry irrelevant.

2. Also see, for instance, Dana Stevens: "Given that the footage in question wasn't intended for a film but for Jackson's own archive, it seemed inevitable that the result would be an exploitative, thrown-together mishmash, a random bunch of murky home-video snippets padded out with sentimental talking-head interviews and montages of too-often-seen bits of old MTV videos and tabloid news headlines."

3. The complete film title is *Michael Jackson's This Is It*. Throughout the essay I simply refer to the title as *This Is It*, since this is how the film is often referred to even by its own creative team, and it's much simpler.

4. During the verse, Jackson sings the lyric "I'm the light of the world," a self-aggrandizing line that rubbed some critics the wrong way.

5. See "A World of Hits" in the *Economist* as a response to Gladwell and Anderson.

6. See "A Universal Movie: Found Footage Films," in Atkinson (103–15).

7. A *Los Angeles Times* article discusses videographer Tim Patterson's odyssey to emerge as the editor of the feature film: "Every night after work, he transferred hours of video shot by himself and collaborator Sandrine Orabona to two hard drives in his home office. The afternoon that Jackson died, Paul Gongaware, a producer of the concert and movie, called him with an urgent request: The footage, which had suddenly become uniquely valuable, had to be delivered to AEG's downtown offices immediately" (Fritz).

AFRO-SONIC FEMINIST PRAXIS

Nina Simone and Adrienne Kennedy in High Fidelity

Little Women

Let's take it back to 1974, when a tiny cinematic maelstrom ensued underneath the cultural radar, perhaps obscured by the blaxploitation noise still lingering in the streets. That year, while few were looking and surely even fewer were listening, comedian Jackie "Moms" Mabley brought her trademark bass-driven, politically trenchant civil rights comedy to the screen in what would sadly turn out to be her first and last Hollywood starring vehicle, *Amazing Grace*, released one year before her death at the age of eighty-one.

Witness the "small acts" of tactical resistance on display in an astonishing scene of the film—astonishing for multiple reasons: first because the scene features Mabley engaging in a nimble game of vaudevillian "Who's on First" antics with fellow veteran Hollywood actress Butterfly McQueen, best known of course for having played the role of Prissy in *Gone with the Wind*. Here Mabley, as the title character Grace, a cinematic extension of her politically progressive stand-up persona, calls up McQueen's character Clarisse, searching for a way to contact a third woman who might assist Grace with her plans to infiltrate the office of Baltimore's racially repressive mayor thus paving the way for a black candidate to triumph in the upcoming election.

Never before and never since in modern cinema—not even in Jennifer Hudson's celebrated *Dreamgirls* tour de force—has a scene so richly showcased the resonating complexities of black female vocality in social space.

McQueen and Mabley's lively two-minute conversation, in fact, takes voice and black female identification(s) as its subject in question and pushes the formalistic limits of communicative convention by interfacing the high and low registers of Grace's and Clarisse's voices, and by stressing the polyrhythmic, polyvocal dimensions of black female phonic subjectivity. I would suggest, in fact, that we think of these characters as "little women"—*not* as an homage to Louisa May Alcott, but as allusively linked to the woman that black studies critic Nicholas Boggs argues is at the center of Ralph Ellison's classic essay "Little Man at Chehaw Station."

In that landmark work of cultural criticism and critical memoir, Ellison reflects on the sage advice that he receives from his Tuskegee music teacher, cosmopolitan classical pianist Hazel Harrison. In the essay, it is Harrison who imparts the famous, transformative riddle to her young charge to "always play your best, even if it's only in the waiting room at Chehaw Station because in this country there'll always be the little man behind the stove." Her advice sets young Ellison on a journey to figure out, among other things, the meaning of performative virtuosity as well as the recognition of cultural hybridity in America.

Much black studies scholarly attention has focused on the figure of the little man as a symbol of the listener who sits (quite literally) at "the crossroads," at Chehaw Station, and who thus serves as a reminder of the importance of performing bilingually—playing, writing, singing in both classical and vernacular idioms (because you never know who might be listening). But as Boggs contends, this focus on the "little man" has come at the expense of considering Harrison's instructive role in guiding Ellison toward an understanding of the meaning of cultural polyvalence in the first place. As he argues, few have taken note of Harrison's sphinxlike presence as the core interventionist figure who, through musical proverb, teaches her student a lesson not only about heterogeneous black subjectivity in American culture but about the critical meaning of black womanhood itself. Harrison is, Boggs suggests, the "little woman" who guides Ellison toward embracing the exigencies of sonic expression as the complex articulation of self.

Let us think then of *our* women in *Amazing Grace*, Mabley and McQueen, as capable of teaching us all a lesson about the (sonic) meaning of black womanhood as well as the way the sonic means for black women. Think, for instance, of how voice is everything in this witty repartee which finds an acerbic Grace vowing to "get a pair of pliers and fix this woman's *voice*" as she rings up Clarisse, all aflutter, on the other end of the line. The two let loose with a furious exchange of punning misidentifications ("This is Grace." "Grace who? . . . It could have been the kind of grace someone says before eating") and (pseudo) homonymic miscommunications ("I want to know who do day work for the mayor?" "Mare? Why a mare is a lady horse!"), clear evidence of each actress's veteran comic skills culled from the TOBA (Theatre Owners Booking Association) black vaudeville circuit.

Situated in the midst of a larger film narrative about black enfranchisement, political mobilization, racial authenticity politics, and black female social, political, and domestic audibility, Grace mediates these concerns by going in search of an ally whom she can only identify by skills manifest in her voice and someone whom she can only seek out by going toe to toe with her linguistic, phonic, and social foil. But aside from reveling in the sheer deliciousness of seeing these two veteran performers more vibrant than ever and on screen together in their golden years, I want to think of this scene as establishing three critical paradigms in my discussion of disruptive black female vocalities, and I want to ultimately suggest that we consider the sound methods that these paradigms offer for reading the cacophonous drama of Adrienne Kennedy and the equally excoriating, blacker-than-blue notes of Nina Simone in a charged, formalistic dialectic with one another.

First, with regard to our aforementioned little women, we might listen to the ways that Clarisse's extreme harmonics tangle with Grace's "fundamental black female vocal bass," in turn producing something akin to musicologist Olly Wilson's "heterogeneous sound ideal," here reflected (and refracted) in black female musical speech. With her class aspirational politics rooted firmly in the tongue, speaking the "King's English," Clarisse declares: "Nadine does the day work for the mayor." To which Grace inquires, "The same one that sings the high part in 'Just a Closer Walk'?" "Oh no," says Clarisse. "This is the Nadine that sings the alto in 'Come Ye, Disconsolate.' But she used to sing second solo in 'Yield Not to Distemper.' And before that she sang the lead on 'Abide with Me.' And before that she sang the higher part on 'Just a Closer Walk with Thee.'"

Nadine, the absent polyvocal phenom, here generates an elaborate process of black female (mis)recognition between Clarisse and Grace that can seemingly only be resolved by Clarisse's ventriloquization of her (singing) parts. By referencing Nadine's multiple range of roles in the choir (second solo, lead, the higher part), she provides Grace, albeit circuitously, with the information she needs to carry out her political subterfuge within the plot. Here and elsewhere, the film drives home the centrality of multiple and varied black female voicings in the pursuit of political mobilization.

Just as important, Clarisse's rehearsal of Nadine's range of vocalities emerges here in concert with Grace's signature, low-end wisecracks, and it is the comingling of their voices that, I want to suggest, can be read as a provocative musical metaphor. Think, for instance, of Olly Wilson's influential definition of "the heterogeneous sound ideal in African-American music," the "tendency to create a high density of musical events within a relatively short musical time frame—*a tendency to fill up all the musical space*" (Wilson, 328).

Through "a kaleidoscopic range of dramatically contrasting qualities of sound," through a "fundamental bias for contrast of color" and a "usage of a diversity of vocal nuances," black music, Wilson contends, often privileges "a musical texture in which individual voices are discerned within a mass of sound," varying "in tempo, melodic contour, and vocal nuances that range from speech to song" (Wilson, 329, 334). Hear, then, how Mabley and McQueen's dutiful sparring resonates with the "collective improvisations" of black musical ensembles, evoking in their chatter a rumbling difference within that fills up space and traverses the limits of Clarisse's hot pink phone line.

Second, we might think of this conversation, too, as evincing some of the key aesthetics of black women's discursive practices that Mae Gwendolyn Henderson outlines in her landmark Bakhtinian study of black feminist glossolalia and heteroglossia, "Speaking in Tongues." The "simultaneity of discourse" evoked in this scene is itself suggestive of the formalistic and ideological conventions that, as Henderson famously argues, are fundamentally constitutive elements of black women's writing, "its interlocutory, or dialogic character reflecting . . . the plural aspects of self that constitute the matrix of black female subjectivity." "Black women writers," she continues, "are 'privileged' by a social positionality that enables them to speak in dialogically racial and gendered voices to the other(s) both within and without" (Henderson, 118, 119). Their discursive practices are constitutive of both a Bakhtinian model of "adversarial . . . verbal communication" and "Gadamerian" notions of language as "consensus" and "communality." These (dis)identifications, Henderson suggests, compete with and complement each other in the production of black women's narrativity.

Mabley and McQueen here literally manifest the polyphonic dimensions of Henderson's theories, but just as well, their exchange—both contesting and collaborative—performs the soundtrack of what I'd like for us to think of as a kind of Afro-sonic feminist noise, a kind of sound composed of heteroglossic gestures that articulate "the ability to speak in diverse [musical] languages" here, as well as glossolaliac desire to forge, maintain, and take pleasure in a black women's musical subculture that is "outside the realm of public discourse and foreign to the known tongues of humankind" (Henderson, 122). Together and in concert with one another, the Grace and Clarisse characters articulate the heterogeneity of black female expressive subjectivity that exists on another frequency from the hegemonic order.

But I am most interested in how these differing voices signal and riff upon the presence of blackness as excess and excessive presence in the musical and discursive operations of black female cultural producers. Mabley and McQueen's exchange in fact depends on a range of asymmetrical black female vocalities that mix speech and song and that, to be sure, generate what Fred Moten might call a kind of "chromatic saturation" emanating from the unpredictable excesses of the black female voice in play (Moten, "Chromatic Saturation").

In an extraordinary forthcoming essay, Moten's brilliant, fugitive, critical reimagining of this musicological concept moves from Susan McClary's notions of the profligate "feminine ending" in classical music through Charles Rosen's reading of Schoenberg as producing compositions that "fil[l] out . . . the chromatic scale" to a point approaching "total saturation" (Rosen, 58). For Moten, the "metaphor of chromatic 'space' . . . denote[s] the theoretical coexistence of all possible notes that can be played." In this "regime of uncut musical differences . . . in which regulation and resolution are rendered spectral im/possibilities," in which "all the notes" are present, he declares, "let's call this other version of chromatic saturation black/ness so that we might consider more fully what it is for a normative musical matrix to be overrun by metrical promiscuity, by profligate madrigal, by accidental, unwritten, black notes." In "music," he continues, "blackness indicates chromaticity as a potentially unregulated or profligate internal difference, an impurity derived from the mixture of modes (major/minor) or of scales (diatonic/chromatic); it can be situated between an unwritten but aurally performed abundance or improvisational excess derived from textual implication or a kind of visual overload of black marks on the page" (Moten, "Chromatic Saturation," 9, 10, 12).

Moten's cogent claims provide us with a third way, then, to think about this key scene and its relation to black women's re-sounding subterfuge. His points help us to conceptualize and hear the ways that black female performers have utilized "the metaphor of chromatic space" as a site for saturation and excess, as a place to play many notes or, perhaps just as accurately, many roles all at once, to "overrun a normative musical" or narrative "matrix" with "metrical promiscuity" that confounds audiences and readers alike. Where his work takes us is to the situation and the place where the voices of women like McQueen and Mabley, as well as Nina Simone (who, like Mabley, exploited the intensities of her lower register) and playwright Adrienne Kennedy, thrive, to "a registral space for a [black female artist] that is not commonly visited," to borrow music theorist Ellie Hisama's words (Hisama, 115).

Below, what I intend to do is to think through the theoretical and methodological "loop" of Wilson, Henderson, and Moten as a means to consider how black women's sonic performances and phonic expression are dialectically and dialogically engaged with black women's discursive and dramaturgical acts.

My aim is to use Nina Simone's sonic vocabulary as a way to stretch our readings of the work of her avant-garde contemporary Adrienne Kennedy. Kennedy's discursive and theatrical gestures, I argue, create a noisy chatter with Simone's mid-1960s work, not unlike that of Grace and Clarisse's boisterous conversation. Think of these two artists, then, in hermeneutic stereo with one another, generating sonic interpretative paradigms that mark a rupture in cultural expectations of putatively normative black female social audibility.

The Black Keys: Figurative Atonality and the Funnyhouse of Nina

The end is the beginning is the end on Nina Simone's classic "Four Women" (1965), a house-on-fire torch song battle cry for the ages. If I could, I'd hold that oddly abrasive, inscrutably piercing very last note of the song—the one that finds Simone delivering an at-once crude and yet oh-so-shrewd meta-joke that rings in your ears—I'd hold that note forever, until the end of the world, until time turned back on itself, until history bled to death. One could say that this is what Simone is aiming for in stanza four as she closes her tale of black female exploitation and abjection handed down like an atavistic slur from one generation to the next.

Murder, she wrote—or rather, scores here for her listeners, tightening, and then stretching and pulling apart the nickname that stereotypically binds black women to a legacy of the street, a legacy of being "outdoors" as Toni Morrison might call it, disinherited from patrilineal wealth and plenitude and reduced to a saccharine sweet pet name.

As is the case in so much of her work, Simone's trademark musicality defamiliarizes sociocultural expectations of where and how black women should *sound* in song. Having recorded her first album, *Little Girl Blue* (1957), against the backdrop of a popular music landscape awash with black female artists' distinct vocal innovations in blues (think of Bessie Smith's power), jazz (think of Billie Holiday's cool, intelligent phrasings), and gospel (think of Rosetta Tharpe's "hot," sacredly profane melismas), Nina Simone produced a cluster of mid-1960s songs (from "Mississippi Goddam" to "Four Women") that broke open a new sonic syntax of black womanhood in popular music culture that ran boisterously alongside the political bebop of Abbey Lincoln.

Like those of Lincoln, Simone's asymmetrical gestures—vocal, generic, compositional—repeatedly thwarted listeners from losing themselves in what Farah Griffin has termed "the romance of the black female singing voice" (Griffin, 107). These kinds of (dissonant) aesthetics are especially apparent in "Four Women," one of the—if not the most—trenchant and well-known black feminist musical interrogations of African American women's material histories of subjugation and corporeal exploitation ever recorded.

The work of several key scholars animates my thinking about "Four Women" in crucial ways. Following Griffin's pathbreaking work on black women's vocalities, I am interested in the way the black female singing voice "tells tales; the form in which it relays the message. The tone of the voice, its inflections, its register, the cadence, the pauses and silences" (Griffin, 107). I'm interested in paying attention to the "details" of Simone's sound here, the ways that the closing note on "Four Women" goes "beyond words when [words] are no longer capable of rendering meaning" (Griffin, 108). Like Susan McClary, I want to treat Simone's "entire complex [of form] as content—[as] social, historically contingent form" (McClary, 7). And more to the point still, I want, like Moten, to pay attention to "radical forms of aurality that upset normative definitions of meaningful speech and conventional musical [structures]" (Moten, "Chromatic Saturation").

As many a black feminist scholar has noted, Simone takes us on a journey through the transhistorical reification of black womanhood in "Four Women." Lyrically, she profiles a series of paradigmatic figures in this, her colored museum, in turn creating a musical litany that is mirrored by the ostinato pattern of the song, a repeated set of notes played by the piano and bass that reinforces the cyclical historical repetition of this "accretion of names" and "confounded identities" like the ones that Hortense Spillers would replay in the famous opening of her essay "Mama's Baby, Papa's Maybe." Spillers, of course, had Simone's track in mind when she opened her extended rumination on the "New World" diasporic plight of the captive body in forced migration by alluding to the "rhetorical wealth" attached to "black womanhood": "Peaches, Brown Sugar, Sapphire, Earth Mother, Aunty, Granny," which is of course, at the same time, an evisceration of black female subjectivity (Spillers, 65). Hear, then, more fully how Simone sounds this crisis in what drama scholar Aida Mbowa described to me in a conversation as the sound of a "stripping down and a bursting out."

The compositional structure of "Four Women" manifests what musicologist Guy Ramsey has helpfully identified for me in a conversation as an embellished minor blues form: twelve bars with a four-bar tag on each chorus. Ramsey calls "Four Women" a moderate hard bop from the bebop family of styles, one that holds the remnants of Latin beats that were very popular among hard bop musicians of the 1950s. I hear a hint of calypso in the framework of the composition as well (but that could just be me!). Broadly, we might think of the track as Afro-diasporic, agitprop folk jazz with Simone on piano, Bobby Hamilton on drums, Lisle Atkinson on bass, and Rudy Stevenson on guitar and flute creating a rhythmic atmosphere of "same-as-it-ever-was" formalistic paradigms that Simone in her role as the singer will dialogically oppose—first gently and then forcefully as the song unfolds.

From Aunt Sarah, who countenances the brutalities of bondage, to the yellow-skinned, long-haired "mulatto" of tragedy Saffronia, the product of racialized, sexualized violence in slavery, and tan-skinned Sweet Thing, selling her "trade" for anyone who can afford it, Simone generates for us a musical narrative of what Ramsey terms "overdetermined nominative properties." These properties historically bind black women to a legacy of corporeal abjection, only to lyrically and sonically undo that legacy in the final stanza, where "Peaches" emerges with four hundred years' worth of bad attitude and hardscrabble posturing to boot. And on that note, we might listen again to the all-important final stanza, this time paying even closer attention to the sound and not just the words—the phono and not just the graph—of "Four Women"'s infamous denouement.

"Four Women" is in the key of A, but as Simone reaches her climax she begins to "sing the tonic so flat as if to suggest an emotionally weighted strain" (Ramsey), ending on the tonic but under much affected duress. It's a gesture that defamiliarizes the rhythmic litany of the track. And so listen yet again for the "grain," as Roland Barthes would of course have it, for what Simone "bodies" forth as her voice rises into her nose, as she reaches her final crescendo. Listen to the ways that she uses her chest voice to ascend, nearly grating the vocal cords. Listen to the ways that she tightens the throat, and uses chest and nasal voice to disrupt the flow of breath. Something is breaking, pulling apart, splintering and fragmenting, coming undone here, like the phonographic trace of the historically frozen black female body: open, public, and exposed—here disintegrating in the throat of our heroine, who wears and discards an excess of masks.

Hear, on "Four Women," the way that Simone recapitulates that body in pain: "black skin," "yellow skin," "tan skin," "brown," "wooly hair," "long hair," "strong back," "inviting hips," and a "mouth like wine." Disassembling it, stripping it down to its core, to the embodied voice that refuses its own abjection. Hear the ways in which she reassembles that body—hair, skin, back, mouth, hips—cutting and pasting like pieces of a brutal yet lovely Romare Bearden collage. This "form of disruption," as Mae Henderson contends of black women's ability to speak in tongues, can be read as a "departure or a break with conventional semantics and/or phonetics." It is a kind of "rupture . . . followed by" a re-sounding "of the dominant story or a 'displacement' that shifts attention 'to the other side of the story'" (Henderson, 136).

What is it about that note, that tenacious A that rounds out Simone's anti-aria? Perhaps it is this key in which we hear Simone singing, sounding, "claim[ing] the monstrosity" that Spillers calls for as a way to "strip down," as Mbowa reminds me, the gross histo-political insult of those names. This is the note that amplifies the exigencies of breaking free of how and where black women *sound* in social space and the cultural imaginary. This is the note that we might instead think of as a kind of figurative atonality—so having less to do with the actual sound of a late Schoenberg piece in all its tricked-out wonder, but having much in common with the disruptive ideological work that the "new music" set out to do.

As Adorno (that anti-fan of jazz) argues, "among the shocks that this music delivers . . . is its denial, for the listeners, of the feeling of inclusion, the spatial embrace. It sounds, to state it bluntly, like a beating" (Adorno, 150). "Atonal music," as Richard Leppert writes in his examination of Adorno's body of work, "engages both tonality and the immanent history it embeds, up-ends established convention, but at the cost of easy comprehensibility—which ironically is symptomatic of the very need the new music seeks to address" (Leppert, 94). It "radically denaturalize[s], stakes out a position counter to aesthetic and social norms alike. It demands attention; it isn't easily relegated to the background by audiences accustomed to a seamless homology between music and life" (Leppert, 94).

On the one hand, the sound Simone generates in "Four Women" that culminates in her "Peaches" crescendo is clearly reminiscent of some of the "overriding characteristics" of African American singing that popular music studies scholar Richard Middleton has noted: "the permeable boundary between 'song' and 'speech' modes . . . the insistence on 'distortion,' inflection and constant variation and [that] love of heterogeneity of sound" to which I referred earlier (Middleton, 30).

In an *Ebony* magazine article from 1968, Simone referred to her work as "black classical music." But Simone's vocal performance here, her decision to interpolate what Middleton might even call a "blues and rock" throat vocal as the exclamation mark for "Four Women," transforms the generic economy of the song, shifting it into "a blues strand where emotional tension tightens the throat" in ways not unlike Robert Johnson or Big Mama Thornton and anticipating the preening, affected screech of the masculinized white male rock vocals of folks like Mick Jagger and Robert Plant (vocals that were, in fact, derivatives of black women's blues vocalities all done up in stadium-rock excess). If the black female singing voice is expected to do a certain kind of work—"to heal a crisis in national unity," as Griffin puts it, to nurture, to "embrace," or to sound out a wounding in a particular way—Simone's note defies the conventional logic of black female vocality, and in this sense her work should make us think of other experimental black female artists like Lincoln who were stretching their repertoire of soundings in the context of civil rights activism.

But I would also suggest that that last note that Simone delivers is the one where her voice moves out of the threnodial cadences, out of the "semantic affective field" of the song and into an/other space, a space that fills up the "normative musical matrix" of the composition by overrunning it at its end with what we might call "gestural promiscuity" (Middleton, 29). It's a note more Brecht than experimental bebop, more Fluxus than fusion jazz, because Simone has essentially performed a pre–Suzi Parks theater piece with an ending as unsettling as anything out of *In the Blood*.

Perhaps in a musical context, then, the Nina on "Four Women" is more of a spiritual, maybe even an ideological, cousin to (wait for it . . .) Yoko Ono, the unheralded queen of avant-garde rock whose work was notoriously "difficult and formed from a wellspring of knotty conceptual impulses decidedly not the stuff of simple pop dreams" (Berger, 245). Simone and Ono spent the sixties and seventies composing their own unique forms of musical "refusals," inasmuch as a "refusal" constitutes what Dick Hebdige would call a form of subcultural style that stresses the sonic poetics of "deformity" and "transformation." Theirs is a kind of "noise" that operates as a "challenge to symbolic order." Think of this noise, as Hebdige suggests, "as the flip-side to Althusser's 'teeth-gritting harmony,'" a contradiction to "ruling ideology" executed obliquely in sonic style (Hebdige, 133).

If, as Jacques Attali influentially maintains, institutional order aims to "ban subversive noise because it betokens demands for cultural autonomy" as well as "support for differences or marginality," then I want, through this extended rumination on Nina's "deep blue note" and dirty tone, to push our understanding of what "noise" can sound like for black women and the work it can do for them in sociocultural contexts (Attali, 8).

More broadly, through this work my intention is to encourage new ways to consider the syntax of musicality in relation to black women's literary production. Arnold Rampersad, Robert O'Meally, and others have shown us the centrality of jazz as an aesthetic and ideological force in the work of Ralph Ellison, and Harry Elam and others have shown us the ways that Bessie Smith and the blues shaped August Wilson's vision of black theater. I want to suggest that we, as critics, have much to discover as well about the intersections between black women's musical aesthetics and discursive texts. We have new and exciting terrain to cross in exploring the "structural and symbolic element" of music in black women's literary works, following the lead of Hazel Carby, Mendi Obadike, and others.

And so now I'd like to engage in what critic Alexander Weheliye might refer to as "thinking sound" and "sound thinking" in relation to a crucial dramatic text in the African American literary canon. I want to consider the ways that we might begin to read Adrienne Kennedy's classic drama *Funnyhouse of a Negro* (1964) in "the key of Nina" so as to hear the dimensions of this text through the prism of what Weheliye refers to as "Afrosonic modernity."

As Weheliye points out in his cogent study *Phonographies*, "the sonic remains an important zone from and through which to theorize the fundamentality of Afro-diasporic formations to the currents of Western modernity, since this field remains," as he sees it, "the principal modality in which Afro-diasporic cultures have been articulated" (Weheliye, 5). Where though, specifically, does the black female singing voice fit into the rubric of "sonic Afro-modernity"? How does it move? What kind of space does it take up? And how do the poetics of space, movement, and location in these vocalities perhaps translate and transmit transatlantic black female histories in particular?

Ahead, my aim is to listen for the noise that Kennedy's play is making and look for the shapes that that noise takes. Put another way, I want to consider the ways that Simone's sonic gestures that I've been discussing may in fact be dialectically and dialogically engaged with the content as well as the formal economy of *Funnyhouse of a Negro*, a play that appeared just one year before the recording of "Four Women." Simone may have seen or heard a dramaturgical sole/soul sister in Kennedy (and we know that, as I've suggested elsewhere, Simone was intrigued by the avant-garde musicals of Bertolt Brecht and Kurt Weill as well as the civil rights drama of her good friend Lorraine Hansberry). My argument, in part, here though is that the qualities of their voices in these two texts are luxuriously, turbulently, stubbornly entwined with one another, and so we might try to sample some key portions of Kennedy's landmark drama so as to better hear Nina's noise (as well as Mom's and Butterfly's) clattering around at the center as well as the edges of this dark, dark fun house.

Heavy Mettle: The Acoustic Disturbances of Adrienne Kennedy

It's all about the body in *Funnyhouse of a Negro*, a play first produced during the advent of the civil rights era and one that parades a series of psychically and corporeally wounded figures across the stage as both a kind of surrogated exorcism and a tormented purgatory for its "tragic mulatta" archetypal lead character. In *Funnyhouse*, Kennedy's treatise on postcolonial trauma and black female interiority, the playwright examines the depths of the central figure "Negro-Sarah's" violent fragmentations of consciousness. Seven other Em-bodied characters populate the stage at various times, with four that are each specifically described as "ONE of [Negro-Sarah's] selves."

Four "selves" [Queen Victoria, the Duchess of Hapsburg, Jesus, and Patrice Lumumba] prowl about Sarah's room—shedding hair, carrying heads, and confronting one another with abstruse declarations about the sexual violence of Sarah's interracial genealogy (that, unlike Simone's "Saffronia," her "darkest of the dark" father has raped her "light-skinned" mother), about the shame attached to "blackness," and about the visceral horrors of social and psychological alienation resulting from the brutalities of bearing black skin and white masks. Impossible supplications and inscrutable confrontations ensue between the characters roaming the landscape that *is* Sarah as she searches for a way to cauterize the wounds of racialized psychic fragmentation born out of slavery's legacies. The play ends with Sarah's suicidal hanging, her body discovered by her landlady and her Jewish boyfriend Raymond.

It is true that, as my colleague feminist theater critic Tamsen Wolff has pointed out to me, an abundance of marvelous work has been done on the ways that this play, like no theatrical work before it, engages the racially and gender marked body as a site of wounding and "national abjection," as Karen Shimakawa might put it. Kennedy's work reveals the ways in which the black female body operates as a critical site for interrogating the "national promiscuity" of forced migration. *Funnyhouse* recycles that overdetermined black female body for its audiences, all pixilated and out of whack and resonating with the affective dimensions of slavery's lingering scenes of subjection. As Marc Robinson observes in his important exploration of Kennedy's plays, her characters "scrutinize their bodies and the places their bodies have lain for the keys to self-knowledge that their minds and spirits have lost" (Robinson, 117). And Elin Diamond observes as well that "in this theater of identification . . . Kennedy's Negroes are doubled, split" and generate a "postmodern ecstasy of alienation" (Diamond, 120).

I want to add to these conversations about Kennedy's work and *Funnyhouse* in particular by thinking just a bit about how voice as well as body matters in this play and more to the point how sonic forms dialogically contest and further complicate the dissonant content of her drama. If, as Robinson observes of Kennedy's play *Sun*, the "body may disperse, but the voice survives it, as does the imagination," and if "the voice" in Kennedy's drama *Sun* "carries over the din of cataclysm, as if reluctant to stop sounding," then what are we hearing in *Funnyhouse* and how does sound as a concept further the ideological arc of the narrative (Robinson, 117)? This is a noisy play, I argue, but it manifests the kinds of expansive modalities of noise that cultural critic and pop music scholar Simon Reynolds identifies in his manifesto on the subject in which he argues for ways of opening up that term for critical usage.

According to Reynolds, "noise is best defined as interference, something which blocks transmission, jams the code, prevents sense being made." In postmodern popular music culture it is often associated, he continues, with "subject matter that is anti-humanist—extremes of abjection, obsession, trauma, atrocity, possession" (Reynolds, 55). Reynolds maintains, however, that this kind of noise (which surely alludes to some of the major themes that both Kennedy and Simone address in their respective works) has "driven itself to dead(ening) end" in the late twentieth-century rave culture of which Reynolds has written extensively (Reynolds, 57). Noise as "dark, unmanageable . . . horror and sickness," he argues, has limited efficacy in a cultural economy that "confer[s] the status of value upon excess and extremism" so as to "bring these things back within the pale of decency" (Reynolds, 56).

Nonetheless, because of these limited and limiting definitions of noise, Reynolds proposes three new ways to escape the trap of what he calls the "noise/horror aesthetic," three ways of thinking about noise that, I want to suggest, might also reanimate our readings of *Funnyhouse*. First, he identifies "inconsistency" as a defining category: in noise studies, we need (he suggests) to listen for "dips, swerves, lapses, use of space and architecture . . . antagonist ambiences and idioms, sampled from random points in pop history. The effect is psychedelia, dispersing consciousness as any pure din" (Reynolds, 57).

"Pure din." Perhaps this is what we're seeing as well as hearing in a play that makes use of a wide range of vocal and rhythmic inconsistencies from start to end. At its core, *Funnyhouse* is an antiphonal play with characters repeating and revising their own lines and each other's lines, which are, in fact, all primarily Sarah's lines: says the Duchess, "My mother looked like a white woman, hair as straight as any white woman's" (Kennedy, 335). To which Victoria later resounds, "My mother was the light. She was the lightest one. She looked like a white woman." Victoria here amplifies the pitch, the key of the Duchess's lament, the longing for an approximated whiteness ("she looked like a white woman"), impossible to inhabit but burning bright like the sun and scorching Sarah's "selves" as they wander the stage.

These nomadic figures have "no place" in the world, only Sarah's "funnyhouse," as she declares, a surrogat(ed) space where voices carry (Kennedy, 337). Indeed, as Tamsen Wolff maintains, Kennedy's drama is perhaps all the more compelling to think about as a work in which the voice is thrown, generating perpetually "antagonistic ambience," producing the psychedelic (sound) effect of "dispersed consciousness" (Wolff, pers. comm.).

An exchange between "Funnyman" boyfriend Raymond and the Duchess in which the two trade brutal riffs about Sarah's father (the father who is "arriving" according to the Duchess, "arriving from Africa" according to Raymond) intensifies and builds. Says the Duchess, "He is an African who lives in the jungle. He is an African who has always lived in the jungle. Yes, he is a nigger who is an African who is a missionary teacher and has now dedicated his life to the erection of a Christian mission in the middle of the jungle. He is a Black man." Says Funnyman, "He is a black man who shot himself when they murdered Patrice Lumumba."

Their dialogue, all reverb and distortion, is interrupted by the Duchess's "scream," the first of many in the play, a "break," as Moten might have it, that ruptures an already fractured narrative, a "swerve" that redirects our focus back to the fraying female body, here re-presented in the form of the Duchess's "fallen hair," which she "draws from a red paper bag" (Kennedy, 338). Fundamental to the structure of *Funnyhouse* is this reliance on rhythmic "swerves" as well as syncopated "drives," what music critic David Wondrich argues are the two key elements of American "hot music," music derived from improvisational musical idioms born out of black and white musical encounters in minstrelsy, taking shape in ragtime, running wild in blues, jazz, and rock and roll.

Wondrich argues that "we can define drive as the quality that gives a piece of music momentum, that pulls you in and makes your body want to move with the music. . . . Usually drive involves some kind of syncopation, whereby the accent is shifted off the strong beats of the measure without losing them altogether." "The swerve," he continues, "is what makes life possible—without it, all is static, permanent, sterile. One little bend, completely without premeditation or plan, just because—call it God, love, free will, anarchy, whatever your name for the unknowable" (Wondrich, 3, 5).

Drive and swerve. New world "noise" that makes the world go 'round. These are the sounds we're hearing, the rhythms that we're feeling in Kennedy's theater. One need only think of that incessant "knocking" called for in stage directions throughout the text to grasp the askew "rhythms" of Kennedy's language that serve as the pulse of her narrative. These knocks announce the entrance of "selves," and by the play's crescendo, we are told that knocking is the sound Sarah's dead "black" father makes at her door: knocking as syncopation as interruption as "blackness," the black noise that shakes the house of Sarah to her very foundations.

These "inconsistencies" are paired with a kind of "textual luxury" that constitutes yet another form of expansive "new noise" that Reynolds describes. "Textual luxury," he argues, is the work that multiple instruments other than the mere fetishized sound of the rock-and-roll guitar can generate "to produce filthy noxious tones" that startle and dismay (Reynolds, 56). Disembodied "screams," floating laughter, create additional sonic layers of atmospheric internal dialogue in *Funnyhouse of a Negro*, a textual luxury that creates a dense tonality in the play. Voices intertwine, speak in unison, stumble over one another—subtly at first but "reaching" what the stage directions call "a loud pitch" in the final scene, where the speeches of "Patrice Lumumba, the Duchess" and "Victoria" "are mixed and repeated by one another" as her selves "wander about," "shouting," "laughing," "chanting," and contemplating those persistent "knocks."

This scene, set "in the jungle" with "red sun, flying things, wild black grass," is, we are told in the text, "unlike the other scenes" set "over the entire stage." It is, we are told, "the longest scene in the play and is played the slowest, as the slow, almost standstill stages of a dream" (Kennedy, 342). Black female chromaticity slowly erupts here as all the keys of Sarah are played, as "unregulated," "profligate internal difference" yields to "improvisational excess" in a darkly luxurious "jungle" of sonic encounters.

And "dark" is indeed the word most often used to describe *Funnyhouse*. But it is the relationship that we might consider between "darkness" and black female vocality that leads me to the final category of revisionist noise outlined by Simon Reynolds that intrigues me most, and it is the point on which I'd like to end. In his essay, Reynolds urges readers to reconsider the voice itself as an instrument capable of generating the most minute kinds of noises, "tiny breakages and stresses dispersed all over the surface of music, all kinds" of popular music in which, he continues, invoking Barthes, "you can hear a surplus of form over content, of genotext over phenotext, semiotic over symbolic . . . 'grain' . . . over technique. Of 'telling' over 'story'" (Reynolds, 57).

What if we think, then, of *Funnyhouse* as the dramaturgical enactment of a kind of "noise" that constitutes the "grain" of black female vocality? As a kind of register that we associate with black women's vocal stylings? What if we consider the timbre of this play—not just its vocal colorings but also the registral category in which it is situated? What if we think of Kennedy's drama as a contralto piece, and what if we think of the register of the contralto as a space where black women artists—from Nina to Marian Anderson, from Moms Mabley to Meshell Ndegeocello—revise and convert the hegemonically constructed discourses of "suffering" associated with black womanhood into creative agency?

The contralto. "The lowest female voice or voice part, intermediate in range between soprano and tenor."[1] The contralto—a register that everyone from Lauryn Hill to Amy Winehouse dares to occupy. Here we might listen closely as well to the "wordless" work of a woman's lower vocal registers as it records and reanimates what Moten refers to as "the complex, dissonant, polyphonic affectivity of the ghost, the agency of the fixed but multiply apparent shade, an improvisation of spectrality" (Moten, *In the Break*, 196). The "ghostly matters" of the black contralto are such that her soundings are often likened to an ineffable history that haunts and yet remains opaque (Gordon). Paradoxically, she archives the ephemeral dimensions of legacies of subjugation that perpetually and spectrally transfigure in cultural memory and yet which simultaneously accrue a kind of sprawling density by virtue of their very elusiveness. It is in the figure of the contralto where cultural notions of scale, mass, sound, vision, race, and gender oddly converge, where a woman's voice can be likened to that which is mystically "veiled" (as is the case in Pauline Hopkins's epic *Of One Blood* [1903]) and yet can also assume the role of carrying "the Weight" that, for instance, Mavis Staples holds in what was anything but her *Last Waltz*.[2] These types of singers are both of their bodies and elsewhere, perceived as evoking through sound a kind of material thickness that is still, however, evocative of "unspeakable" histories which instead must be sung. Their voices compress and translate suffering and sobbing into acousmatic dreamscapes of black historical memory remixed and re-sounded.[3] They are the figures most often conflated with the "sonic blackness" that voice theorist Nina Eidsheim describes as "a perceptual phantom projected by the listener; a vocal timbre that happens to match current expectations about blackness; or the shaping of vocal timbre to catch current ideas about the sound of blackness" (Eidsheim, 663–64).

These women of the lower registers, like their brothers up high, push our imagination, our desires, our quotidian needs to engage with the traces of suffering by challenging us through sound to go to (other) extremes and border regions, to tarry in the boundaries of the elsewhere. By way of their location on these "lower frequencies," they "speak for" us.[4]

"Blackness" and suffering are equated with each other in the content of *Funnyhouse*. We are told by the landlady that Sarah is "suffering." The Duchess declares that "my father is a nigger who drives me to misery. Any time spent with him evolves into suffering" (Kennedy, 338). The very tragic dimensions of Negro-Sarah's literal fate in the narrative have weighted this play with what some critics read as a kind of grim certitude about the inevitability of black abjection.

But interpreting this text as a contralto piece would necessitate that we think of Kennedy's work as *resembling* suffering but like the contralto's mighty vocal cords, ultimately affirming the "troubling" resistances of the black female artist, in this case Kennedy, who herself executes the production of this play in the aesthetically fecund register of the "duende," a kind of "dark sound" not limited to the contralto register but certainly characteristic of that timbre.

In his classic and much cited work "Theory and the Play of the Duende," Federico García Lorca excavates "the buried spirit of saddened Spain" as "dark sounds" that generate "a mysterious force that everyone feels and no philosopher explains," like that of a "medieval mourner" who "begins to sing with scorched throat, without voice, breath, colour, but with duende." And, as Robinson makes clear, Lorca was a figure whose "dark, complex vision was thrilling and comforting to Kennedy" (Robinson, 117).

Duende, Lorca insists, "is not IN the throat"; it is "not a question of skill, but of style," style "defeating inadequate content." Duende's "rhythm, pauses and intensity . . . give life and knowledge to bodies devoid of expression" (Lorca, quoted in Mackey, 183). It is, as Nathaniel Mackey has influentially argued in relation to black musical forms, "a kind of gremlin, a gremlin like troubling spirit." To Mackey, duende is "something beyond technical virtuosity. It is something troubling. It has to do with trouble, deep trouble." Duende is "the taking over of one's voice by another voice." Its opacity is thus due in part to its "polysemous" dimensions that cannot be contained. Mackey likens this sound to the "surge, a runaway dilation, a quantum rush one hears in [Coltrane's] music" (Mackey, 183, 186, 191).

When we see the hanging figure of Negro-Sarah as the curtain comes down on Kennedy's play, we might read the thick, ominous, dark possibilities of this event. We might listen for the sound of troubling style of which Simone sings the fugitive grace note, and we might hear the way that *Funnyhouse* reignites a conversation with the dead, the "gone but not forgotten" selves of Sarah sacrificed here in the name of generating postmodern black womanhood.

Funnyhouse does so by "stretch[ing]" its voices "and passionately reach[ing]" back into the history of a complexly opaque Marian Anderson solo, and future forward into a sumptuous Atlantic Records Aretha Franklin melisma, into a fractured Tina Turner howl, into a grating Betty Davis funk screech—creating volatile black feminist noise for the next generation of little women who sit at the crossroads of new epistemic possibilities.

Notes

For Fred Moten and in memory of Lodell Brooks Matthews. Many thanks to Eric Glover for research assistance with this project.

1. *American Heritage Dictionary of the English Language*, 4th ed. (Boston: Houghton Mifflin, 2009).

2. Contralto soul legend Mavis Staples and the Staple Singers accompany the Band on their anthem "The Weight" in Martin Scorsese's film *The Last Waltz* (1978).

3. Mendi Obadike theorizes the politics of "acousmatic blackness" in her dissertation on the subject. See also Lordi; Radano.

4. Invisible Man's parting words are instructive in the case of black (con)tralto singers: "Who knows but that, on the lower frequencies, I speak for you?" (Ellison, 581). Gayle Wald considers the ways that Marian Anderson's historic performances on the steps of the Lincoln Memorial "registe[r] and projec[t] a collective presence through sound" (Wald, 673–96).

To be clear, what I'm interested in here differs from the "cry break" and the "pharyngealized tone" that Aaron Fox outlines in his study of country music singing. Fox describes how country singers "evoke key affective gestalts through distinctive changes in the site and manner of voice production. A pharyngealized tone . . . can be iconic of the ravaged voice of a character textually narrated as 'crying.' 'Crying' itself can be iconically represented with specific inflections known categorically as 'cry breaks'— sharp deformations of the melodic line effected through intermittent falsetto or nasalization, glottal or diaphragmatic pulsing of the airstream and thus the melodic line, or the addition of articulatory 'noise' to an otherwise timbrally 'smooth' vocal tone'" (Fox, 276). Instead, I am interested in the melancholic atmospheric and spatial resonances associated with vocalists of this register. Descriptions of iconic black contralto singers consistently invoke references to power and depth, as when the *New York Times* describes "the surging force" combined with the "deep sincerity" of Mahalia Jackson's voice ("Mahalia Jackson Sings"). Similarly, Anderson makes a "deep and abiding impression" on some critics, yet the same critics find that she is equally capable of "sudden change to the calm disembodied tones of Death's reply" in her rendition of "Divinités du Styx" from the opera *Alceste* by Gluck ("Marian Anderson in Closing Recital"). Thanks to Jody Kreiman and to Marti Newland for their generous insight, and my sincerest thanks to Nina Eidsheim for being the ultimate "sounding board" and for her tremendously helpful feedback with regard to these points. Thanks also to Francisco Robles for his tireless research assistance in this project. I take up this discussion at greater length in my essay "'Bring the Pain.'"

HIP-HOP HABITUS v.2.0

The conditionings associated with a particular class of conditions of existence produce *habitus*, systems of durable, transposable dispositions, structured structures predisposed to function as structuring structures, that is, as principles which generate and organize practices and representations that can be objectively adapted to their outcomes without presupposing a conscious aiming at ends or an express mastery of the operations necessary in order to attain them.

—Pierre Bourdieu, *The Logic of Practice*, 53

By now, hip-hop dance and its myriad articulations constitute a constellation that engages entertainment, competitions, social networking, concert performance, and expressions of social justice. Still, many academic studies rely on narratives that foreground African American and Latino wellsprings for hip-hop dance styles without considering shifts in circulation that surround these movement forms. This chapter explores the slippage from Africanist performance histories to global hip-hop corporealities. How does hip-hop dance "sound" in locations without obvious connection to an Africanist movement legacy? Does some singular notion of hip-hop "do" something recognizable, or consistent, in its various movement manifestations? How has a "global hip-hop" shifted its ideological possibilities from an Africanist sensibility? How has hip-hop become a habitus recognizable to youth and attendant audiences worldwide?

Everyman's Rhapsody

A young skinny white guy emerges from the shower drying himself off. He walks from a large, airy bathroom into the living room of what

must be a shared rental domicile—it's too big and established to be his prop-
erty, and he's too moist and dewy, literally, to have organized himself into this
level of home ownership. Besides, there's a smiling female pop starlet cooing an
anti-love song at a baby grand piano in the living room, a feature only avail-
able in a fantasy. Never mind; he pulls on a T-shirt and, with a towel wrapped
around his legs, moves to the remote control for the large flat screen facing
the couch. The starlet's gaze—a white and happy gaze—follows him, seem-
ingly intent on maintaining his interest. Too late; with no remorse or concern,
our everyman changes the channel. Starlet disappears, her song rejected mid-
phrase. Suddenly a black hip-hop trio appears, clad in skinny jeans, designer
tees, millennium baseball caps, and dookie chains, microphones in hand; a
small suggestion of a stage area and theatrical lights framing them. White ev-
eryman grimaces into an appropriately warrior-masculine mask of intent and
begins to move to the electronic pulsations alongside the conjured blackness.
His body jerks, twitches, and heaves to the beat, weight directed downward
and insistent, pushing against imagined forces of binding. The cool performers
move as they rhyme on their Mr. Mic machines, stressing rhythmic accents
with displacements of weight more lateral than vertical, but surely as regularly
shaped, in temporal accord, as everyman's. Everyman shakes his head, still
damp and seemingly happy, in this dance moment, to be among the Cool Kids.[1]

This commercial for Rhapsody digital music service intends to sell conve-
nience and variety, diversity of musical taste, and the possibility of an endless musical mood. No vanishing point here; choose whatever music suits
your shifting emotional state. Changing channels might be as easy as wiping
the water off your back or the dirt off your shoulder, unlimited access to an
endless variety of sound available for a low monthly fee.

In corporealizing the encounter of our young everyman with the bodies
of his temporary interest, the Rhapsody ad confirms an interchangeability of
physical approaches to being. Bodies are present and absent simultaneously,
topologies flattened, winsome instantly transformed to forceful, female to
male, white to black, lyrical to percussive. The ad denigrates the performative impulse at the heart of music-making. What the artists hope to convey
may be evacuated by the consumer's desire to receive at will. In this ad (and
it may be worth noting that there are other versions of the same ad campaign
in circulation that offer different narratives) our everyman chooses to consume and construct by his movements in response to their music, the cool.

Of course, the cool kids drive the marketplace. In *The Tipping Point: How
Little Things Can Make a Big Difference* (2000), Malcolm Gladwell describes
the lengths to which advertising agencies go in order to predict trends that

will influence future markets. Hiring information "mavens" to make sense of shifting economies of cool, advertising agencies compete to align their clients with impossibly ambiguous terms of desirability. The cool kids—the ones who swim against the streams of normalcy, who stand out because of their "maverick" flexibility in the face of the everyday—constitute the relied-upon information sources. Cool coheres; it reflects and recognizes itself; and its agents perform its presence—and allow it to be marketed—through their affiliations. The cool kids get together, and the rest of us try to assemble among their number.

Gladwell's book is often referred to as psychology (of a popular sort), and his gestures toward the marketplace align cool easily with a state of mind that can be recognized, packaged, and consumed. This may be so, but cool is also a performative, an approach to movement or dance that we value as embodied abstraction. Cool replenishes imagination, and surely we all crave its access. But in approaching the performance of cool we run the risk of misstepping (usually via excess) and possibly falling, with a thud, somewhere in the realm of clown. Our rhapsodic everyman almost gets his cool groove on, but we're not quite sure that he actually embodies his own movements: after all, he had to conjure the Cool Kids in order to find his dance. Really cool kids don't need other cool kids to be cool.

The derisive irony of calling oneself a cool kid doesn't escape note. The Cool Kids emcees, from Chicago, emerge from a playful, self-created my/ space that could counterbalance even their very uncool appearance in the Rhapsody television commercial. These cool kids dress odd, ride BMX, and seem to mock their attempts at hip-hop celebrity while simultaneously pursuing it. The simulacra shimmer, and they are and aren't cool, even as they can only be identified as such by name.

My favorite Cool Kids song of the 2000s is "Bassment Party," an uptempo dance track with a crackling backbeat and several well-constructed rhythmic breaks. Depending on your speakers or headphones, you might appreciate the tune title variously: the insistent bass tones only resonate with a good sound system, while the lyrical call to an adolescent house party may strike you as hapless, thrilling, or just silly. This bassment party is cool in the Kanye West ironic mold; clownish and ineffective at the performative transcendence of balance that usually characterizes cool, it becomes cool by violating principles of the concept. The Cool Kids tend to record in two modes: up-tempo party, or slow, plodding, "lean back" beats. In either mode the bass drives the track, and the emcees flow in opposition to its inevitable return. Is this cool? Possibly. Is this hip-hop? Possibly. Are the everyman's movements to their music recognizable as hip-hop corporeality?

A larger question surrounding what hip-hop might be wonders at what hip-hop can do, and the borders of its possibilities as resistance expression. At first, many older folks thought hip-hop dances too brash to be considered black popular culture and tried to label them the renegade practice of a few. But the academy broke, and hip-hop came to be theorized in line with a progressive social politic, typically narrated as a response by working-class young people of color to rising tides of economic inequities in the post–civil rights era. In this vaguely functionalist analysis, hip-hop fulfilled a need for expressive flexibility as an outlet for speaking truth to power. Hip-hop can be narrated as a return to the real in its aggressive rhythmicity, its lyrical directness, and its physical abundance of heavily accented movements. These performance qualities of hip-hop (echoed in graphic stylings of visual arts associated with the genre) suggested a truthfulness of expressive gesture that predicted possibilities of communication across boundaries of race, class, and location, if not gender, sexuality, or age group. For hip-hop's first generation of scholars and journalists, hip-hop claimed expansive space as a necessary voice of expression for the disenfranchised; for its second-generation interpreters, it became a connectivity for youth across geography, practiced locally.[2]

Some scholars tentatively cited the production of black pleasure, or even radical black joy, within hip-hop dances. Whether or not we found ways to talk about hip-hop in these terms that aligned black expressive culture with social justice and pleasure simultaneously, it continued its largest trajectory as a source of unmarked popular pleasure quickly made available to global populations of youth. In the early to mid-1980s, at site after site, young people witnessed some aspect of hip-hop expressivity through mediated or live performance and found themselves drawn to its forms.

Dancers in France, Australia, and Japan seized hip-hop's performative idioms, and breaking crews propagated. While DJ-ing, emceeing, and graffiti writing found devotees over time in local language, hip-hop dance accumulated committed performers almost immediately as popping and breaking became expressive weapons of choice available to young men, and some women, worldwide. Clearly, hip-hop dances encouraged social organization along axes of burgeoning masculinities, physical strength/control/endurance, physical imagination, and expressive communication. But analytic narratives that aligned hip-hop's physical movements to collective action foundered. As often occurs when considering the power of the body, hip-hop dances came to be discussed as embodiments of collective action only to the extent that their performance could generate economic exchange within the frame of the festival circuits. The many breakdance festivals of the 1990s allowed product marketing for consumable goods (videotapes, travel, sports gear, alcohol) to function at the center of these social activities. Hip-hop dance stylings—and this includes b-boying and b-girling—came to refer to themselves and the individuals who performed them, a gathering notion of individuality within a group dynamic, but one aimed only reflexively at its own contents. If breaking and b-girling had been conceived to speak physical truth to oppressive forces that would deny the presence of young people of color, by the 1990s these forms stood largely as referents to resistance co-opted by a nimble marketplace eager to commodify the cool.

So, where did the possibilities for collective action within hip-hop movements go? Are these possibilities subsumed by the ability of hip-hop movement to be cool?

Habitus

> The *habitus*, a product of history, produces individual and collective practices—more history—in accordance with the schemes generated by history.
> —Bourdieu, *The Logic of Practice*, 54

Because social dance has had so little theoretical capacity in Europeanist discourses, and has been so pervasive as to be ubiquitous and practically disposable in Africanist discourses, its border transgressions as an agent of social change have gone under-acknowledged. Hip-hop dances have fared no better than swing dances or soul-era dances in terms of theoretical scrutiny that could illuminate the unrelenting popularity of black social-dance practice across cultural boundaries. But surely these dances create an identifiable alignment of black performance and cool that becomes part of a network of social situation worth recovery. A review of the literature specific to hip-hop dance is quickly achieved. One of the two manuscript-length texts in English devoted to hip-hop dance—Carla Stalling Huntington's *Hip Hop Dance: Meanings and Messages*—focuses much of its text on functional historical explications that align particular movements with historical African American dance forms, and speculative descriptions of dances that interpret, again, with a functionalist bent, how particular dances refer to narratives of black oppression. Huntington, like other Africanist scholars of hip-hop globalization including Halifu Osumare (*Africanist Aesthetic in Global Hip Hop: Power Moves*), interpret hip-hop's emergence from working-class communities of color as evidence of the desirability of a shared black past, one that is inevitably referenced and rearticulated through hip-hop expressive discourse in any location. Hip-hop dances are "supposed" to refer, rhetorically, to a black past, and their performance unifies youth movements around themes of dispossession reclaimed through expressive physical labor. Hip-hop dances embody linguistic ideologies (Huntington) or offer possibilities for "connective marginalities" (Osumare) that allow youth to acknowledge their common subordinate subject locations.

But how might hip-hop dances constitute a habitus of physicality that refers to aesthetic creativity? And can aspects of physical creativity construct, say, joy—in any subject location—recognizable to young people in a way that aligns that construction with the aesthetic imperatives of hip-hop? What might be lost through a consideration of pleasure and its dispersal, or the embodiment of cool, within hip-hop social dances? Is the pleasure within the engagement of these corporealities part of what undermines their social force or impact?

Ethnographer Joseph G. Schloss explores these questions in his full-length study *Foundation*, based on fieldwork that he conducted as a b-boy in New York from 2003 through 2008 (Schloss). Schloss affirms that post-millennial b-boying mobilizes its participants to recognize each other, dance together, and affirm a common history—even if the details of that history are contentious and widely debated.[3] In Schloss's study, the community that breakers recognize is self-selecting and hermetically sealed; for one to materially participate in the culture of the dance, one must become "of" the dance and its culture through extensive training, apprenticeship, and participation. While Schloss does allow b-boying to be considered artistic practice by its practitioners, the terms of its creativity are defined by a genealogy that extends back only to post–civil rights era gang activity transformed into twenty-first-century competitive dance structures. Dancing offers its participants a safe communal space that mitigates the daily stresses of life for its practitioners. But here, we find little recovery of the political capacities of dance to transfigure an expansive population of attendant witnesses beyond the terms of participation in the cypher.[4]

Sociologist Katrina Hazzard-Donald narrates dance in hip-hop culture as an extension of the earliest African American dance practices, all born of cultural adaptations that secured presence in an American marketplace. These practices include an exceptional "cyclical" iteration in which dances appear, go underground, or seem to die out, and then "emerge twenty or so years later as a 'new' dance." For Hazzard-Donald, this cycling reflects the U.S. commodity market, within which African American culture has surely developed, and which "continually demands new dance material" (Hazzard-Donald, 220, 221). Hazzard-Donald also notes an "influential exchange of dance material between vernacular-popular-folk dances and the black professional performance tradition," a dialectic that predicts a detachable, performative quality of motion that could allow its movement across geographic, class, and aesthetic boundaries.

Taken together, these volumes and essays affirm that hip-hop corporealities cohere, and their particular practices emerge within particular genealogical contexts. The detailed studies of dance practice within core communities of b-boys or hip-hop devotees suggest a granularity of knowledge far more developed than the passing familiarity of mediated hip-hop dance that circulates globally today. That passing familiarity is not usually structured around following the rules of b-boying, or knowing a history of dance families; rather, a growing global populace recognizes these physical ways of being in the world as our everyman does—as playful, fizzy, millennial fun that can open spaces of belligerent cool. So how is it that social-dance forms so deeply imbued with meanings and historical contexts crucial to their core participants float in a contemporary mediascape without grounding in the Africanist aesthetics that gave rise to them?

> Because the *habitus* is an infinite capacity for generating products—thoughts, perceptions, expressions and actions—whose limits are set by the historical and socially situated conditions of its production, the freedom it provides is as remote from the creation of unpredictable novelty as it is from simple mechanical reproduction of the original conditioning.
> —Bourdieu, *The Logic of Practice*, 55

I'm hinting at the limits of understanding pleasure, aesthetic physical activity, and power relations among diverse cultural systems. Surely we veer toward cool physicalities because they "feel good" in their alignment of energy, individual expression, and perceived connection to a larger social group. Black social dances offer pleasure to those who engage them because they encourage cool aesthetic approaches; they confirm careful organization of the body in relation to discourses of physical ability and ingenuity. Hip-hop dances thrive in the production of *corporeal orature*, or body talking; in their aggressive rhythmicity, they encourage muscular engagements that underscore dynamism, power, and control.[5] Not all black social dances operate in this way; buck and wing dances (of the nineteenth century), swing dancing (of the 1930s), and footworking (of the 2000s), for example, are not explicitly concerned with the enactment of power and strength in the way that breaking, popping, and whacking styles are. These hip-hop styles demonstrate power as often as not; in this, an affiliation of power and pleasure at the center of these forms may seem politically regressive. After all, a feminist analysis could easily discard the seemingly inevitable affiliations of strength, domination (in hip-hop's myriad competitive strains), and masculinized pleasure of hip-hop to focus more favorably on the more welcoming and flexible possibilities of other black social-dance forms. For example, partner forms including swing dance, disco, and Chicago stepping highlight interpersonal communication toward a unified goal of movement in a way that hip-hop surely does not.

To be clear, here, I mean to align pleasure with aesthetic purpose as well as social function. What hip-hop dance styles manage to do, in their organization of physicalities and dispersals of energy, is to combine the joy of controlling an emotional and physical self in a blankly powerful manner that suggests social dynamism. Hip-hop dancers "hit it hard" whether breaking or popping; when combining genres to include movements from ballet or house dancing, hip-hoppers tie a persistent weightiness to the pleasure of bringing it down to the ground. Hip-hop dancing gathers energy as it broadens its contours and revels in its own accomplishment as an aggressive, masculinist style that conditions its dancers to demonstrate their power. In the contexts of its emergence, hip-hop dances demonstrated the abilities of its practitioners among peer groups, to confirm social status and creative facility. For young people discovering an awareness of their own physical, emotional, and desirous capacities, hip-hop dances combine the need to explore along each of these axes to a demonstration of strength and control bound up with unprecedented pleasure—a pleasure not to be found in other aspects of daily life. Hip-hop dances answer a need for creative release that allows aesthetic contemplation to young people who could then recognize each other's artistry in process.

Not surprisingly, hip-hop shows up on global theatrical stages with great regularity. In these circumstances, by 2014, the social component of these moves have been carefully evacuated; these are dances created in careful rehearsal to reveal aesthetic qualities and contest fixed subjectivities in theatrical situations. Two thumbnail examples: in July 2008 dancer Kentaro offered a solo performance of his hip-hop stylings extended into an hour-long theatrical form.[6] Kentaro spent as much time not dancing as moving, as he tested space in luxuriant slow motion and explored geometric form via hip-hop-inspired physicality, but the whole was danced to pop music, staged with rock-concert-styled lighting effects and jokey films that he made with some friends projected in between dance segments. The performance included only one or two sections of flat-out spontaneous movement invention; for the most part, Kentaro carefully controlled the release of energy; he seemingly allowed himself to limit the possibility of us seeing him directly through a context of hip-hop. In August 2008, Compagnie Accrorap presented *Petits Histoires*, a work for five men that aligned hip-hop dance with memories of the performers' fathers and grandfathers, stories related in monologue recited between segments of dance.[7] This grand theatrical spectacle included radio-controlled airplanes and cars, inexplicable props that traveled across the back of the stage on a clothesline, a sequence staged on a wheeled sofa, and a "funky chicken" locking dance performed by a man dressed in a chicken costume. The dancing in *Petits Histoires* ranged through several idioms: strong floor work and popping sequences interspersed with comedic episodes, and segments of masculine bravado undercut by unexpected theatrical effects. In one scene, the chicken dancer was shot by an offstage hunter; the dancer disappeared in a lighting blackout, to be replaced by a clutch of chicken feathers floating to the ground in his absence.

Hip-hop, then, proves its flexibility as a constellation of dance idioms that can be reconstituted in various circumstances, and by 2014 these possibilities are exploited in every direction imaginable. Here, the promise of flexibility, often cited as a key component of black performative cultures, fulfills itself as dancers claim hip-hop lineage. Kentaro, the men of Accorap, and anonymous young men in the South Bronx a generation or two earlier share their approach to physicality and embodied representation. We can recognize that these are hip-hop dances in these different venues; the form allows for many to engage its physical ideologies. And audiences assemble for a taste of that release of palpably powerful energy; Kentaro's large audience of teenage girls and Accrorap's legions of families and teenage boys gather to witness the ends of physical challenge that hip-hop can engender. Performative flexibility is akin to the communicative tradition of signifyin' that enlarges realms of meaning-making by shifting the context of recognition available to a word, phrase, or vocal tonality. In performance circumstances, this flexibility assumes relations between hip-hop and other forms of dance; it assumes that Korean teenagers have an access to the physical imperatives of hip-hop, as do teens from Houston, Texas. Black social-dance forms emerge from particular social spaces, but are constructed with an aesthetic resilience that allows them to transform and suit other performative contexts.

And yet, in the movement of movement across geographies and social spaces, how that movement signifies shifts. The qualitative flexibility that allows the form to speak variously to various communities parasitically diminishes its own core values of derisiveness. As signifying practice, black social dances tend toward the space of derision; dancers tease those who are not dancing (or not dancing well) through their gestures. These dances of derision—and of course Robert Farris Thompson included them as an entire aesthetic category of West African invention (Thompson, "Dance and Culture")—lose their capacity to function outside localized social spaces: they don't translate from Lexington to Lyon. In social and theatrical contexts, hip-hop has not yet become able to speak convincingly with derision to a global audience.

Disarmed, unmoored from the progressive social possibilities of staging derisive masculinities or narratives of strength and control, what can hip-hop dances do? What sorts of narratives can their gestures inspire? Kentaro's performance suggests that expressive control might be something contained by a hip-hop body, but released only sparingly and in isolation from other hip-hop genres. (On his website, Kentaro claims to want to draw connections between hip-hop and techno and rock; for him, hip-hop emceeing and DJ-ing have exhausted their potential to generate movement.) The dancers of Accrorap explicitly align hip-hop with comedy, in the process constructing the spectacle of hip-hop virtuosity as something necessarily undercut by gestures of self-deprecation. The Accrorap dancers are modern clowns, who engage hip-hop to encourage a mutable masculinity, one that directs its agents toward a vanishing point of irrelevancy beyond the moment of performance. As comic enactment, hip-hop becomes something like pantomime on steroids, with an insistent rhythmic pulse: the dancers amuse their audience with their abilities, but stop far short of suggesting that these movements hold the potential for social action alongside the pleasures of their production. In each case, the dancers address the performance of cool, and that cool seems to be a lot of fun to engage.

> The *habitus*—embodied history, internalized as a second nature and so forgotten as history—is the active presence of the whole past of which it is the product.
> —Bourdieu, *The Logic of Practice*, 56

Where, then, has hip-hop gone? In traveling the world, hip-hop coheres in its movement ideologies—Kentaro and Accrorap offered exciting popping and locking demonstrations—but it contracts, perhaps, in its communicative resonances. An American audience probably can't decode Kentaro's commentary on gender and sexuality that responds to his large female fan base. Japanese audiences may miss out on physical references to immigrant strife in France, corporealized in gestures by the largely Algerian-born French dancers of Accrorap. And French audiences may not understand an American skepticism surrounding the Cool Kids' commercial appearance, a skepticism that hints at "sellout" even before the Kids have released an album. When hip-hop loses its ability to sound derisive notes, what can it do—beyond entertain?

Consider the mashup DJ stylings of Girl Talk (Gregg Michael Gillis), who too often places emcee rhymes over favorite beats. Here, aspects of hip-hop become part of a flyby landscape, a constantly shifting immersive environment that evacuates historicizing aesthetics central to black musics in favor of a cumulative singularity. Building on black expressive culture's rhetorical strategies of flexibility, which are, after all, at the heart of hip-hop DJ-ing, Girl Talk poaches from any source that will produce an effective whole. How the fragments he chooses functioned in different contexts before now does not matter; listener-dancers are encouraged to take inventory of the number of samples that are recognizable, but only for a fleeting moment. Hip-hop becomes linked to a purpose of celebration, with only the vestiges of a small rhetorical stance against the marketplace that might restrict this sort of construction.

Girl Talk evidences skill in the way he constructs tracks; like any good DJ in the house tradition, he works with sturdy underpinnings of rhythmicity and bass tonality. At times, listening/dancing to his music, I wonder at the compulsion to work with so much information at all times. For decades, house DJs have constructed musical environments that provoke dance with far less sonic information than Girl Talk employs. House music also tends to work with sparingly articulated referents, evocative lyrical hooks that are open-ended enough to repeat over several minutes without significant elaboration. In this expressive space that values repetition over change, details of harmonic and rhythmic structural shifts matter greatly. More than anything, house music relies upon the movement of the bass to generate sonic drama. House music, born, like hip-hop, in the American crucible of black expression of the post–civil rights era, has become variegated in its soundings (trip, drum and bass, garage, chill, classic, detroit, electro, etc.), but never achieved the global popularity of hip-hop. House dancing, less concerned with the competitive possibilities or blankly aggressive physicalities of hip-hop, has not yet found a global youth movement able to conjure cool at the rhapsodic push of a remote control button.

Girl Talk, like our Rhapsody everyman, loves music in several varieties and hopes to compress his infatuation into a manageable singularity—something we might call popular culture. Along the way, certain rhetorical roadblocks are ignored, and the sensibilities that might allow these passions to be marked as love for black popular culture diminish. Everyman has access to an aggressive rhythmical movement, and he can change the channel.

Girl Talk can raid the digital frequencies for portions of recordings that appeal, to compile a document that means only what it can physically provoke for a listening dancer.[8]

> The *habitus* tends to protect itself from crises and critical challenges by providing itself with a milieu to which it is as pre-adapted as possible, that is, a relatively constant universe of situations tending to reinforce its dispositions by offering the market most favourable to its products.
> —**Bourdieu, *The Logic of Practice*, 61**

Some argue convincingly that dance disappears in the moment of its emergence. So then, it may also always be potential. This truism may be part of how social dance recurs, even when we seem to engage so little discourse beyond that recurrence. What social dances can do shifts dramatically after their appearance in a local space. Strangely, what coheres to those dance forms—from their wide-ranging constructions of physical preparedness, emotional expressiveness, gestures toward social justice, realignments of sex and sexuality, or narratives of class mobility—tends to be the embodied possibilities for unmarked rhythmical pleasure. Broad categories of movement ideologies fall away in the shift from a local black public space to a global public space. "Krumping" loses its framing as a response by marginalized kids—within a homophobic black adolescent space—designed to physically prepare those kids to deal with daily tauntings, and becomes a dance taught at strip mall dance studios. Purpose shifts, even before purpose has become clear.

How is it that hip-hop physicalities become a means for young people to recognize themselves in space? How are some dances chosen, and why do others fall away? If social dance generates only small bits of analytic public discourse, how do we decide what dances to do when? Can we look to the African American expressive *imperative to innovate* to discuss aspects of taste?

An abiding aesthetic imperative to innovate fits directly into narratives of spectacular display that allow social dance to function in the current reality television–game show mediascape. Public dance competitions change the idiom and its possibilities. The pleasures of dance cohere and reproduce themselves across landscapes and bodies; of course, this is how hip-hop dances have gained such broad practitioner bases. But in black communities, pleasure must be aligned with aesthetic purpose and social function of one sort or another. Global stages overwhelm social function beyond their local identities: dancers at the international hip-hop "Event of the Year" or on MTV's "America's Best Dance Crew" seek celebrity that needn't be aligned with sexual identity, local community histories, family hierarchies, social identity, and so on. Competitors in these public arenas dance to win and then possibly transfer their celebrity to a local context. Because dance, following neoliberal discourses, has so little cachet beyond the space of pleasurable individualized motion, we assume that pleasure drives the practice of this dance. In the context of performance that invites scrutiny without participation, pleasure can become the alpha and omega of a conversation about dance. Here, it may be enough to enjoy the sight of uninterrupted flow or controlled releases of physical impulses to decide where the ground of the dance begins. Watching the mediated networked dance competition, we learn little of the complex interactions that inform movement choices. And yet, these tiny choices, navigated in practice sessions and then again throughout the performance of social dance, deflect singular appraisals of performance as "joyful" or "strong" or "good." Encountered in context, shifts in tonality or approach; weight and attack of gesture; dispersal of energy and the construction of flow all shape the experience of social-dance performance. The pleasure of the doing is but part of the event.

Notably, the pleasurable recognition of physical flow is seldom enough to account for value within the aesthetic structures that give rise to these dances. In one analysis, the dances themselves are constructed against a ground that considers their presence to be derisive, impossible, unprecedented, radical. Each of these aspects may be visible in hip-hop dance: the dance that is practiced incessantly to ultimately reveal its languageable teasing of another; its unexpected, outrageous movements that defy the visible. When the body can be coaxed into dancing beyond what can be seen, this achievement accepts a truly radical capacity, a potentially unlimited capacity for innovation and creative expressivity. This capacity defies the boundaries laid out for black people in the New World, people for whom, generations earlier, dancing in shackles was intended to be a final condensing of social exchange into physical potential enabled, by slavery, for the marketplace. Hip-hop dances surely arise from this tradition of dance that defies expectation, dances that confirm something beyond reach (freedom?) but present within the capacity of the physicality of doing. In the performance of these dances, dancers strive for a cool stance afforded through persistent practice and refinement. These rehearsals allow dancers a pleasure of recurrence, enhanced by the unexpected flash palpable in performance. The pleasure of repeated rehearsal as a feature of social exchange enabled by the dance gives way to the pleasure of execution—the aesthetic action underscored by the coolness of preparation. The pleasure of hip-hop dance practice is always visible in performance. This pleasure is aligned with accuracy of performance, with the execution of aesthetic action well done.

Hip-hop dance has few impermeable rules of engagement within the spheres of its recognition; you can't really dance *wrong* here so much as *poorly*.[9] That recognition includes the *imperative to innovate*; dancers in this idiom must reveal something unprecedented for the dance to arrive with conviction. The revelation of individual innovation—inevitable in convincing hip-hop dance—is acknowledged by all as the fullest capacity of dance to demonstrate subjectivity. Here, hip-hop dance proceeds from an assumption that each individual dancer will fulfill herself through an unprecedented alignment of desire, intention, and action. Because black performance aesthetics tend to be fed by this alignment of invention—rather than some need to master or preserve preexisting regulations—these dance practices hold special significance in identity formation and social development. Black aesthetics prize working as an individual within a group dynamic; surely this arrangement appeals to adolescents developing expressive voice for their emotional, physical, and communicative energies.[10]

This energy in transformation—the *delta* of a person's being that dance performance activates—becomes the visible marker of hip-hop dance fulfillment. This *fulfilled* performance cannot be entirely preplanned or rehearsed into superfluousness; it must come into being in real time and register a delta of change perceptible to its attendant witnesses. In this requirement, hip-hop dance, like jazz musicianship, becomes a barometer of individual capacity, an action that reveals the possibility of the unprecedented. When hip-hop dance fulfills itself, witnesses and dancers recognize the change that occurs through the alignment of desire and aesthetic action. The pleasure of this temporary transformation becomes palpable through the dance.

And to be sure, pleasure drives the rehearsal and performance of hip-hop dances. The layered pleasure of subtle alignments released by the dancer among witnesses who can recognize these fluctuations of capacity drives the continued circulation of hip-hop as black performance. Like jazz musicianship, hip-hop dance demands palpable effort that is produced, and then rechanneled toward a quality of cool that effectively undermines the visibility of effort. Cool is a sensibility and an aesthetic achievement consistently experienced as pleasurable by actors and witnesses alike. We enjoy the sensations of cool because they confirm a multilayered awareness of energy and its distribution. Moments of transformation—the delta of change—are inevitably tied to an abiding affect of cool, produced by labor that can balance these contrasting performative tendencies. In the best hip-hop dance, clarity of intention, desire to transform, purposefulness of action, and their organization within the context of cool aesthetics form the core of vast appeal.

Hip-hop dance also enjoys a privileged position as a product of the marketplace with the credible appearance of resisting the authority of the markets that produced it. Of course, aesthetics are not outside of the marketplace, and hip-hop as a practice emerged in determined affiliation to political and economic circumstances that surrounded its emergence. Hip-hop's transformation, from a creative constellation that satisfied Africanist performance imperatives for youth of color into a market-recognized dance practice that could feed television, Internet, and film markets hungry for representations of young people engaged in aesthetic action, completes a feedback loop in which the system inspires creative practice that then validates the system. Hip-hop emerged as a resistant aesthetic practice that provided beauty and joy—aspects necessary for human development—to its participants outside of mainstream markets; it continues to provide these aspects to young people simultaneously within and without marketplace support. In this, hip-hop straddles, often uncomfortably, its own capacities as resistant and compliant practices that allow its practitioners to work within and without normalizing narratives of social order. For dancers who hope to claim creative presence from the margins of local social order, hip-hop suggests an upending of common logics surrounding dance and expression with its downward-driven weightiness, its impossible fragmentation of the body in gestures of robotic precision, and its unlikely earthbound manipulations of directionality. But these dances are also available for those who dance on opera house stages, or participate in market-driven media exercises, such as *So You Think You Can Dance*. Hip-hop carries its markings as "street culture"—creative expression in reference to marginalized, minoritarian life—into venues far removed from its mythic roots.

From the margins, hip-hop dance operates in a persistent present, without regard for its own futurity or capacity as commerce. Dancers engage the corporeal practices of hip-hop to tie their physical pleasure to something immediate and entirely social; dance as a tactic to express and survive, to imagine future sociabilities outside of commodity exchange. In the mainstream, though, hip-hop might be more of a strategy to corral black performance toward its minoritarian boundaries. Over time, hip-hop dance, like jazz musicianship, has become a nearly empty referent to politicized expression that thrives without access to the politicized implications that originally created the form. The aesthetic structures survive, honed by exposure and engagement with ever-expanding publics, but with their relationship to social expression limited by the commercial sphere. Dancers in the mediaplace enjoy limited capacity to inspire social mobility, if only because the media-place requires the possibility for repetition, incessant and public rehearsal, and narratives of predictable, predetermined achievement. Robbed of their potential to register transformation, these dances exist in an eternal place of nostalgia and already-done-ness; audiences enjoy the commitment to dance that these forms demand, but think little of their potential beyond their dispersal as product.

But what of the dancers who engage hip-hop dances within the mediated marketplace in order to achieve social and commodity mobility? Is the expressive capacity of the form necessarily eclipsed by the need for rehearsal and obvious narratives of "overcoming the odds" to arrive as a dancer in the mainstream? Probably. The delta of dance capacity is likely not mediable; it is an experience in time and skin, smell and place, vision and presence. The mediaplace resists, and even denies, the sensates of smell, skin, and presence; but these aspects of performance are bound up with recognition of the dance. Dancers in the mediaplace compromise their engagement with the dance to suit the visual requirements of the simulated dance. Creative innovation does happen here, delimited by the overwhelming need to construct pre-palatable contexts for dance. And when the dance cannot register transformation, it becomes something other than itself: its copy, or maybe just something else.

> The *habitus* is the principle of a selective perception of the indices tending to confirm and reinforce it rather than transform it, a matrix generating responses adapted in advance to all objective conditions identical to or homologous with the (past) conditions of its production; it adjusts itself to a probable future which it anticipates and helps to bring about because it reads it directly in the present of the presumed world, the only one it can ever know.
> —Bourdieu, *The Logic of Practice*, 64

The mass distribution of hip-hop corporealities via media transforms what hip-hop does in the world. Of course these physicalities don't retain their shape or presence across the space and time that media distribution makes possible, and how these ways of being "mean" to groups of people changes rapidly. In general, black social dances distributed by the mediaplace veer toward familiar spectacles of excessive activity and hyperkinetic impossibilities. The three major documentaries dedicated to these modes of dance practice—Mura Dehn's *The Spirit Moves* (released 1986), Jennie Livingston's

Paris Is Burning (1990), and David LaChapelle's *Rize* (2005)—can be characterized by their outside-the-dance attitudes that move from fascination through explication to exploitation. This sequencing mirrors the relationship of black social dances as minoritarian aesthetic practices across historical eras, from the fascination with black structures of feeling associated with civil rights activism (Dehn), through a more ethnographically shaped accounting of black modes of survival in the era of Reagan (Livingston), to the blankly commodity-driven constructions of the millennium (LaChapelle). Surely these three white authors of black-dance mediaplace subjectivity are interested in the teleology of the dances they capture in their films. And yet, the terms of aesthetic achievement represented in these films become undermined through these acts of mediation, to become so easily reduced to the dynamism of the outward shapes of their performance. While the two later documentaries focus on the contextualizing narratives of the lives of dancers of color to some degree, how any single performance resounds for these individuals escapes discussion. Dance becomes a practice that is accessible and repeatable by an absent and unknown (unknowable?) viewer, and in the process, the dance becomes predictable and reducible to the spectacle of its sight. Its power to release unprecedented transformations of energy through performance is tamed by the insensate camera's lens and the process of digital mediation.

When documentarians of black corporeality operate inside the structures they film—as in Israel's *The Freshest Kids: A History of the B-Boy* (2002)—discussions and demonstrations of transformative capacities of dance ensue. To a large degree, the creative team examining hip-hop dance here draws on its layered understanding of the history and trajectory of these ways of moving. Where LaChapelle, Livingston, and Dehn necessarily position themselves outside of the dance cultures they capture, Israel and executive producer Quincy Jones III claim close familiarity with black modes of being. The resulting document arrives as a particular history of the idiom, something of a "how-to" manual coded in the commentary of mature dancers in reflection on how to allow these dances to speak through varying social registers. The film offers evidence of the capacity of these dances to transform in discussions of singular historical events, and the capturing of singular performances not to be repeated or commodified beyond the terms of this DVD representation.

In these films, the place where the dance happens can be artificially constructed. Many phantasmagoric shadow sequences of *The Spirit Moves* were filmed in Dehn's studio; at times, *Rize* and *The Freshest Kids* took dances out of social context in order to effectively capture their contents. This shift of location predicts the displacement of these dances that is reiterated by the circulation of the films themselves. The dances are moved to a "neutral" place to be mediated; the newly minted, mediated corporealities can then be mass-distributed to be reassembled in a fragmentary manner by consumers.

As documentaries, these films place dance among a web of activities and social exchange; filmmakers use the dance as a central "fixing agent" to discuss gender, sexuality, class, location, age, ability, and race. Dance binds the film subjects and offers evidence to understand other dimensions of identity claimed by participants. The place of sex and gender deserves special attention here. While each of these documentary films includes women among its subjects, they spend very little time exploring the place of the feminine within narratives of black social-dance physicality. The feminine exists as a category in *The Spirit Moves* and *Paris Is Burning*, as the space for the partner of male dancers in World War II–era dances, and as the aspirational identity of queens—male and some female—walking the balls in New York in the 1980s. But the hip-hop-inspired movements of *The Freshest Kids* and *Rize* make no distinction that allows an alternative to the aggressive actions inevitably configured as masculine. The feminine here is absorbed by the context of visibly powerful, weighted movements that suggest a blockish, superhero-styled resistance to empathy. While women certainly perform hip-hop dances—Ana Rokafella Garcia's *All The Ladies Say . . .* (2009) features vibrant documentation of these movements—the idiom has been circumscribed by the mediaplace as a masculinist pursuit. Women in hip-hop "man up" to achieve narratives of transcendence; they engage the strength and balance regimes that allow performance of the most flamboyant moves that distinguish hip-hop from other forms of black social dance. And yet, the presence of the feminine is routinely abrogated in discourses of hip-hop physicality.

Rather, hip-hop has become something of a FEMA trailer for youth, a place to congregate and triage amid battles for identity and resources in the world at large. Locked within articulations that deny the human connectivity at the core of black performance—the sensate registration of affect that occurs as part of transformation through performance—hip-hop corporeality stands as a reference to emergent youthful masculinity; a stand-in for individual power and cool; a referent of access to the marginalized, to minoritarian politics through the assumption of its shapes, rhythms, and weightinesses. In the FEMA trailer we can see each other for a moment and recognize our attendant cool poses, our ability to assume the postures of the cool kids, and in that moment access something like group connectivity. Even if we are alone at home with a computer mouse or smartphone in our hand. But then what? And what of the aesthetic imperative of sociability to recognize effort and transformation?

A FEMA trailer indeed, because hip-hop dance in and of itself may be unsustainable as a physical practice. We triage, to recover from the shifting storms of time that predict our changed capacity to approach hip-hop corporealities. We step out from the center of the dance circle, to allow other, more nimble energies, the recognition of placement in the spotlight. Hip-hop in the mediaplace, though, is popular culture creating its own centered spotlight in a vicious feedback loop without the need for provocation from gathered witnesses of the dance.

And yet. Pleasure, and maybe something we can recognize as *Black Joy*, become aspects that are potentially uncommodifiable in this discussion. These dances surely enlarge access to a purposeful fizzy creativity that we could align with a historically situated black joy born within spaces of marginalized resistance and aesthetic innovation. Do we need corporeal orature as a means to recognize this joy? Or could the joy exist outside of its direct recognition as communication? Could the pleasure of engaging these dances allow us access to some globally available (quasi-*universal*) kinetic space, at times outside of commodity exchange? Would this distributed space be aligned with something of the "racial sincerity" that John L. Jackson Jr. theorizes, one that "stresses its excesses, its visible and invisible overflow, the elements of self not totally expressed in social phenotype" (Jackon, *Real Black*, 227)?[11] What might it mean if we were to all dance hip-hop?

Hip-Hop Habitus

The habitus, sociologist Pierre Bourdieu's constructed categories of being that govern actions of the everyday, becomes the place where hip-hop's masculinist qualities are practiced by an international cohort of youth regardless of place, class, gender, race, sexuality, or, in some cases, ability. (We can look to the wheelchair-bound character on television's *Glee* for representation of an impaired youth engaged, at times, in hip-hop physicalities.) Hip-hop corporealities cohere, as in the Rhapsody commercial, to define and perpetuate ways of being. They become orderly, entirely sociable on a blank, repeatable scale that allows their repetition in the mediaplace. The political import of hip-hop corporealities—so central to their emergences on the bodies of youth of color in the years leading up to Reagan's urban America—is displaced and evacuated so that the gestures can become protected patterns of motion produced spontaneously and without reflection. These are the terms of the habitus, that it produces and protects itself without hesitation.

And a physical hesitation in hip-hop would be very uncool.

Notes

Thank you to the Choreography and Corporeality working group of the International Federation for Research in Theatre convened by Philipa Rothfield, to the Princeton reading group organized by Daphne Brooks, to Ian Condry of Comparative Media Studies at MIT, to members of the ASTR working group (2008) organized by Katherine Mezur, and especially to members of the Black Performance Theory working group.

1. "Rhapsody Commercial Cool Kids and Sara Bareilles." Rapmusic.tv.

2. This logical progression follows from the first-generation situated sociological approach of Tricia Rose in *Black Noise*, which valorized hip-hop approaches to creativity as emblematic of life in New York City, followed by a slew of cultural studies renditions of global sites for hip-hop, including *Global Noise: Rap and Hip Hop Outside the USA*, edited by Tony Mitchell, and more specialized studies, such as Ian Condry's *Hip-Hop Japan: Rap and the Paths of Cultural Globalization*.

3. Schloss's subjects disagree on particular narratives of breaking history in terms of who did what where and when; Schloss documents a remarkable circumspection in terms of claiming master origin stories for b-boying among early practitioners of the form.

4. To be sure, Schloss documents testimonial statements about the power of dance to transform aspects of life beyond the dance. But b-boying is depicted essentially as a hobby activity that finds devotees in uneasy, always tension with professional identity; it is dancing as a permanent subaltern status.

5. For an overview of the concept of corporeal orature, see "The Black Beat Made Visible."

6. Performance in Tokyo, Japan; see "Kentaro!! Profile," http://www.kentarock.com/profileeng.html, for an overview of Kentaro's works.

7. Performance in Lyon, France; see "Compagnie Accrorap," http://www.accrorap.com/, for an overview of the company's operations. Photographs of the production can be accessed at http://www.flickr.com/photos/fredbeaubeau/sets/72157622611268104/.

8. Mechanical engineer by day, touring DJ by night, Girl Talk embodies the mythic "everyman" persona as an ultimate unlikely cool kid.

9. Schloss details ways that breakers are deemed inappropriate or poorly prepared for battling; still, according to his interview subjects, space is invariably made in b-boy ciphers for participation by all.

10. This analysis differs mightily from Schloss's conclusions. In that study, b-boys are quick to police the boundaries of acceptable or tasteful dance practice.

11. In my reading, Jackson's articulations of racial authenticity and sincerity line up with global b-boy and b-girl desires to authenticate the dance and its history even as it moves further and further from its originating aesthetic capacities and social purposes.

BIBLIOGRAPHY

"Abercrombie's 'Look Policy' under Fire." CBSNews.com, June 24, 2009. http://www
.cbsnews.com/stories/2009/06/24/business/main5109462.shtml?tag=topnews.

Adorno, Theodor W. "On the Commentary Relationship of Philosophy and Music."
In *Essays on Music: Selected, with Introduction, Commentary, and Notes by Richard
Leppert*, edited by Richard Leppert, translated by Susan H. Gillespie, 135–61.
Berkeley: University of California Press, 2002.

Agamben, Giorgio. *The Coming Community*. Theory out of Bounds. Vol. 1. Minneapolis: University of Minnesota Press, 1993.

Alexander, Elizabeth. "'Can You Be BLACK and Look at This?': Reading the Rodney
King Video(s)." In *Black Male: Representations of Masculinity in Contemporary
American Art*, edited by Thelma Golden, 91–110. New York: Whitney Museum of
American Art, 1994.

Allen, James, John Lewis, Leon F. Litwack, and Hilton Als. *Without Sanctuary: Lynching Photography in America*. Santa Fe, NM: Twin Palms, 2000.

Althusser, Louis. "Ideology and Ideological State Apparatuses." In *Lenin and Philosophy and Other Essays*, 127–86. New York: Monthly Review, 1971.

Amazing Grace. Stan Lathan, director. MGM Pictures, 1974.

Anbinder, Tyler. *Five Points: The Nineteenth-Century New York City Neighborhood
That Invented Tap Dance, Stole Elections, and Became the World's Most Notorious
Slum*. New York: Penguin Books, 2002.

Anderson, Chris. *The Long Tail*. New York: Hyperion Books, 2006.

Appiah, Kwame Anthony. *The Ethics of Identity*. Princeton, NJ: Princeton University
Press, 2005.

Atkinson, Michael. *Ghosts in the Machine: The Dark Heart of Pop Cinema*. New York:
Proscenium, 2004.

Attali, Jacques. "Noise and Politics." In *Audio Culture: Readings in Modern Music*,
edited by Christoph Cox and Daniel Warner, 7–9. New York: Continuum, 2006.

Awkward, Michael. "'Unruly and Let Loose': Myth, Ideology, and Gender in *Song of
Solomon*." *Callaloo* 13, no. 3 (1990): 482–98.

Badejo, Diedre. *Oshun Séégesi, the Elegant Deity of Wealth, Power and Femininity*.
Trenton, NJ: Africa World Press, 1996.

Baker, Houston A., Jr. *Blues, Ideology, and Afro-American Literature: A Vernacular
Theory*. Chicago: University of Chicago Press, 1984.

Baldwin, James. *The Fire Next Time*. New York: Vintage International, [1963] 1991.

———. "Notes of a Native Son." In *The Art of the Personal Essay: An Anthology from the Classical Era to the Present*, edited by Phillip Lopate, 587–603. New York: Anchor, 1997.

Barker, Andrew. "Jackson's Talent Alive and Well in *This Is It*." *Variety* 416, no. 12 (November 2–8, 2009): 64.

Baron, Zach. "*This Is It*: Michael Jackson Goes Out with a Whimper." *Miami New Times*, November 5, 2009.

Barthes, Roland. "The Grain of the Voice." In *Image, Music, Text*, translated by Stephen Heath, 179–89. New York: Hill, 1977.

Bartlett, Andrew. "Airshafts, Loudspeakers, and the Hip Hop Sample: Contexts and African American Musical Aesthetic." *African American Review* 28, no. 4 (1994): 639–52.

"BART Police Shoot and Kill Man at Fruitvale BART Station: Indybay." *San Francisco Bay Area Independent Media Center*. Indymedia, the San Francisco Bay Area Independent Media Center, January 3, 2009. http://www.indybay.org/newsitems/2009/01/03/18558098.php.

Bataille, Georges. *The Accursed Share*. Vol. 1: *Consumption*. New York: Zone Books, 1989.

Batiste, Stephanie Leigh. *Darkening Mirrors: Imperial Representation in Depression-Era African American Performance*. Durham, NC: Duke University Press, 2011.

Bean, Annemarie, James V. Hatch, and Brooks McNamara, eds. *Inside the Minstrel Mask: Readings in Nineteenth-Century Blackface Minstrelsy*. Hanover, NH: Wesleyan University Press, 1996.

Bederman, Gail. *Manliness and Civilization: A Cultural History of Gender and Race in the United States, 1880–1917*. Chicago: University of Chicago Press, 1995.

Belchem, John. "Comment: Whiteness and the Liverpool-Irish." *Journal of British Studies* 44, no. 1 (2005): 146–52.

Benhabib, Seyla. *Critique, Norm, and Utopia: A Study of the Foundations of Critical Theory*. New York: Columbia University Press, 1986.

Berger, Arion. "Yoko Ono." In *Trouble Girls: The Rolling Stone Book of Women in Rock*, edited by Barbara O'Dair. New York: Random House, 1997.

Bernstein, Nina. "City of Immigrants Fills Jail Cells with Its Own." *New York Times*, January 1, 2012. http://www.nytimes.com/2008/12/27/us/27detain.html?_r=1.

Bessire, Aimée. "Iké Udé's Beyond Decorum: The Poetics and Politics of Fashionable Selves." In *Beyond Decorum: The Photography of Iké Udé*, edited by Mark H. C. Bessire and Lauri Firstenberg, 8–9. Cambridge, MA: MIT Press, 2000.

Best, Stephen. *The Fugitive's Properties: Law and the Poetics of Possession*. Chicago: University of Chicago Press, 2004.

Biskind, Peter. "The Last of Heath." *Vanity Fair* 51, no. 8 (August 2009). http://www.vanityfair.com/culture/features/2009/08/heath-ledger200908.

Blake, Susan L. "Folklore and Community in *Song of Solomon*." *MELUS* 7, no. 3 (1980): 77–82.

Boggs, Nicholas. "A Grammar of Little Manhood: Ralph Ellison and the Queer Little Man at Chehaw Station." *Callaloo* 35, no. 1 (2012): 245–66.

Bourdieu, Pierre. *The Logic of Practice.* Translated by Richard Nice. Stanford, CA: Stanford University Press, 1990.

Bowles, Scott. "The Biggest Concert Film of All Time: *This Is It*; Jackson's $101M Surpasses Cyrus." *USA Today,* November 2, 2009, D1.

Bradley, Ben. "29 People Shot over Weekend, at Least 6 Killed." ABCNews WLS Chicago, April 20, 2001. http://abclocal.go.com/wls/story?section=news/local&id =6091348.

Bridges, Flora W. *Resurrection Song: African-American Spirituality.* Maryknoll, NY: Orbis Books, 2001.

Brody, Jennifer DeVere. "The Blackness of Blackness . . . Reading the Typography of *Invisible Man*." *Theatre Journal* 57 (2005): 679–98.

———. *Punctuation: Art, Politics, and Play.* Durham, NC: Duke University Press, 2008.

Brooks, Daphne A. "'Bring the Pain': Post-soul Memory, Neo-soul Affect, and Lauryn Hill in the Black Public Sphere." In *Taking It to the Bridge: Music as Performance,* edited by Nicholas Cook and Richard Pettengill. Ann Arbor: University of Michigan Press, 2013.

Brown, Jayna. *Babylon Girls: Black Women Performers and the Shaping of the Modern.* Durham, NC: Duke University Press, 2008.

Burnard, Trevor. "'Do Thou in Gentle Phibia Smile': Scenes from an Interracial Marriage, Jamaica, 1754–86." In *Beyond Bondage: Free Women of Color in the Americas,* edited by David Barry Gaspar and Darlene Clarke Hine. Urbana: University of Illinois Press, 2004.

Burns, Sean. "*This Is It*." *Philadelphia Weekly,* November 4–10, 2009, 52.

Cabezas, Amalia L. "Discourses of Prostitution: The Case of Cuba." In *Global Sex Workers: Rights, Resistance, and Redefinition,* edited by Kamala Kempadoo and J. Doezema. New York: Routledge, 1998.

———. *Economies of Desire: Sex and Tourism in Cuba and the Dominican Republic.* Philadelphia: Temple University Press, 2009.

———. "On the Border of Love and Money: Sex and Tourism in Cuba and the Dominican Republic." In *Labor versus Empire: Race, Gender, and Migration,* edited by Gilbert G. Gonzalez, Raul A. Fernandez, Vivian Price, David Smith, and Linda Trinh Vo. New York: Routledge, 2004.

Cabrera, Lydia. *Yemayá y Ochún.* Madrid: C.R., 1974.

Carey, H. C., and I. Lea. *Map of the District of the Columbia, 1822.* Digital image. David Rumsey. http://www.davidrumsey.com/luna/servlet/detail/RUMSEY~8~1~7 42~70016:Geographical,-Historical,-And-Stati.

Carroll, Patrick J. *Blacks in Colonial Veracruz: Race, Ethnicity and Regional Development.* Austin: University of Texas Press, 1991.

Cashmere, Paul. "Interview: Sandrine Orabona, Videographer for *This Is It*." Undercover.com, November 2009. http://www.undercover.com.au.

Castillo Gómez, Amranta Arcadia. "Los estereotipos y las relaciones interétnicas en la Costa Chica oaxaqueña." *Revista Mexicana de Ciencias Políticas y Sociales* 46, nos. 188–89 (2003): 267–90.

Catanese, Brandi Wilkins. *The Problem of the Color[blind]: Racial Transgression and the Politics of Black Performance.* Detroit: University of Michigan Press, 2011.

Chasteen, John Charles. "A National Rhythm: Social Dance and Elite Identity in Nineteenth-Century Havana." *Critical Studies: Music, Popular Culture, Identities* 19, no. 1 (August 2002): 55–73.

Chatterjea, Ananya. *Butting Out: Reading Resistive Choreographies through Works by Jawole Willa Jo Zollar and Chandralekha.* Middletown, CT: Wesleyan University Press, 2004.

Chude-Sokei, Louis. *The Last "Darky": Bert Williams, Black-on-Black Minstrelsy, and the African Diaspora.* Durham, NC: Duke University Press, 2006.

Clarke, Kamari Maxine, and Deborah Thomas, eds. *Globalization and Race: Transformation in the Cultural Production of Blackness.* Durham, NC: Duke University Press, 2006.

Cocuzza, Dominique. "The Dress of Free Women of Color in New Orleans, 1790–1840." *Dress* 27 (2000): 78–87.

Colbert, Soyica Diggs. *The African American Theatrical Body: Reception, Performance, and the Stage.* Cambridge: Cambridge University Press, 2011.

Colbert, Stephen, et al. "Debra Dickerson." colbertnation.com, February 8, 2007. http://www.colbertnation.com/the-colbert-report-videos/81955/february-08-2007/debra-dickerson.

Condry, Ian. *Hip-Hop Japan: Rap and the Paths of Cultural Globalization.* Durham, NC: Duke University Press, 2006.

Conquergood, Dwight. "Lethal Theatre: Performance, Punishment, and the Death Penalty." *Theatre Journal* 54, no. 3 (2002): 339–67.

———. "Rethinking Elocution: The Trope of the Talking Book and Other Figures of Speech." In *Opening Acts: Performance in/as Communication and Cultural Studies,* edited by Judith Hamera, 141–62. Thousand Oaks, CA: Sage, 2006.

Cook, Raymond Allen. *Fire from the Flint: The Amazing Careers of Thomas Dixon.* Winston-Salem, NC: J. F. Blair, 1968.

Corbett, John. *Extended Play: Sounding Off from John Cage to Dr. Funkenstein.* Durham, NC: Duke University Press, 1994.

Crazy Horse, Kandia. *Rip It Up: The Black Experience in Rock 'N' Roll.* New York: Palgrave, 2004.

Cripps, Thomas. *Slow Fade to Black: The Negro in American Film, 1900–1940.* New York: Oxford University Press, 1977.

Cruz Carretero, Sagrario, Alfredo Martínez Maranto, and Angélica Santiago Silva. *El Carnaval en Yanga: Notas y comentarios sobre una fiesta de la negritud.* Mexico City: Consejo Nacional para la Cultura y las Artes, 1990.

Cunard, Nancy, ed. *Negro: An Anthology.* London: Wishart, 1934.

Curtis, L. Perry, Jr. *Apes and Angels: The Irishman in Victorian Caricature.* Washington, DC: Smithsonian Institution Press, 1971.

Dagan, Esther A., ed. *The Spirit's Dance in Africa: Evolution, Transformation and Continuity in Sub-Sahara*. Westmount, QC, Canada: Galerie Amrad African Arts Publications, 1997.

Daniel, Yvonne. *Dancing Wisdom: Embodied Knowledge in Haitian Vodou, Cuban Yoruba, and Bahian Candomblé*. Chicago: University of Illinois Press, 2005.

———. *Rumba: Dance and Social Change in Contemporary Cuba*. Bloomington: Indiana University Press, 1995.

Davis, Tracy C., and Thomas Postlewait, eds. *Theatricality*. New York: Cambridge University Press, 2003.

de Certeau, Michel. *The Practice of Everyday Life*. Translated by Steven Rendall. Berkeley: University of California Press, 1984.

DeFrantz, Thomas F. "The Black Beat Made Visible: Hip Hop Dance and Body Power." In *Of the Presence of the Body: Essays on Dance and Performance Theory*, edited by André Lepecki, 64–81. Middletown, CT: Wesleyan University Press, 2004.

———. "Foreword: Black Bodies Dancing Black Culture—Black Atlantic Transformations." In *Embodying Liberation: The Black Body in American Dance*, edited by Dorothea Fischer-Hornung and Alison D. Goeller, 11–16. Piscataway, NJ: Transaction, Rutgers University, 2001.

Deleuze, Gilles, and Félix Guattari. *Anti-Oedipus: Capitalism and Schizophrenia*. Translated by Robert Hurley, Mark Seem, and Helen R. Lane. Minneapolis: University of Minnesota Press, 1983.

Derrida, Jacques. "The Law of Genre." *Critical Inquiry* 7, no. 1 (1980): 55–81.

Dery, Mark. "Black to the Future: Interviews with Samuel R. Delany, Greg Tate, and Tricia Rose." *South Atlantic Quarterly* 92, no. 4 (1992): 735–38.

Diamond, Elin. *Unmaking Mimesis: Essays on Feminism and Theater*. London: Routledge, 1997.

Douglass, Frederick. *Narrative of the Life of Frederick Douglass*. New York: Signet, 1968.

Dray, Philip. *"At the Hands of Persons Unknown": The Lynching of Black America*. New York: Random House, 2002.

Dr. Dre. *The Chronic*. Interscope Records, 1992.

Dubey, Madhu. *Signs and Cities: Black Literary Postmodernism*. Chicago: University of Chicago Press, 2003.

Duffy, Damian, and John Jennings. *The Hole: Consumer Culture*. Vol. 1. New York: Front Forty Press, 2008.

Early, Gerald Lyn. *One Nation under a Groove: Motown and American Culture*. Revised and expanded ed. Ann Arbor: University of Michigan Press, 2004.

Ebert, Roger. "Jackson's *This Is It* a Fitting Finale." *Chicago Sun Times*, October 30, 2009.

Ebner, Mark. *Six Degrees of Paris Hilton: Inside the Sex Tapes, Scandals, and Shakedowns of the New Hollywood*. New York: Simon Spotlight Entertainment, 2009.

Eckholm, Erik. "Murders by Black Teenagers Rise, Bucking a Trend." *New York Times*, December 29, 2008. http://www.nytimes.com/2008/12/29/us/29homicide.html?_r=1.

Edwards, Brent Hayes. "Introduction." *Callaloo* 25, no. 1 (2002): 5–7.

———. "The Uses of *Diaspora*." *Social Text* 19, no. 1 (2001): 45–73.

Eidsheim, Nina. "Marian Anderson and 'Sonic Blackness' in American Opera." *American Quarterly* 63, no. 3 (2011): 663–64.

Elam, Harry Justin, and David Krasner, eds. *African-American Performance and Theater History: A Critical Reader*. New York: Oxford University Press, 2001.

Ellison, Ralph. *Invisible Man*. New York, Vintage, 1980.

———. "The Little Man at Chehaw Station: The American Artist and His Audience." *American Scholar* 47, no. 1 (winter 1978): 25–48.

Emery, Lynne Fauley. *Black Dance from 1619 to Today*. Palo Alto, CA: National Press Books, 1972.

English, Daylanne. *Unnatural Selections: Eugenics in American Modernism and the Harlem Renaissance*. Chapel Hill: University of North Carolina Press, 2004.

Eribon, Didier. *Insult and the Making of the Gay Self*. Translated by Michael Lucey. Durham, NC: Duke University Press, 2004.

Eshun, Kodwo. *More Brilliant than the Sun: Adventures in Sonic Fiction*. London: Quartet Books, 1999.

Esquerita. *Sock It to Me Baby*. Bear Family Records, Vollersode, Germany, 1989.

Everett, Anna. "Lester Walton's *Écriture Noir*: Black Spectatorial Transcodings of 'Cinematic Excess.'" *Cinema Journal* 39, no. 3 (spring 2000): 30–50.

Fanon, Frantz. *Black Skin, White Masks*. Translated by Charles Markmann. New York: Grove, 1967.

———. *The Wretched of the Earth*. Translated by Richard Philcox. New York: Grove, 2004.

Fielding-Stewart, Carlyle, III. *Black Spirituality and Black Consciousness*. Trenton, NJ: Africa World Press, 1999.

Fischer-Lichte, Erika. *The Semiotics of Theater*. Edited and translated by Jeremy Gaines and Doris L. Jones. Indianapolis: Indiana University Press, 1992.

Fisher, Mark. "Michael Jackson's This Is It." *Sight and Sound* 20, no. 1 (January 2010): 66–67.

Foner, Eric. *A Short History of Reconstruction*. New York: Harper Perennial, 1990.

Foster, Susan L. "Choreographies of Gender." *Signs* 24, no. 1 (1998): 1–33.

———. *Reading Dancing: Bodies and Subjects in Contemporary American Dance*. Berkeley: University of California Press, 1986.

Foster, Thomas. *The Souls of Cyberfolk: Posthumanism as Vernacular Theory*. Minneapolis: University of Minnesota Press, 2005.

Fox, Aaron. *Real Country: Music and Language in Working-Class Culture*. Durham, NC: Duke University Press, 2004.

Freud, Sigmund. "On Narcissism: An Introduction." Translated by James Strachey. *The Standard Edition of the Complete Psychological Works of Sigmund Freud*, vol. 14, 67–104. London: Hogarth, 1914.

Fritz, Ben. "'*This Is It*' as His Personal Thriller; Commercial Director Tim Patterson Can Savor His Start-to-Finish Role in Making the Film on Michael Jackson." *Los Angeles Times*, November 3, 2009, D1.

Fryer, Peter. *Staying Power: The History of Black People in Britain*. London: Pluto, 2010.

Fusco, Coco. "Hustling for Dollars: Jineterismo in Cuba." In *Global Sex Workers: Rights, Resistance, and Redefinition*, edited by Kamala Kempadoo and Jo Doezema. New York: Routledge, 1998.

Garland-Thomson, Rosemarie. *Staring: How We Look*. New York: Oxford University Press, 2009.

Gaspar, David Barry, and Darlene Clarke Hine, eds. *Beyond Bondage: Free Women of Color in the Americas*. Urbana: University of Illinois Press, 2004.

Gates, Henry Louis, Jr. *The Signifying Monkey: A Theory of African-American Literary Criticism*. New York: Oxford University Press, 1989.

———. "The Trope of a New Negro and the Reconstruction of the Image of the Black." *Representations* 24 (fall 1998): 129–51.

Gates, Racquel. "Reclaiming the Freak: Michael Jackson and the Spectacle of Identity." *Velvet Light Trap* 65 (April 1, 2010): 3.

Gilmore, Glenda. *Gender and Jim Crow: Women and the Politics of White Supremacy in North Carolina, 1896–1920*. Chapel Hill: University of North Carolina Press, 1996.

Gilroy, Paul. *Against Race: Imagining Political Culture Beyond the Color Line*. Cambridge, MA: Harvard University Press, 2000.

———. *The Black Atlantic: Modernity and Double Consciousness*. Cambridge, MA: Harvard University Press, 1993.

———. "Wearing Your Art on Your Sleeve: Notes toward a Diaspora of Black Ephemera." In *Small Acts: Thoughts on the Politics of Black Cultures*, 237–57. London: Serpent's Tale, 1993.

Gladwell, Malcolm. "The Science of the Sleeper." *New Yorker* 75, no. 29 (October 4, 1999): 48.

———. *The Tipping Point: How Little Things Can Make a Big Difference*. New York: Back Bay Books, 2000.

Goffman, Erving. *Stigma: Notes on the Management of Spoiled Identity*. Englewood Cliffs, NJ: Prentice-Hall, 1963.

Gomez, Michael A. *Exchanging Our Country Marks: The Transformation of African Identities in the Colonial and Antebellum South*. Chapel Hill: University of North Carolina Press, 1998.

Gonzalez, Gilbert G., Raul A. Fernandez, Vivian Price, David Smith, and Linda Trinh Vo, eds. *Labor versus Empire: Race, Gender, and Migration*. New York: Routledge, 2004.

González, Reynaldo. *Contradanzas y Latigazos*. Havana, Cuba: Letras Cubanas, 1983.

Gonzales-Day, Ken. *Lynching in the West, 1850–1935*. Durham, NC: Duke University Press, 2006.

Gordon, Avery F. *Ghostly Matters: Haunting and the Sociological Imagination*. Minneapolis: University of Minnesota Press, 1997.

Gottschild, Brenda Dixon. *The Black Dancing Body: A Geography from Coon to Cool*. New York: Palgrave Macmillan, 2003.

———. *Digging the Africanist Presence in American Performance: Dance and Other Contexts*. Westport, CT: Praeger, 1996.

Griffin, Farah Jasmine. "When Malindy Sings: A Meditation on Black Women's Vocality." In *Uptown Conversation: The New Jazz Studies*, edited by Brent Hayes Edwards, Farah Jasmine Griffin, and Robert G. O'Meally, 102–25. New York: Columbia University Press, 2004.

Grimké, Angelina Weld. "'Rachel' The Play of the Month: Reason and Synopsis by the Author" [1920]. In *Lost Plays of the Harlem Renaissance*, edited by James V. Hatch and Leo Hamalian, 424–26. Detroit, MI: Wayne State University Press, 1996.

Guevara, Gema R. "Inexacting Whiteness: Blanqueamiento as a Gender-Specific Trope in the Nineteenth Century." *Cuban Studies* 36 (December 2005): 105–28.

Guevara Sanginés, Maria. "Guanajuato colonial y los Afroguanajuatenses." In *Memoria del III Encuentro Nacional de Afromexicanistas*, edited by Luz Maria Martínez Montiel and Juan Carlos Reyes G. Colima: Consejo Nacional para la Cultura y las Artes, 1993.

Guillory, Monique. "Some Enchanted Evening on the Auction Block: Quadroon Balls of New Orleans." PhD dissertation, New York University, 1999.

———. "Under One Roof: The Sins and Sanctity of the New Orleans Quadroon Balls." In *Race Consciousness: African-American Studies for the New Century*, edited by Judith Jackson Fossett and Jeffrey A. Tucker, 67–92. New York: New York University Press, 1997.

Guins, Raiford, and Omayra Zaragoza Cruz. "Prosthetists at 33 1/3." In *The Prosthetic Impulse: From a Posthuman Present to a Biocultural Future*, edited by Marquard Smith and Joanne Morra, 221–36. Cambridge, MA: MIT Press, 2006.

Gunning, Sandra. *Race, Rape, and Lynching: The Red Record of American Literature, 1890–1912*. New York: Oxford University Press, 1996.

Hall, Jacquelyn Dowd. "'The Mind That Burns in Each Body': Women, Rape, and Racial Violence." In *Powers of Desire: The Politics of Sexuality*, edited by Ann Snitow, Christine Stansell, and Sharon Thompson, 328–49. New York: Monthly Review Press, 1983.

Hamilton, Marybeth. "Sexual Politics and African-American Music; or, Placing Little Richard in History." *History Workshop Journal* 46 (1998): 161–76.

Hanger, Kimberly S. *Bounded Lives, Bounded Places: Free Black Society in Colonial New Orleans, 1769–1803*. Durham, NC: Duke University Press, 1997.

———. "'Desiring Total Tranquility' and Not Getting It: Conflict Involving Free Black Women in Spanish New Orleans." *Americas* 54 (April 4, 1998): 541–56.

Harris, A. Leslie. "Myth as Structure in Toni Morrison's *Song of Solomon*." MELUS 7, no. 3 (1980): 69–76.

Harris, Trudier. *Exorcising Blackness: Historical and Literary Lynching and Burning Rituals*. Bloomington: Indiana University Press, 1984.

Hartman, Saidiya. *Lose Your Mother: A Journey along the Atlantic Slave Route*. New York: Farrar, Straus and Giroux, 2007.

———. *Scenes of Subjection: Terror, Slavery and Self-Making in Nineteenth-Century America*. Oxford: Oxford University Press, 1997.

Hazard, Samuel. *Cuba in Pen and Pencil*. Hartford, CT: Hartford Publishing Company, 1871.

Hazzard-Donald, Katrina. "Dance in Hip Hop Culture." In *Droppin' Science: Critical Essays on Rap Music and Hip Hop Culture*, edited by William Eric Perkins, 220–35. Philadelphia: Temple University Press, 1996.

Hebdige, Dick. *Subculture: The Meaning of Style*. New York: Routledge, 1979.

Heidegger, Martin. *Basic Writings*. Edited by David Farrell Krell. New York: HarperCollins, 1993.

———. *Being and Time*. Translated by John Macquarrie and Edward Robinson. New York: Harper, 1962.

Henderson, Mae Gwendolyn. "Speaking in Tongues: Dialogics, Dialectics, and the Black Woman Writer's Literary Tradition." In *Reading Black, Reading Feminist: A Critical Anthology*, edited by Henry Louis Gates Jr., 116–42. New York: Meridian, 1990.

Hill, Errol G., and James Hatch. *A History of African American Theatre*. Cambridge: Cambridge University Press, 2003.

Hisama, Ellie M. "Voice, Race, and Sexuality in the Music of Joan Armatrading." In *Audible Traces: Gender, Identity, and Music*, edited by Elaine Barkin and Lydia Hamessley, 115–32. Zurich: Carciofoli Verlagshaus, 1999.

"HIV among African Americans." Department of Health and Human Services, Centers for Disease Control, November 8, 2011. http://www.cdc.gov/hiv/topics/aa/resources/factsheets/aa.htm.

Honeycutt, Kirk. "This Is It." *Hollywood Reporter* 412 (October 29, 2009): 20.

Hopkins, Pauline. *Contending Forces: A Romance Illustrative of Negro Life North and South*. 1900. New York: Oxford University Press, 1988.

———. "Of One Blood, or The Hidden Self." In *The Magazine Novels of Pauline Hopkins*, edited by Hazel Carby. New York: Oxford University Press, 1988.

———. "Prospectus of the New Romance of Colored Life, *Contending Forces*." *Colored American Magazine* 1, no. 4 (September 1900): n.p.

Horkheimer, Max, and Theodor W. Adorno. *Dialectic of Enlightenment*. London: Verso, 1997.

Hughes, Langston, and Arna Bontemps. "All God's Chillen Had Wings." In *The Book of Negro Folklore*, edited by Langston Hughes and Arna Bontemps, 62–65. New York: Dodd, Mead, 1958.

Hull, Gloria T. *Color, Sex, and Poetry: Three Women Writers of the Harlem Renaissance*. Bloomington: Indiana University Press, 1987.

Huntington, Carla Stalling. *Hip Hop Dance: Meanings and Messages*. Jefferson, NC: McFarland, 2007.

Hurston, Zora Neale. "Characteristics of Negro Expression." In *Negro: An Anthology*, edited by Nancy Cunard, 8–46. London: Wishart, 1934.

Ignatiev, Noel. *How the Irish Became White*. New York: Routledge, 1995.

Jackson, Blair. "'Michael Jackson's This Is It'." *Mix* 33, no. 12 (December 2009): 42.

"Jackson Concert Film in the Works." BBCNews, August 6, 2009. http://news.bbc.co.uk/2/hi/8186995.stm.

Jackson, John L., Jr. *Real Black: Adventures in Racial Sincerity*. Chicago: University of Chicago Press, 2005.

Jackson, Kennell. "Introduction: Traveling While Black." In *Black Cultural Traffic: Crossroads in Global Performance and Popular Culture*, edited by Harry J. Elam Jr. and Kennell Jackson, 1–42. Ann Arbor: University of Michigan Press, 2005.

Jackson, Michael. "My Childhood, My Sabbath, My Freedom." Beliefnet.com, December 2000. http://www.beliefnet.com/Faiths/2000/12/My-Childhood-My -Sabbath-My-Freedom.aspx.

Jiménez Román, Miriam. "Mexico's Third Root." In *Africa's Legacy in Mexico: Photographs by Tony Gleaton*, edited by the Smithsonian Institution. Washington, DC: Smithsonian Institution, 1993.

Johnson, E. Patrick. *Appropriating Blackness: Performance and the Politics of Authenticity*. Durham, NC: Duke University Press, 2003.

———. "Black Performance Studies: Genealogies, Politics, Futures." In *The Sage Handbook of Performance Studies*, edited by D. Soyini Madison and Judith Hamera, 446–63. Thousand Oaks, CA: Sage, 2006.

Johnson, E. Patrick, and Mae G. Henderson, eds. *Black Queer Studies: A Critical Anthology*. Durham, NC: Duke University Press, 2005.

Jones, Gayl. *Corregidora*. New York: Random House, 1975.

———. *Liberating Voices: Oral Tradition in African American Literature*. Cambridge, MA: Harvard University Press, 1991.

Jones, LeRoi. "The Revolutionary Theatre." In *Home: Social Essays*, 210–15. New York: William Morrow, 1966.

Jones, Meta Du Ewa. "Jazz Prosodies: Orality and Textuality." *Callaloo* 25, no. 1 (2002): 66–91.

Jones, Omi Osun (Joni L.), Lisa L. Moore, and Sharon Bridgforth, eds. *Experiments in a Jazz Aesthetic: Art, Activism, Academia, and the Austin Project*. Austin: University of Texas Press, 2010.

Jones, Steve. "Michael Jackson's 'This Is It': Consensus Is 'It's Not Bad.'" *Miami Times*, 87, no. 8 (October 21–27, 2009): 1C.

Kelley, Norman. *R&B, Rhythm and Business: The Political Economy of Black Music*. New York: Akashic, 2002.

Kempadoo, Kamala, and J. Doezema, eds. *Global Sex Workers: Rights, Resistance, and Redefinition*. New York: Routledge, 1998.

Kennedy, Adrienne. *Funnyhouse of a Negro*. In *Black Theatre USA: Plays by African Americans from 1847 to Today*, vol. 2, edited by James V. Hatch and Ted Shine. New York: Free Press, 1996.

Kerr, Paulette A. "Victims or Strategists? Female Lodging-House Keepers in Jamaica." In *Engendering History: Caribbean Women in Historical Perspective*, edited by Verene Shepard, Bridget Brereton, and Barbara Bailey. New York: St. Martin's, 1995.

King, Jason. "Form and Function: Superstardom and Aesthetics in the Music Videos of Michael and Janet Jackson." *Velvet Light Trap* 44 (1999): 80–96.

Kiviat, Barbara. "10 Questions for Kanye West." *Time*, December 20, 2004. http:// content.time.com/time/magazine/article/0,9171,1009743,00.html.

Knight, Arthur. *Disintegrating the Musical: Black Performance and American Musical Film*. Durham, NC: Duke University Press, 2002.

Knowles, Ric. *Reading the Material Theatre*. Cambridge: Cambridge University Press, 2004.

Kristeva, Julia. *Desire in Language: A Semiotic Approach to Literature and Art*. New York: Columbia University Press, 1980.

Kutzinski, Vera M. *Sugar's Secrets: Race and the Erotics of Cuban Nationalism*. Charlottesville: University Press of Virginia, 1993.

Lane, Jill Meredith. *Blackface Cuba, 1840–1895*. Philadelphia: University of Pennsylvania Press, 2005.

Last Waltz, The. Martin Scorsese, director. MGM Pictures, 2002.

Lawal, Babatunde. "The African Heritage of African American Art." In *Black Theatre: Ritual Performance in the African Diaspora*, edited by Paul Carter Harrison, Victor Leo Walker II, and Gus Edwards, 39–63. Philadelphia: Temple University Press, 2002.

Lee, Chris. "For Michael, 'This Is It' Had Many Meanings." *Gainesville Sun*, October 29, 2009.

Lee, Dorothy H. "Song of Solomon: To Ride the Air." *Black American Literature Forum* 16, no. 2 (1982): 64–70.

Leppert, Richard. "Commentary." In *Essays on Music: Selected, with Introduction, Commentary, and Notes by Richard Leppert*, by Theodor W. Adorno, edited by Richard Leppert, translated by Susan H. Gillespie. Berkeley: University of California Press, 2002.

Leroy, Dan. "MF Doom." allmusic.com. http://www.allmusic.com/cg/amg.dll?p=amg&searchlink=MF|DOOM&sql=11:wifixq9jld6e~T1.

Levin, Alan. "Experience Averts Tragedy in Hudson Landing." *USA Today*, June 8, 2008. http://www.usatoday.com/news/nation/2009-06-08-hudson_N.htm.

Levine, Lawrence W. *Black Culture and Black Consciousness*. New York: Oxford University Press, 1978.

Lewis, Julinda. "Reggie Wilson's Fist and Heel Performance Group: DTW's Bessie Schonberg Theater." *Dance Magazine*, February 9–12, 1995, 67.

Lewis, Theophilus. "Survey of the Negro Theater—Ill." *Messenger*, October 8, 1926, 301–2.

Lhamon, W. T. *Deliberate Speed: The Origins of a Cultural Style in the American 1950s*. Washington, DC: Smithsonian Institution Press, 1990.

Li, Stephanie. "Resistance, Silence and Placées: Charles Bon's Octoroon Mistress and Louisa Picquet." *American Literature* 79, no. 1 (2007): 85–112.

Light, Alan. "The Resurrection of Michael Jackson: How 'This Is It' Restores an Icon's Magic." msn.com, 2009. http://music.msn.com/music/article.aspx?news=453340.

Lincoln, Eric, and Lawrence H. Mamiya. *The Black Church in the African American Experience*. Durham, NC: Duke University Press, 1990.

Lindfors, Bernth. *Ira Aldridge: The African Roscius*. Rochester Studies in African History and the Diaspora. Rochester, NY: University of Rochester Press, 2007.

Little Richard. *The Specialty Sessions*. Audio CD. Specialty, 1989.

Logan, Rayford. *The Betrayal of the Negro*. 1965. New York: Da Capo, 1997.

Lomax, Alan. *Negro Folk Songs as Sung by Lead Belly*. New York: Macmillan, 1936.

Longworth, Karina. "Trash Humpers at NYFF." 2009. http://blog.spout.com/2009/10/02/trash-humpers-at-nyff.

Lordi, Emily. *Black Resonance: Iconic Women Singers and African American Literature*. New Brunswick, NJ: Rutgers University Press, 2013.

Lott, Eric. "Blackface and Blackness: The Minstrel Show in American Culture." In *Inside the Minstrel Mask: Readings in Nineteeth-Century Blackface Minstrelsy*, edited by Annemarie Bean, James Hatch, and Brooks McNamara, 3–32. Hanover, NH: Wesleyan University Press, 1996.

——. *Love and Theft: Blackface Minstrelsy and the American Working Class*. New York: Oxford University Press, 1993.

MacGregor C., José Antonio, and Carlos Enrique García Martínez. "La negritud en Queretaro." In *Memoria del III Encuentro Nacional de Afromexicanistas*. Colima: Consejo Nacional para la Cultura y las Artes, 1993.

Mackey, Nathaniel. *Paracritical Hinge: Essays, Talks, Notes, Interviews*. Madison: University of Wisconsin Press, 2005.

Madison, D. Soyini. "The Labor of Reflexivity." *Cultural Studies↔Critical Methodologies* 11, no. 2 (2011): 129–38.

——. "Performing Theory/Embodied Writing." *Text and Performance Quarterly* 19, no. 2 (April 1999): 107–24.

"Mahalia Jackson Sings: Rouses Town Hall Audience to a Cheering Fervor." *New York Times*, December 23, 1957.

Mahon, Maureen. *Right to Rock: The Black Rock Coalition and the Cultural Politics of Race*. Durham, NC: Duke University Press, 2004.

Marcus, Greil. *Lipstick Traces: A Secret History of the Twentieth Century*. Cambridge, MA: Harvard University Press, 1989.

Margolick, David. *Strange Fruit: The Biography of a Song*. New York: Ecco, 2001.

"Marian Anderson in Closing Recital; 'Divinites du Styx' Offered in Program Presented at Carnegie Hall." *New York Times*, May 13, 1937.

Marlantes, Liz. "Could an Inexperienced Pilot Put You at Risk?" ABCNews.com, February 2, 2008. http://abcnews.go.com/GMA/BusinessTravel/story?id=4232878.

Marshall, Emily Zobel. "From Messenger of the Gods to Muse of the People: The Shifting Contexts of Anansi's Metamorphosis." *Society for Caribbean Studies Annual Conference Papers* 7 (2006): 1–14.

Martinez Montiel, Luz Maria. *Presencia Africana en Mexico*. Mexico City: Consejo Nacional para la Cultura y las Artes, 1994.

Martínez Montiel, Luz Maria, and Juan Carlos Reyes G., eds. *Memoria del III Encuentro Nacional de Afromexicanistas*. Colima: Consejo Nacional para la Cultura y las Artes, 1993.

Marx, Karl. *Early Writings*. Translated by Rodney Livingstone and Gregor Benton. London: Penguin, 1975.

Mason, John. *Black Gods: Spirituality in the New World*. New York: Yoruba Theological Archministry, 1985.

———. *Olóòkun: Owner of Rivers and Seas*. New York: Yoruba Theological Archministry, 1996.

———. *Orin Orisa: Songs for Sacred Heads*. New York: Yoruba Theological Archministry, 1992.

Mbiti, John. *Introduction to African Religion*. New York: Praeger, 1975.

McAllister, Marvin. *White People Do Not Know How to Behave at Entertainments Designed for Ladies and Gentlemen of Colour*. Chapel Hill: University of North Carolina Press, 2003.

McCaskill, Barbara, and Caroline Gebhard, eds. *Post-Bellum, Pre-Harlem: African American Literature and Culture, 1887–1919*. New York: New York University Press, 2006.

McClary, Susan. *Conventional Wisdom: The Content of Musical Form*. Minneapolis: University of Minnesota Press, 1991.

McClintock, Anne. *Imperial Leather: Race, Gender and Sexuality in the Colonial Contest*. New York: Routledge, 1995.

McHenry, Elizabeth. *Forgotten Readers: Recovering the Lost History of African American Literary Societies*. Durham, NC: Duke University Press, 2002.

McLeod, Ken. "Space Oddities: Aliens, Futurism and Meaning in Popular Music." *Popular Music* 22, no. 3 (2003): 337–55.

McRuer, Robert. *Crip Theory: Cultural Signs of Queerness and Disability*. New York: New York University Press, 2006.

Mena, Luz. "Stretching the Limits of Gendered Spaces: Black and Mulatto Women in 1830s Havana." *Cuban Studies* 36 (December 2005): 87–104.

Mercer, Kobena. *Welcome to the Jungle: New Positions in Black Cultural Studies*. New York: Routledge, 1994.

Meserve, Walter J. *An Outline History of American Drama*. New York: Feedback Theatrebooks and Prospero Press, [1966] 1994.

"Metropolitan Area Employment and Unemployment Summary." Bureau of Labor Statistics. July 30, 2013. http://www.bls.gov/news.release/metro.nro.htm.

"Michael Jackson—Jackson Movie Uses Old Material." Contactmusic.com, November 16, 2009. http://www.contactmusic.com.

Middleton, Richard. "Rock Singing." In *The Cambridge Companion to Singing*, edited by John Potter. Cambridge: Cambridge University Press, 2000.

Miller, Paul D. *Rhythm Science*. Cambridge, MA: MIT Press, 2004.

Mitchell, Gail. "Music Biz Insiders Say Sony–Jackson Deal Makes Sense." *Billboard*, March 19, 2010.

Mitchell, Koritha. "(Anti-)Lynching Plays: Angelina Weld Grimké, Alice Dunbar-Nelson, and the Evolution of African American Drama." In *Post-Bellum, Pre-Harlem: African American Literature and Culture, 1877–1919*, edited by Barbara McCaskill and Caroline Gebhard, 210–30. New York: New York University Press, 2006.

———. *Living with Lynching: African American Lynching Plays, Performance, and Citizenship, 1890–1930*. Urbana: University of Illinois Press, 2011.

Mitchell, Tony, ed. *Global Noise: Rap and Hip Hop Outside the USA*. Hanover, NH: Wesleyan University Press, 2002.

Moore, Robin D. *Nationalizing Blackness: Afrocubanismo and Artistic Revolution in Havana, 1920–1940*. Pittsburgh, PA: University of Pittsburgh Press, 1997.

Morrison, Toni. *Beloved*. New York: Knopf, 1987.

———. *Playing in the Dark: Whiteness and the Literary Imagination*. New York: Vintage, 1992.

———. *Song of Solomon*. New York: Vintage, 1977.

Moten, Fred. "Chromatic Saturation." Unpublished paper.

———. *In the Break: The Aesthetics of the Black Radical Tradition*. Minneapolis: University of Minnesota Press, 2003.

Mullen, Harryette. "African Signs and Spirit Writing." *Callaloo* 19, no. 3 (1996): 670–89.

———. "Miscegenated Texts and Media Cyborgs: Technologies of Body and Soul." *Poetics Journal* 9 (June 1991): 36–43.

Muñoz, Jose Esteban. *Disidentifications: Queers of Color and the Performance of Politics*. Minneapolis: University of Minnesota Press, 1999.

Murphy, John M. *Working the Spirit: Ceremonies of the African Diaspora*. Boston: Beacon, 1994.

Myers, Gerald E. "Spirituality in Modern Dance." *Dance and Spiritual Life*. Program, 651 Arts Center, November 21, 1998, 3–4.

Nassy Brown, Jacqueline. *Dropping Anchor, Setting Sail: Geographies of Race in Black Liverpool*. Princeton, NJ: Princeton University Press, 2005.

Neal, Mark Anthony. *Soul Babies: Black Popular Culture and the Post-soul Aesthetic*. New York: Routledge, 2002.

Nelson, Alondra, Thuy Linh N. Tu, and Alicia Headlam Hines, eds. *Technicolor: Race, Technology, and Everyday Life*. New York: New York University Press, 2001.

Nettl Ross, Rosa Margarita. "La población parda en la provincia de Colima a fines del siglo XVIII." In *Memoria del III Encuentro Nacional de Afromexicanistas*, edited by Luz Maria Martínez Montiel and Juan Carlos Reyes G. Colima: Consejo Nacional para la Cultura y las Artes, 1993.

Newman, Bruce. "'Cloverfield' Mantra: If It's Scary, Get It on Video." *Oakland Tribune*, January 18, 2008, 1.

Obadike, Mendi. "Low Fidelity: Stereotyped Blackness in the Field of Sound." PhD dissertation, Duke University, 2005.

Olmsted, Frederick Law. *The Cotton Kingdom: A Traveler's Observations on Cotton and Slavery in the American Slave States*. New York: Knopf, 1953.

Ortega, Kenny. "That Was It; *This Is It* Director Kenny Ortega Recalls His Good Friend Jacko." *Times*, February 20, 2010, 11.

O'Shea, Gary. "Jacko . . . This Isn't It; Exclusive: Film Songs Trick." *Sun*, November 16, 2009, 21.

Osumare, Halifu. *The Africanist Aesthetic in Global Hip-Hop: Power Moves*. New York: Palgrave Macmillan, 2007.

———. "The New Moderns: The Paradox of Eclectism and Singularity." In *African American Genius in Modern Dance*, edited by Gerald E. Myers, 26–29. Durham, NC: American Dance Festival, 1993.

Ovid. *Metamorphoses*. Translated by Charles Martin. New York: W. W. Norton, 2004.

Palmer, Colin. *Slaves of the White God: Blacks in Mexico 1570–1650*. Cambridge, MA: Harvard University Press, 1976.

Palmer, Landon. "Culture Warrior: Found Footage Filmmaking." FilmSchoolRejects .com. October 12, 2009. http://www.filmschoolrejects.com/features/culture -warrior-found-footage-filmmakinglpalm.php.

Pareles, Jon, and Jon Caramanica. "A Jackson Song Arrives, and the Discussion Begins." *New York Times*, October 13, 2009, C3.

Parliament. *Mothership Connection*. Universal Music and Video Distribution, 2003.

Pasteur, Alfred B., and Toldson, Ivory L. *Roots of Soul: The Psychology of Black Expressiveness*. Garden City, NY: Anchor Press / Doubleday, 1982.

Patterson, Orlando. *Rituals of Blood: Consequences of Slavery in Two American Centuries*. Washington, DC: Civitas / CounterPoint, 1998.

Perkins, Kathy A., and Judith L. Stephens, eds. *Strange Fruit: Plays on Lynching by American Women*. Bloomington: Indiana University Press, 1998.

Perrone, Pierre. "A Marketable Mystique That the Living Can't Match." *Independent*, March 17, 2010, 10.

Phelan, Peggy. *Unmarked: The Politics of Performance*. New York: Routledge, 1993.

Pollock, Della. "Performing Writing." In *The Ends of Performance*, edited by Peggy Phelan and Jill Lane, 73–103. New York: NYU Press, 1998.

Radano, Ron. *Lying Up a Nation: Race and Black Music*. Chicago: University of Chicago Press, 2003.

Ramsay, Paulette. "History, Violence, and Self-Glorification in Afro-Mexican *corridos* from Costa Chica d Guerrero." *Bulletin of Latin American Research* 23, no. 4 (2004): 446–64.

Reynolds, Simon. "Noise." In *Audio Culture: Readings in Modern Music*, edited by Christoph Cox and Daniel Warner, 55–58. New York: Continuum, 2006.

"Rhapsody Commercial Cool Kids and Sara Bareilles." Rapmusic.tv. http://www .youtube.com/watch?v=8bXXxx1HeWk.

Richardson, Gary. *American Drama from the Colonial Period through World War I: A Critical History*. New York: Twayne, 1993.

Rickey, Carrie. "Michael Jackson's Moves Are the Star of 'This Is It.'" *Philadelphia Inquirer*, October 30, 2009, W4.

Riis, Thomas L. "The Experience and Impact of Black Entertainers in England, 1895–1920." *American Music* 4, no. 1 (1986): 50–58.

Roach, Joseph. *Cities of the Dead: Circum-Atlantic Performance*. New York: Columbia University Press, 1996.

Robb, Brian J. *Heath Ledger: Hollywood's Dark Star*. 2nd ed. Medford, NJ: Plexus Publishing, 2010.

Roberts, Rosemarie A. "Radical Movements: Katherine Dunham and Ronald K. Brown Teaching toward Critical Consciousness." PhD dissertation, City University of New York. Ann Arbor, MI: University Microfilms International, 2005.

Robinson, Marc. *The Other American Drama*. Cambridge: Cambridge University Press, 1994.

Rockwell, David, with Bruce Mau. *Spectacle*. New York: Phaidon, 2006.

Rodríguez, Francisco Camero. *Canto a la Costa Chica*. Chapingo, Mexico: Universidad Autónoma Chapingo, 2006.

Rose, Tricia. *Black Noise: Rap and Black Music in Contemporary America*. Hanover, NH: Wesleyan University Press, 1994.

Rosen, Charles. *Arnold Schoenberg*. Chicago: University of Chicago Press, 1996.

Rosen, Hannah. *Terror in the Heart of Freedom: Citizenship, Sexual Violence, and the Meaning of Race in the Postemancipation South*. Chapel Hill: University of North Carolina Press, 2009.

Rucker, Walter, and James Upton, eds. *Encyclopedia of American Race Riots*. New York: Greenwood, 2007.

Rudder, Christian. "How Your Race Affects the Messages You Get." *OkTrends*, October 5, 2009. http://blog.okcupid.com/index.php/your-race-affects-whether -people-write-you-back/.

Samuels, Gertrude. "Why They Rock 'N' Roll—and Should They?" *New York Times Magazine*, January 12, 1958.

Sappol, Michael. *A Traffic of Dead Bodies: Anatomy and Embodied Social Identity in Nineteenth-Century America*. Princeton, NJ: Princeton University Press, 2002.

Sartre, Jean Paul. *Being and Nothingness: A Phenomenological Essay on Ontology*. Translated by Hazel Barnes. New York: Pocket, 1966.

Savannah Unit, Georgia Writers' Project, Works Projects Administration. *Drums and Shadows: Survival Studies among the Georgia Coastal Negroes*. Athens: University of Georgia Press, 1940.

Scaggs, Austin. "Kanye West." *Rolling Stone*, November 15, 2007. http://www.rolling-stone.com/music/news/kanye-west-the-40th-anniversary-interview-20071115.

Schechner, Richard. *Between Theater and Anthropology*. Philadelphia: University of Pennsylvania Press, 1985.

Schloss, Joseph G. *Foundation: B-Boys, B-Girls, and Hip-Hop Culture in New York*. New York: Oxford University Press, 2009.

Scott, Anna Beatrice. *A Fala Que Faz: Words That Work*. Saarbrücken, Germany: VDM, 2010.

"Selma-to-Montgomery March." National Park Service. http://www.nps.gov/history /nr/travel/civilrights/al4.htm.

"Selma to Montgomery National Historic Trail—History and Culture (U.S. National Park Service)." *U.S. National Park Service—Experience Your America*. http://www .nps.gov/semo/historyculture/index.htm.

Serlin, David. "The Other Arms Race." In *The Disability Studies Reader*, edited by Lennard J. Davis, 49–65. New York: Routledge, 2006.

Sharpe, Jenny. *Ghosts of Slavery: A Literary Archeology of Black Women's Lives*. Minneapolis: University of Minnesota Press, 2004.

Sheffield, Rob. "Kanye West: Late Registration." *Rolling Stone*, September 8, 2005. http://www.rollingstone.com/music/albumreviews/late-registration-20050825.

Shepard, Verene, Bridget Brereton, and Barbara Bailey, eds. *Engendering History: Caribbean Women in Historical Perspective*. New York: St. Martin's, 1995.

Shimikawa, Karen. *National Abjection: The Asian American Body Onstage*. Durham: Duke University Press, 2002.

Simpson, Mark W. *Introduction, Jumping the Broom, [untitled]*, Performance Program, Yerba Buena Arts Center, April 30, 2007.

Skerrett, Joseph T., Jr. "Recitation to the Griot: Storytelling and Learning in Toni Morrison's *Song of Solomon*." In *Conjuring: Black Women, Fiction, and Literary Tradition*, edited by Marjorie Pryse and Hortense J. Spillers, 192–202. Bloomington: Indiana University Press, 1985.

Small, Stephen. "Racialised Relations in Liverpool; A Contemporary Anomaly." *New Community* 17, no. 4 (July 1991): 511–37.

Smallwood, Stephanie E. *Saltwater Slavery: A Middle Passage from Africa to American Diaspora*. Cambridge, MA: Harvard University Press, 2007.

Smith, Shawn Michelle. "The Evidence of Lynching Photographs." In *Lynching Photographs*, 10–41. Berkeley: University of California Press, 2007.

———. *Photography on the Color Line: W. E. B. DuBois, Race, and Visual Culture*. Durham, NC: Duke University Press, 2004.

Smith, Susan Harris. *American Drama: The Bastard Art*. New York: Cambridge University Press, 1997.

Smith, Valerie. *Self-Discovery and Authority in Afro-American Narrative*. Cambridge, MA: Harvard University Press, 1987.

Soergel, Matt. "Long Live King of Pop: Michael Jackson Film Is a Triumph in an Unsentimental, Exuberant, Musical Way." *Florida Times Union*, October 30, 2009, J6.

Solomons, Jason. "Heath Is Where the Heart Is: A Posthumous Oscar Seems to Be Already on the Cards but, Asks Jason Solomons, Does Heath Ledger's Joker Justify the Hype?" *Observer*, July 20, 2008, 3.

Southern, Eileen. *The Music of Black Americans: A History*. New York: W. W. Norton, 1971.

———. "The Origin and Development of the Black Musical Theater." *Black Music Research Journal* 2 (1981–82): 1–14.

Spillers, Hortense J. "Mama's Baby, Papa's Maybe: An American Grammar Book." In "Culture and Countermemory: The 'American' Connection," special issue, *Diacritics* 17, no. 2 (summer 1987): 64–81.

Spivak, Gayatri Chakravorty. "Echo." In *The Spivak Reader*, edited by Donna Landry and Gerald McClean, 175–202. New York: Routlege, 1996.

Stearns, Marshall, and Jean Stearns. *Jazz Dance: The Story of American Vernacular Dance*. New York: Schirmer, 1968.

Stern, Peter. "*Gente de Color Quebrado*: Africans and Afromestizos in Colonial Mexico." *Colonial Latin American Historical Review* 3, no. 2 (1994): 185–205.

Stevens, Dana. "The Last Moonwalk: Michael Jackson's Incredibly Moving *This Is It*." *Slate*, October 28, 2009. http://www.slate.com/id/2233842.

Storey, Olivia Smith. "Flying Words: Contests of Orality and Literacy in the Trope of the Flying Africans." *Journal of Colonialism and Colonial History* 5, no. 3 (2004): 1–22.

Stuckey, Sterling. "Christian Conversion and the Challenge of Dance." In *Dancing Many Drums: Excavations in African American Dance*, edited by Thomas F. De-Frantz, 39–58. Madison: University of Wisconsin Press, 2002.

Sublette, Ned. *Cuba and Its Music: From the First Drums to the Mambo*. Chicago: Chicago Review Press, 2007.

Suisman, David. "Co-workers in the Kingdom of Culture: Black Swan Records and the Political Economy of African American Music." *Journal of American History* 90, no. 4 (2004): 1295–324.

Swartz, Tracy. "Tracking Homicides in Chicago." *Red Eye*. http://homicides .redeyechicago.com/.

Tate, Claudia. "Toni Morrison." In *Black Women Writers at Work*, edited by Claudia Tate, 117–31. New York: Continuum, 1983.

Tate, Greg. "The Man in Our Mirror." *Village Voice* 54, no. 27 (July 1–7, 2009): 13.

Taylor, Diana. *The Archive and the Repertoire: Performing Cultural Memory in the Americas*. Durham, NC: Duke University Press, 2003.

This Is It. Kenny Ortega, director. Columbia Pictures, 2009.

Thomas, Susan. "Lo Más Femenino De Los Géneros: Gender, Race, and Representation in the Cuban Zarzuela, 1927–1944." PhD dissertation, Brandeis University, 2002.

Thompson, Robert Farris. "Dance and Culture, an Aesthetic of the Cool: West African Dance." *African Forum* 2 (1966): 85–102.

———. *Flash of the Spirit: African and Afro-American Art and Philosophy*. New York: Vintage Books, 1984.

Toor, Frances. *A Treasury of Mexican Folkways*. New York: Crown, 1947.

Touré. "Head of the Class." *Rolling Stone*, April 29, 2004. http://web.ebscohost.com /ehost/detail?vid=3&hid=109&sid=ff2cc78b-5d25-4c9a-93c9-df9eb76f86c2%40 sessionmgr109.

"Transcript—Barack Obama's Inaugural Address." *New York Times*, January 20, 2009. http://www.nytimes.com/2009/01/20/us/politics/20text-obama.html.

Tyrangiel, Josh. "Why You Can't Ignore Kanye." *Time*, August 29, 2005. http://web .ebscohost.com/ehost/detail?vid=3&hid=115&sid=046559fa-2487-4b22-88fc -d46d25ea8664%40sessionmgr109.

Vaudeville: An American Masters Special. Greg Palmer, writer. Thirteen / WNET, KCIT, Palmer/Fenster, 1997.

Vinson, Ben, III. *Bearing Arms for His Majesty: The Free-Colored Militia in Colonial Mexico*. Stanford, CA: Stanford University Press, 2001.

Waddell, Ray. "That Was That and *This Is It*." *Billboard* 121, no. 44 (November 7, 2009): 24.

Wald, Gayle. "Soul Vibrations: Black Music and Black Freedom in Sound and Space." *American Quarterly* 63, no. 3 (2011): 673–96.

Wall, Cheryl A. *Worrying the Line: Black Women Writers, Lineage, and Literary Tradition*. Chapel Hill: University of North Carolina Press, 2005.

wa Thiong'o, Ngugi. *Penpoints, Gunpoints, and Dreams: Towards a Critical Theory of the Arts and the State in Africa*. Oxford: Clarendon, 1998.

Weheliye, Alexander G. *Phonographies: Grooves in Sonic Afro-modernity*. Durham, NC: Duke University Press, 2005.

Weinberg, J. "Things Are Queer." *Art Journal* 55, no. 4 (1996): 11–14.

Wells, Ida B. *Southern Horrors: Lynch Law in All Its Phases*. 1892. In *Southern Horrors and Other Writings: The Anti-lynching Campaign of Ida B. Wells, 1892–1900*, edited by Jacqueline Royster, 49–72. New York: Bedford, 1997.

Welsh-Asante, Kariamu. "Commonalities in African Dance: An Aesthetic Foundation." In *Moving History / Dancing Cultures: A Dance History Reader*, edited by Ann Dils and Ann Cooper Albright, 144–51. Middletown, CT: Wesleyan University Press, 2001.

West, Cornell. "Black Spiritual Strivings in a Twilight Civilization." In *The Future of the Race*, edited by Henry Louis Gates Jr. and Cornel West, 53–114. New York: Vintage, 1996.

West, Kanye. *College Dropout*. Universal Music and Distribution Group, 2004.

Wheeler, Brad. "Paul Anka and the Mystery of the Jackson Jive." *Globe and Mail*, October 17, 2009, A13.

White, Charles. *The Life and Times of Little Richard*. New York: Da Capo, 1994.

White, Shane, and Graham White. *Stylin': African-American Expressive Culture, from Its Beginnings to the Zoot Suit*. Ithaca, NY: Cornell University Press, 1999.

White-Dixon, Melanye. "Telling Stories, Keepin' It Real: A Conversation with Ronal K. Brown." *Attitude Magazine* 14, no. 4 (2000): 6–11.

Wiegman, Robyn. *American Anatomies: Theorizing Race and Gender*. Durham, NC: Duke University Press, 1995.

Wilentz, Gay. *Binding Cultures: Black Women Writers in Africa and the Diaspora*. Bloomington: Indiana University Press, 1992.

———. "If You Surrender to the Air: Folk Legends of Flight and Resistance in African American Literature." *MELUS* 16, no. 1 (1990): 21–32.

Williams, Ben. "Black Secret Technology: Detroit Techno and the Information Age." In *Technicolor: Race, Technology, and Everyday Life*, edited by Alondra Nelson, Thuy Linh N. Tu, and Alicia Headlam Hines, 154–76. New York: New York University Press, 2001.

Wilson, Olly. "The Heterogeneous Sound Ideal in African-American Music." In *New Perspectives on Music: Essays in Honor of Eileen Southern*, edited by Samuel A. Floyd Jr. and Josephine Wright. Warren, MI: Harmonie Park Press, 1992.

Winters, Lisa Ze. "Spectacle, Specter and the Imaginative Space: Unfixing the Tragic Mulatta." PhD dissertation, University of California, Berkeley, 2005.

Woll, Allen. *Black Musical Theatre: From "Coontown" to "Dreamgirls."* New York: Da Capo, 1989.

Wondrich, David. *Stomp and Swerve: American Music Gets Hot, 1843–1924*. Chicago: Chicago Review Press, 2003.

Woodard, Josef. "Last Rites for the 'It' Man." *Santa Barbara Independent* 23, no. 199 (November 12, 2009): 77.

"A World of Hits." *Economist* 393 (November 28, 2009): 79.

Wright, Michelle M. *Becoming Black: Creating Identity in the African Diaspora*. Durham, NC: Duke University Press, 2004.

Wynter, Sylvia. "Beyond Miranda's Meanings: Un/Silencing the 'Demonic Ground' of Caliban's Women." In *Out of the Kumbla: Caribbean Women and Literature*, edited by Carole Boyce Davies and Elaine Savory Fido, 355–72. Trenton, NJ: Africa World Press, 1990.

Ybarra, Patricia. *Performing Conquest: Five Centuries of Theater, History, and Identity in Tlaxcala, Mexico*. Ann Arbor: University of Michigan Press, 2009.

Young, Harvey, Jr. "The Black Body as Souvenir in American Lynching." *Theatre Journal* 57, no. 4 (December 2005): 639–57.

———. *Embodying Black Experience: Stillness, Critical Memory, and the Black Body*. Detroit: University of Michigan Press, 2010.

Zangrando, Robert. *The NAACP Campaign against Lynching, 1909–1950*. Philadelphia: Temple University Press, 1980.

Zawia, Alexandra. "Harry Belafonte on Capitalism, Media Moguls and His Disappointment with Jay-Z and Beyonce (Q&A)." *Hollywood Reporter*, August 7, 2012.

CONTRIBUTORS

Thomas F. DeFrantz is professor of African and African American studies, dance, and theater studies at Duke University. He is the director of SLIPPAGE: Performance, Culture, Technology, a research group that explores emerging technology in live-performance applications, in residence at Duke University (www.slippage.org). Projects include solo tap/technology piece *Monk's Mood: A Performance Meditation on the Life and Music of Thelonious Monk*; *The House Music Project*; and CANE, an immersive environment dance-theater work created in collaboration with Wideman/Davis Dance. He edited *Dancing Many Drums: Excavations in African American Dance* (2002, CHOICE Award and Errol Hill Award) and authored *Dancing Revelations: Alvin Ailey's Embodiment of African American Culture* (2004, de la Torre Bueno Prize). Performances include the *Morton Gould Tap Concerto* with the Boston Pops conducted by Keith Lockhart and the *Duke Ellington Tap Concerto (David Danced)* with the Aardvark Jazz Orchestra conducted by Mark Harvey. DeFrantz served as president for the Society of Dance History Scholars, was book editor for the Dance Critics Association, and organized the dance history program at the Alvin Ailey School for many years. He is always interested in stories, how we tell them, and what we think they might mean.

Anita Gonzalez is a professor of theater at the University of Michigan, Ann Arbor. She has authored two books, *Afro-Mexico: Dancing between Myth and Reality* (2010) and *Jarocho's Soul* (2005), that reveal the influence of African people and their cultural productions on Mexican festival performance. Her essays about multicultural and international performance appear in several edited collections including *The Community Performance Reader* (Kuppers, ed.), *Festive Devils* (Riggio, Segura, and Vignola, eds.), and the *Oxford Handbook of Dance and Theatre* (George-Graves, ed.). She has published articles in the *Radical History Review*, *Modern Drama*, *Performance Research International*, and *Dance Research Journal*. Gonzalez is also a director and choreographer whose work has appeared on PBS national television and at Dixon Place, the Working Theater, HereArts, Tribeca Performing Arts Center, Ballet Hispanico, and other venues. She has been awarded a residency at Rockefeller's Bellagio Center (2003) and has completed three Senior Scholar Fulbright grants. Gonzalez earned her PhD in Theater/Performance Studies from the University of Wisconsin, Madison (1997). She is an associate member of Stage Directors and

Choreographers and a member of the Dramatists Guild, the National Theatre Conference, and the Players Club as well as the Association for Theatre in Higher Education, the American Society for Theatre Research, and the Society of Dance History Scholars. Dr. Gonzalez enjoys serving as a destination lecturer for Royal Caribbean and Celebrity cruise lines.

Melissa Blanco Borelli is senior lecturer in dance at Royal Holloway University of London. She is the editor of the *Oxford Handbook of Dance and the Popular Screen* and the author of *She Is Cuba: A Genealogy of Mulata Corporeality*. She has been published in *Women and Performance: A Journal of Feminist Theory*, the *International Journal of Performing Arts and Digital Media*, *Brolga: Australian Journal for Dance*, and the *International Journal of Screendance*. Her research interests include feminist/performative ethnography, popular dance on screen, and performative writing. Dr. Blanco Borelli has contributed to the *Feminist Wire* and the *Huffington Post* and, with Sanjoy Roy, dance critic at the *Guardian*, leads workshops on the art of critical writing. Her practical work fuses performance ethnography, cabaret, and Latino social dance to tell stories about women of color.

Daphne A. Brooks is professor of English and African American studies at Princeton University, where she teaches courses on African American literature and culture, performance studies, critical gender studies, and popular music culture. She is the author of two books: *Bodies in Dissent: Spectacular Performances of Race and Freedom, 1850–1910* (Duke University Press, 2006), winner of the 2007 Errol Hill Award for outstanding scholarship in African American theater studies, and *Jeff Buckley's Grace* (2005). She is also the editor of *The Great Escapes: The Narratives of William Wells Brown, Henry Box Brown, and William Craft* (2007) and the performing-arts volume of *The Black Experience in the Western Hemisphere* (Howard Dodson and Colin Palmer, series eds.) (2006). Brooks is a contributing writer for the *Nation*, where she has published articles on Beyoncé, Amy Winehouse, and Whitney Houston. She is currently at work on a new book manuscript titled *Subterranean Blues: Black Women Sound Modernity*.

Soyica Diggs Colbert is an associate professor of African American Studies and Theater and Performance Studies at Georgetown University. She is the author of *The African American Theatrical Body: Reception, Performance and the Stage* (2011), and the editor of the "Black Performance" special issue of *African American Review*. She has published articles and reviews on James Baldwin, Alice Childress, August Wilson, Lynn Nottage, Katori Hall, and Suzan-Lori Parks in *African American Review*, *Theater Journal*, *Boundary 2*, *South Atlantic Quarterly*, and *Theater Topics*, and the collections *Contemporary African American Women Playwrights: A Casebook* and *August Wilson: Completing the Cycle*. Her research interests span the nineteenth through the twenty-first centuries, from William Wells Brown to Beyoncé, and from poetics to performance.

Nadine George-Graves is professor of theater and dance at the University of California, San Diego. Her work is situated at the intersections of African American studies, gender studies, performance studies, theater history, and dance history. She is the author of *The Royalty of Negro Vaudeville: The Whitman Sisters and the Negotiation of Race, Gender, and Class in African American Theater, 1900–1940* and *Urban Bush Women: Twenty Years of Dance Theater, Community Engagement and Working It Out* as well as numerous articles on African American theater and dance. She is currently editing the *Oxford Handbook of Dance and Theater*. She is also an adapter and director. Her recent creative projects include Suzan-Lori Parks's *Topdog/Underdog* and *Anansi the Story King*, an original dance-theater adaptation of African American folk stories using college students, professionals, and fourth graders. George-Graves earned her BA from Yale University and her PhD from Northwestern University. She serves as president of the Congress on Research in Dance (CORD).

Rickerby Hinds is a native of Honduras, Central America, who immigrated to South Central Los Angeles at age thirteen. His visionary creations span the gamut of human emotions and experiences. His play *Daze to Come* debuted in 1989 as one of the first full-length plays to use the founding elements of hip-hop as the primary language of the stage. *Blackballin'*, which received a reading at London's Royal Court Theatre, examines the issue of race and history in American sports and society. The semiautobiographical *Birthmark* explores the social and cultural conflicts of a Spanish-speaking immigrant of African descent forced to choose between the limiting racial categories offered within American society. Among the entities that have supported his works in the form of commissions, grants, and fellowships are the Ford Foundation, the Showtime Television Network, the Geva Theatre in New York, the Mark Taper Forum, the Cornerstone Theatre, the Bay Area Playwrights Festival, the Oregon Shakespeare Festival, and the New LATC (Los Angeles Theater Center). Hinds is currently professor at the University of California, Riverside, and the founder and artistic director of the Califest Hip-Hop Theater Festival.

Jason King is associate professor and the founding faculty member of the Clive Davis Institute of Recorded Music, an innovative leadership training program for aspiring music entrepreneurs at Tisch School of the Arts, New York University, where he has been teaching classes on popular music history, the music business (marketing/branding), and the social aspects of music technology for more than thirteen years. He produced EMP Pop Conferences featuring Amanda Palmer, Esperanza Spalding, and Santigold; "The Making of Afrika Bambaataa and SoulSonic Force's Planet Rock" with Arthur Baker and Fab 5 Freddy; and Motown's fiftieth anniversary series with Leon Ware and Raphael Saadiq. Jason has been a music critic and journalist for publications including *Vibe* (2001–8), the *Village Voice* (2003–6), *Blender*, the *Los Angeles Times*, and the *Root*. He is the author of *The Michael Jackson Treasures*, a Barnes and Noble exclusive biography published in 2009, and a book called *Blue Magic*, on the role of metaphysics and energy in the music of artists like Timbaland, forthcoming from Duke University Press.

D. Soyini Madison is professor and chair in the Department of Performance Studies at Northwestern University with appointments in the Program of African Studies and the Department of Anthropology. Her recent books include *Acts of Activism: Human Rights as Radical Performance* (2010), *Critical Ethnography: Method, Ethics, and Performance* (2nd ed., 2012), and the coedited collection *African Dress: Fashion, Agency, Performance* (2013). As a performance ethnographer, Madison directs non-fiction and ethnographic data for the stage, including *Labor Rites*, a mosaic of the U.S. labor movement; *I Have My Story to Tell*, the oral histories of North Carolina service workers; *Mandela, the Land, and the People*, on the activism of Nelson Mandela; *Is It a Human Being or a Girl?* on religion and gender in Ghana; and *Water Rites*, on public water as a human right.

Koritha Mitchell is a literary historian and cultural critic. Her research centers on African American literature, racial violence in U.S. literature and contemporary culture, and black drama and performance. Her study *Living with Lynching: African American Lynching Plays, Performance, and Citizenship* won book awards from the American Theatre and Drama Society and from the Society for the Study of American Women Writers. Her essay "James Baldwin, Performance Theorist, Sings the *Blues for Mister Charlie*" appears in *American Quarterly*. Her *Callaloo* journal article "Love in Action" draws parallels between racial violence at the last turn of the century and anti-LGBT violence today. Currently an associate professor of English at Ohio State University, Mitchell earned her PhD in English at the University of Maryland, College Park.

Tavia Nyong'o received a BA from Wesleyan University and an MA and PhD in American Studies from Yale University. His research interests include the intersections of race and sexuality, visual art and performance, and cultural history. His book, *The Amalgamation Waltz: Race, Performance, and the Ruses of Memory* (2009), won the Errol Hill Award. His current project investigates race, fabulation, and ecology. He is the coeditor of the journal *Social Text*.

Carl Paris holds an MA in Dance in Higher Education from NYU and a PhD in Dance Studies and Cultural Theory from Temple University. Carl performed with Olatunji African Dance, the Eleo Pomare and Martha Graham Dance companies, and the Alvin Ailey American Dance Theater. He taught and choreographed in Spain and throughout Europe for nearly seventeen years and received the nationally recognized Dance Association of Madrid Award for his work as a teacher in 1995. He has been a guest teacher and choreographer at CalArts, the Alvin Ailey Repertory Company, the Fiorella La Guardia High School of the Performing Arts, and the Martha Graham School. He has taught dance and dance-related courses at New York University and Long Island University as well as courses on African American history and race and ethnicity in American culture at John Jay College of Criminal Justice. He has presented papers at conferences in dance research, and his critical reviews and essays on blacks in concert dance have appeared in several dance publications.

Anna B. Scott performs Afro-futurist conjurations with dance, digital devices, and text onstage, in blogs, in books, and through strategic marketing plans. Scott has worked in arts management, production, performance, research, and education since the late 1980s. Her work and process traverse many genres and roles; she is a convergent human. As a performance scholar trained in ethnography and certified in Human Subjects Research Protocol, Scott has published one book and several articles that examine the impact technological advances exert on memory and therefore performance of identity, paying attention to the repercussions of taking up the brand and branding strategies as new identity markers. She served University of California, Riverside, as an assistant professor of dance history and theory for nine years and continues to work as a thesis and career adviser at large. Her passion for arts-centered analysis energizes innovation in clients and collaborators. It is her pleasure to bring their secret aspirations to fruition through the application of research, storytelling, and prescient data analysis. She is the artistic director of VISCERA Performance Instigation Troupe, a company that performs "high tech" street theater installations. The troupe launched the inaugural performance in the Los Angeles World Airports' and Public Art division of the Department of Cultural Affairs' Ephemeral Art Program with *'Bout to Get On* (http://kineme.blogspot.com).

Wendy S. Walters is associate professor of poetry in the Department of Literary Studies at Eugene Lang College of the New School University and a contributing editor at the *Iowa Review*. Her work has appeared in *Fence, Callaloo, Bookforum*, the *Iowa Review*, and *Harper's* magazine. She is completing a forthcoming book of essays and is the author of two books of poems, *Troy, Michigan* and *Longer I Wait, More You Love Me*.

Hershini Bhana Young is associate professor at SUNY Buffalo, where she teaches classes on gender, sexuality, race, and performance. Her first book, *Haunting Capital: Memory, Text and the Black Diasporic Body*, examines the injured body in literature and art of the African diaspora. Her completed second book project, titled *Illegible Will: Coercive Performances in Southern African Spectacles of Labor*, examines issues around the legibility of historical "will" in various gendered performances across the African diaspora. Looking at historical and fictional representations of women like Saartjie Baartman and South African slave women who killed their children, the book proposes that "will" is a queer relational performance of vulnerability. Her latest publication, titled "'Sound of Kuduro Knocking at My Door': Kuduro Dance and the Poetics of Debility," appears in *African American Review*.

INDEX

"Back and Forth" (Jennings), 57
Badejo, Dierdre, 73
bailes de cuna, 65, 67, 75–80
Baker, Houston A., Jr., 3, 46
Baker, Josephine, 45, 52
"Baker's Burden" (Jennings), *46*
Bakke case, 146
Baldwin, James, 100, 103, 153, 156n19, 202
Banes, Sally, 7
Baraka, Amiri (LeRoi Jones), 3–4
Barthes, Roland, 211, 218–19
"Bassment Party" (Cool Kids), 225
Bataille, Georges, 181–82
Batlett, Andrew, 145
b-boys and b-girls, 227–29, 242n11
B. Brown and His Orchestra, 171
Bearden, Michael, 198, 202
Bearden, Romare, 212
Beatles, the, 190
Belafonte, Harry, ix
Belchem, John, 25
Bell, Kelvyn, 180
Beloved (Morrison), 59
Best, Stephen, 53
Beyond Decorum (Udé), 60
Biggie Smalls, 115–16
Bight of Biafra, 136
"Billie Jean" (Jackson), 188, 201–2
biological essentialism, 38–40. *See also* hybridity; identity; race
Birth of a Nation (Griffith), 94
"black" (name), 2
Black Arts Movement, 142
Black Atlantic, 46. *See also* circum-Atlantic movements
Black Atlantic, The (Gilroy), 81n3, 132
Black Bastards (MF Doom), 59
Black Burlesque (Wilson), 109–10
Black Burlesque (Revisited) (Wilson), 102, 109–113, *110*
Black Cultural Traffic (Elem and Jackson), 5, 132
Black Dancing Body, The (Gottschild), 114n5
blackface, 24–27. *See also* minstrel shows
blackness: abjection and, vii, 59–60, 174, 209, 212, 215; aurality and, 2–3, 13–14, 100–102, 131–37, 180, 185, 198; circula-

tions of, 11–12, 19–32, 64–82, 107–13, 130–33, 142–47, 234–39; citizenship discourses and, 22–23, 36, 53–59, 65–68, 89–98, 152; commodification of, 45–62, 101, 147, 170–83, 227–28, 239–40; definitions of, vii–ix, 1–2; embodiment and, vii–viii, viii–ix, 4–10, 45, 49–51, 68, 99–114, 227–39; essentialisms and, ix, 1–2, 20–32, 37–38, 40–42, 53, 102, 150; expression and, 2–3, 100–114, 158–65, 196–200, 207–8, 225–32; feminism and, 9, 14, 204–22; libidinal economies and, 65–82, 152, 182, 211; minstrelsy and, 21–32, 98; non-black performers and, 20–32; performance theory and, 1–15, 35–36, 131–33, 158–65, 178–203, 225–38; post-humanism and, 45–62; rock 'n' roll and, 170–83; sensibilities of, 1–2, 6–10, 223, 229, 233–36, 241. *See also* circulations; dance; diaspora movements and studies; gender; music; performance; race; sexuality
Black Noise (Rose), 242n2
"Black or White" (Jackson), 200
Black Performance Theory (BPT), vii–ix
Black Popular Culture (Wallace and Dent), 4–5
Black Public Sphere, The (Black Public Sphere Collective), 4–5
Black Public Sphere Collective, 4–5
Black Skin, White Masks (Fanon), 48–49
Black Swan records, 175
Black Umfolosi, 110
Blackwell, Robert, 179
Blair Witch Project, The, 193–94
Blake, Susan L., 148n3
bodies. *See* dance; embodiment; epistemologies; music; performance; practice theory; voice(s)
Boggs, Nicholas, 205
Bontemps, Arna, 135
Boone, Pat, 175, 180–81
Borelli, Melissa Blanco, 12, 63–84
Bourdieu, Pierre, 223, 227, 229, 232, 238, 241
breakdancing, 226–28
Brecht, Bertolt, 214
Bridges, Flora Wilson, 113n1
Brochu, Don, 187
Brody, Jennifer DeVere, 135–36